W9-AVI-124

Fodor's InFocus

BARBADOS
& ST. LUCIA

3rd Edition

Fodor's Travel Publications New York, Toronto, London, Sydney, Auckland
www.fodors.com

Portions of this book appear in *Fodor's Caribbean 2013*

FODOR'S INFOCUS BARBADOS & ST. LUCIA

Editor: Douglas Stallings, *series editor*

Editorial Contributor: Jane E. Zarem

Production Editor: Carrie Parker

Maps & Illustrations: David Lindroth and Mark Stroud *cartographers*; Rebecca Baer, *map editor;* William Wu, *information graphics*

Design: Fabrizio La Rocca, *creative director;* Tina Malaney, Chie Ushio, Jessica Ramirez, *designers;* Melanie Marin, *associate director of photography;* Jennifer Romains, *photo research*

Cover Photo: (The Pitons, St. Lucia) Robert Harding Images/Masterfile

Production Manager: Anglea McLean

COPYRIGHT

3rd Edition

ISBN 978-0-89141-935-8
ISSN 1941-0212

SPECIAL SALES

This book is available for special discounts for bulk purchases for sales promotions or premiums. Special editions, including personalized covers, excerpts of existing books, and corporate imprints, can be created in large quantities for special needs. For more information, write to Special Markets/Premium Sales, 1745 Broadway, MD 3-1, New York, NY 10019, or e-mail specialmarkets@randomhouse.com.

AN IMPORTANT TIP & AN INVITATION

Although all prices, opening times, and other details in this book are based on information supplied to us at press time, changes occur all the time in the travel world, and Fodor's cannot accept responsibility for facts that become outdated or for inadvertent errors or omissions. **So always confirm information when it matters,** especially if you're making a detour to visit a specific place. Your experiences—positive and negative—matter to us. If we have missed or misstated something, **please write to us.** Share your opinion instantly through our online feedback center at fodors.com/contact-us.

PRINTED IN CHINA
10 9 8 7 6 5 4 3 2 1

917.2981
FOD

CONTENTS

DID YOU KNOW?

Sandy Lane's Green Monkey golf course, designed by Tom Fazio, was once a limestone quarry. It's widely considered one of the Caribbean's best courses.

ABOUT
THIS BOOK

Fodor's Ratings
Everything in this guide is worth
doing—we don't cover what
isn't—but exceptional sights,
hotels, and restaurants are recognized with additional accolades.
Fodor's Choice★ indicates our top
recommendations; ★ highlights
places we deem highly recommended. Care to nominate a new
place? Visit Fodors.com/contact-us.

Trip Costs
We list prices wherever possible to
help you budget well. Hotel and
restaurant price categories from **$**
to **$$$$** are noted alongside each
recommendation. For hotels, we
include the lowest cost of a standard double room in high season.
For restaurants, we cite the average price of a main course at dinner
or, if dinner isn't served, at lunch.
For attractions, we always list adult
admission fees; discounts are usu-

ally available for children, students,
and senior citizens.

Hotels
Our local writers vet every hotel to
recommend the best overnights in
each price category, from budget to
expensive. Unless otherwise speci-
fied, you can expect private bath,
phone, and TV in your room. For
expanded hotel reviews, facilities,
and deals visit Fodors.com.

Restaurants
Unless we state otherwise, restaurants are open for lunch and dinner daily. We mention dress code
only when there's a specific require-
ment and reservations only when
they're essential or not accepted.
To make restaurant reservations,
visit Fodors.com.

Credit Cards
The hotels and restaurants in this
guide typically accept credit cards.
If not, we'll say so.

Ratings
★ Fodor's Choice
★ Highly
  recommended
☺ Family-friendly

Listings
⊠ Address
⊠ Branch address
⌂ Mailing address
☏ Telephone
🖷 Fax
⊕ Website

✎ E-mail
🎫 Admission fee
🕒 Open/closed
  times
Ⓜ Subway
⊹ Directions or
  Map coordinates

**Hotels &
Restaurants**
🏨 Hotel
🛏 Number of rooms
🍽 Meal plans

✕ Restaurant
🥢 Reservations
👔 Dress code
⊟ No credit cards
$ Price

Other
⇨ See also
🕮 Take note
🏌 Golf facilities

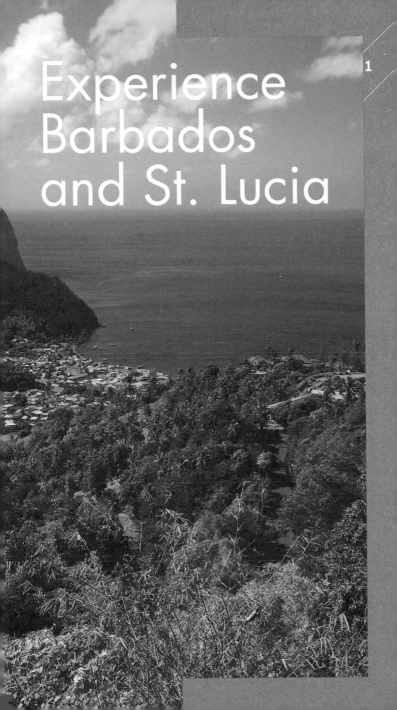

Experience Barbados and St. Lucia

WHAT'S WHERE

Caribbean

1 Barbados. Broad vistas, sweeping seascapes, craggy cliffs, and acre upon acre of sugarcane make up the island's varied landscape. A long, successful history of tourism has been forged from the warm, Bajan hospitality, welcoming hotels and resorts, sophisticated dining, lively nightspots, and, of course, magnificent sunny beaches.

2 St. Lucia. One of the greenest and most beautiful islands in the Caribbean is, arguably, the most romantic. The scenic south and central regions are mountainous and lush, with dense rain forest, endless banana plantations, and fascinating historic sites. Along the west coast some of the region's most picturesque and interesting resorts are interspersed with dozens of delightful inns that appeal to families, as well as lovers and adventurers.

50 mi

50 km

Portsmouth ○ **Dominica**

Roseau ○

W I N D W A R D

St Pierre ○ ○ La Trinité

Fort-de-France ○ **Martinique**

Castries ○

2

St. Lucia

Barbados

Bridgetown ○ 1

Kingstown ○ **St. Vincent**

Bequia

The Grenadines

Carriacou

I S L A N D S

Grenada
○ St. George's

Tobago

○ Scarborough

Port of Spain ○ **Trinidad**

San Fernando ○

VENEZUELA

BARBADOS PLANNER

Island Activities	Logistics
There's always something to do in Barbados, and that's the appeal to most visitors. The soft, white-sand **beaches** await your arrival whether you choose to stay in the millionaire's row of resorts on the west coast or the more affordable south coast.	**Getting to Barbados:** Several airlines fly nonstop to Barbados, or you may have to connect in Miami or San Juan. Grantley Adams International Airport (BGI) is in Christ Church Parish, about 15 minutes from hotels situated along the south coast, 45 minutes from the west coast, and about 30 minutes from Bridgetown.
Exceptional **golf** courses lure a lot of players to the island, but the private courses—notably Royal Westmoreland and Sandy Lane—aren't for anyone with a light wallet.	**Hassle Factor:** Low because of many non-stop flights from airports in the United States.
The island's **restaurant scene** is impressive; you can choose from street-party barbecue to international cuisine that rivals the finest dining on the planet.	**On the Ground:** Ground transportation is available immediately outside the customs area. Some resorts arrange ground transfers if you make arrangements in advance. Otherwise, you can get a taxi. Airport taxis aren't metered, but fares are regulated (about $30 to Speightstown, $20–$22 to west-coast hotels, $10–$13 to south-coast hotels). Be sure, however, to establish the fare before getting into the cab and confirm whether the price quoted is in U.S. or Barbadian dollars.
Getting out on the water is the favored activity, whether that's on a **snorkeling** day sail, in a **mini-sub**, on a **deep-sea fishing** boat, or on a **surfboard** at Bathsheba Soup Bowl.	**Getting Around on the Island:** If you are staying in an isolated area, you may want (or need) to rent a car, but bus service is good throughout the island. Taxis may suffice for travelers staying in busy resort areas.

Where to Stay

Whether you stay on the tony west coast or on the action-packed south coast, you'll have access to great beaches, but the east coast doesn't have easy access to good swimming beaches. Prices in Barbados can be twice as high in-season as during the quieter months. Most hotels include no meals in their rates, but some include breakfast and many offer a meal plan. Some require you to purchase the meal plan in the high season; a few offer all-inclusive packages.

Resorts: Great resorts run the gamut—from unpretentious to knock-your-socks-off—in size, intimacy, amenities, and price. Many are well suited to families.

Villas and Condos: Families and long-term visitors may choose from a variety of condos (from busy time-share resorts to more sedate holiday complexes). Villas and villa complexes range from luxurious to simple.

Small Inns: A few small, cozy inns are located in the east and southeast regions.

Hotel and Restaurant Costs

Prices in the restaurant reviews are the average cost of a main course at dinner or, if dinner is not served, at lunch; taxes and service charges are generally included. Prices in the hotel reviews are the lowest cost of a standard double room in high season, excluding taxes, service charges, and meal plans (except at all-inclusives). Prices for rentals are the lowest per-night cost for a one-bedroom unit in high season.

Tips for Travelers

The minimum legal drinking age in Barbados is 18.

Electricity in Barbados is 110 volts, just as in the United States. No converters or transformers are needed for U.S. appliances.

A 10% service charge is sometimes added to restaurant bills; otherwise, tip 10%–15%. Some hotels add a 10% service charge, as well.

The Barbados dollar is pegged to the U.S. dollar at a rate of Bds$1.98 to US$1. U.S. currency is accepted almost everywhere on the island, so many travelers never change their money into local currency—although change will most often be given in local currency. ATMs are widely available but dispense local currency only.

ST. LUCIA PLANNER

Island Activities	Logistics
The island's **beaches** are certainly inviting—but you won't find long stretches of fine white sand, since St. Lucia is a volcanic island; Reduit Beach, in the north, has golden sand and is considered the island's best. St. Lucia offers excellent **diving**, particularly along its southwest coast near Soufrière. Anse Chastanet, an upscale resort near the Pitons, and Ti Kaye, farther north at Anse Cochon, specialize in beach-access diving. Deep-sea **fishing** is also good. And a **day sail** on a catamaran is one of the best ways to see a good bit of the island and a good way to travel from Castries to Soufrière, or vice versa. St. Lucia's crown jewel is its well-preserved **rain forest,** which is best explored on a guided hike. Climbing one of the twin **Pitons** is a rewarding—if arduous—experience, but you must hire a guide.	**Getting to St. Lucia:** St. Lucia's primary gateway is Hewanorra International Airport (UVF) in Vieux Fort, on the island's southern tip; all large planes land at Hewanorra, which is somewhat more convenient to resorts in the Soufrière area. Some airlines fly smaller aircraft into George F. L. Charles Airport (SLU) in Castries, which is also referred to as Vigie Airport and is more convenient to resorts in the north; it may be worth the hassle to change to a smaller plane in San Juan if you are staying in the Rodney Bay or Marigot Bay areas. The drive between Hewanorra and resorts in the north takes 90 minutes; the trip between Hewanorra and Soufrière takes about 30 minutes. **Hassle Factor:** Medium to high, because of the long drive from Hewanorra International Airport. **On the Ground:** Taxis are available at both airports if transfers are not included in your travel package, but it's an expensive 90-minute ride to the north from Hewanoorra (at least $75). For resorts in the Soufrière area, the 60-minute ride from Hewanorra costs about $55. A helicopter is available to Castries from Hewanorra; it's a costly ($145 per person) but convenient option, cutting the transfer time to about 10 minutes. **Getting Around:** A car is more of a necessity if you are staying at a small inn or hotel away from the beach. If you're staying at an all-inclusive beach resort, taxis are a better bet.

Where to Stay

St. Lucia's resorts and small inns are nearly all tucked into lush, secluded coves, unspoiled beaches, or forested hillsides in three locations along the calm Caribbean (western) coast: Rodney Bay north to Cap Estate, Castries to Marigot Bay, and in and around Soufrière. Only one resort is in the south at Vieux Fort.

Big Beach Resorts: Most people choose to stay in one of St. Lucia's many beach resorts, the majority of which are upscale and fairly pricey. Several are all-inclusive, including three Sandals resorts two Sunswept resorts (The Body Holiday at LeSPORT and Rendezvous); some offer an all-inclusive option.

Small Inns: If you want something more intimate and perhaps less expensive, a locally owned inn or small hotel is a good option, but it may not be directly on the beach.

Villas: Luxury villa communities and independent private villas are a good alternative for families. Many of these are in the north in or near Cap Estate.

Hotel and Restaurant Costs

Prices in the restaurant reviews are the average cost of a main course at dinner or, if dinner is not served, at lunch; taxes and service charges are generally excluded. Prices in the hotel reviews are the lowest cost of a standard double room in high season, excluding taxes, service charges, and meal plans (except at all-inclusives). Prices for rentals are the lowest per-night cost for a one-bedroom unit in high season.

Tips for Travelers

The minimum legal drinking age in St. Lucia is 18.

Electricity in St. Lucia is 220 volts, 50 cycles. U.S. appliances will require a plug adaptor (square, three-pin) and, if they are not dual-voltage, a transformer.

A 10% service charge is usually added to restaurant bills; otherwise, tip 10%–15%. Tip bellboys $1 per bag, maids $2 per night, and taxi drivers 10% of the fare.

The Eastern Caribbean dollar is pegged to the U.S. dollar at a rate of EC$2.67 to US$1. U.S. currency is accepted almost everywhere on the island, but you'll get change in local currency. It's helpful to have some local currency if you plan to shop in smaller markets or ride local buses.

A 15% V.A.T. is added to restaurant bills. An 8% V.A.T. is added to all hotel costs.

TOP EXPERIENCES

Dine in Period Style at Sunbury Plantation House and Museum, Barbados

(A) Period furnishings and a complete, loving restoration after a major fire in 1995 have created a picture-postcard vision of plantation life in the 18th and 19th centuries. A very special, albeit expensive five-course dinner served in the house's period dining room at a long mahogany table is held two nights a week during the high season. Alternatively, come for the buffet lunch.

Tour Diamond Botanical Gardens, St. Lucia

(B) This private botanical garden is still owned and operated by a descendant of the original Devaux brothers, who were deeded the land for their vast estate by King Louis XIV in 1713. It's claimed that Empress Joséphine bathed in the sulfurous waters when she was a girl (and long before she met M. Bonaparte); for an extra fee, you can also take a soak. Hire one of the private guides outside the gates to get the full story; and if you are looking for a souvenir, check out the handmade pieces offered by the wood-carver who is usually stationed in the parking lot.

Spelunk in Style through Harrison's Cave, Barbados

(C) Major renovations completed in 2011 have greatly improved the visitor experience at this extensive and interesting cave system that winds its way through the limestone underneath Barbados. There's even a 40-foot waterfall. This is one of the island's most popular sights, so try to plan around the cruise-ship crowds.

Taste Some Barbados Rum at the Source

(D) Several Barbados rum distilleries offer tours, but Mount Gay Rum (distilled here since 1703) is the world's oldest surviving rum company. A tour of the historic rum distillery includes a tasting, of course, and the opportunity to purchase a bottle or two to take home. The actual distilling process is currently done in a larger, more modern plant in the north of the island.

Take a Picture of the Amazing Pitons, St. Lucia

(E) These twin peaks—which have become a symbol of St. Lucia—rise precipitously from the cobalt-blue Caribbean Sea just south of Soufrière. You can either stay in the Jalousie Plantation resort that stretches between them, climb them (with a certified guide), or just stop to take in the views to get your shot. But this UNESCO World Heritage Site is a don't-miss attraction on the island.

Sail into Marigot Bay, St. Lucia

The island's most beautiful harbor—a secluded bay within a bay—has been a movie location, a popular anchorage for yachts, and now a destination for landlubbers, too. The bay is lined with lovely resorts and villas and even has a small sandy beach. It offers a quiet getaway for the day or a week.

Take a Hike in the Barbados Flower Forest, Barbados

More than 100 species of tropical flora line the pathways of this 50-acre reserve in central Barbados. From the paths you can get a view of Mt. Hillaby (1,100 feet), the highest point on Barbados. It's a

TOP EXPERIENCES

low-key way to relax and recharge when you get tired of the beach.

Play a Round at Sandy Lane, Barbados

(F) On an island with several spectacular courses, this resort has three of the best. Golfers who are not guests at Sandy Lane can play on the Old Nine or the 18-hole Country Club Course. (The famous Green Monkey Course is reserved for resort guests or club members only.) Fees are high, but so is the quality of play.

Buy a Piece of Barbados

(G) If you're looking for a genuine local souvenir to take home, consider a piece of the blue or green pottery from Earthworks Pottery. This family-owned business has been producing beautiful handmade ceramics that are both decorative and usable since

1983. You're welcome to watch the potters at work.

Party with the Locals at the Oistins Fish Fry, Barbados

(H) One of the Caribbean's best street parties takes place in this south-coast fishing village every Friday night. The food is good and inexpensive (about $10 gets you a huge plate of grilled fish or fried chicken, along with rice or fries, salad, and macaroni pie). There's plenty to drink, as well as live music for listening and dancing.

Dine at Dasheene, St. Lucia

(I) If you have the opportunity to dine at the Ladera Resort's wonderful Dasheene restaurant, you'll be mesmerized by the view. Not only is the food good, but looking straight out between the fabulous Pitons is magical. It's a casual and quiet lunch spot that gets more

festive at night and is especially romantic at sunset.

Take It Out to Sea, St. Lucia

(J) The best way to get your first glimpse of the Pitons is on a sailing excursion or boat trip along the island's amazingly beautiful west coast. The sea route is also the best way to get from Rodney Bay or Vigie Cove down to Soufrière. Most of the daylong sailing excursions include some time on land to see the sights in the southern part of the island, as well as a snorkeling stop at a secluded beach.

Dance in the Street at the Gros Islet Jump-Up, St. Lucia

It seems that Fridays bring people out into the streets all over the Caribbean. This popular street party near Rodney Bay brings together both islanders and tourists to enjoy inexpensive barbecue,

dance to the latest music, or just relax and "lime." Don't be surprised if you see a spontaneous dance-off by local youth.

Dive in at Anse Chastanet, St. Lucia

Anse Chastanet, which is just around the bend from the Pitons and has a coral-lined wall right offshore that drops from 20 to more than 140 feet, is one of the island's best beach-entry dive sites. But there are many more opportunities for great diving near the Pitons, at Anse Cochon, or elsewhere on the western shore of the island.

IF YOU LIKE

A Romantic Rendezvous

Both Barbados and (especially) St. Lucia are popular destinations for weddings, honeymoons, second honeymoons, and other intimate getaways. Here are a few of our favorite romantic resorts, hotels, and inns:

The House, Barbados. A candlelit dinner on the beach and spa treatments for two are special treats at this luxurious, adults-only, beachfront enclave on the busy west coast.

Sweetfield Manor, Barbados. Perched on a ridge overlooking Carlisle Bay, this restored manse in a peaceful garden setting is, perhaps, the island's most delightful bed-and-breakfast inn.

Sandals Halcyon, St. Lucia. What's your idea of romantic? Lots of folks find this couples-only resort quite romantic.

Rendezvous, St. Lucia. For couples only, this all-inclusive beachfront resort in Castries offers a variety of accommodations and lots of activities.

Ti Kaye Village, St. Lucia. Quiet and remote, your private cottage peeps out of the hillside high above Anse Cochon.

Great Eating

The culinary experience in Barbados ranges from the finest gourmet dining to simple local fare—and everything in between. On St. Lucia the French influence is strong, but most chefs embrace the creole style. Try these special spots:

The Atlantis, Barbados. Lunch on the deck overlooking the ocean is the perfect choice when touring the east coast.

Daphne's, Barbados. Seafood and Italian fare are the specialties at this chic beachfront restaurant.

Fish Pot, Barbados. This seaside restaurant serves fresh seafood (obviously) and delicious Mediterranean specialties.

Waterside, Barbados. Waves crashing under the dining porch won't distract you from the elegant cuisine.

The Edge, St. Lucia. One of several excellent Rodney Bay restaurant choices, this one features "Eurobbean" cuisine.

Boucan, St. Lucia. Everything on the menu here has chocolate as an ingredient.

Dasheene Restaurant at Ladera, St. Lucia. Dinner at this terrace restaurant is memorable, but the close-up view of The Pitons is breathtaking during lunch or the cocktail hour.

Coal Pot, St. Lucia. The delicious meals prepared by Chef Xavier have been sought after since the early 1960s.

The Water

Both Barbados and St. Lucia offer a number of ways to enjoy the beautiful Caribbean Sea with very little or a whole lot of exertion, but always plenty of fun. Here are some suggestions:

Miami Beach, Barbados. This underrated south coast beach is broad, with white sand and low-to-medium surf; on the west coast beaches can become quite narrow after autumn storms.

Windsurfing, Barbados. Head for the southern tip of the island, one of the prime locations in the world for windsurfing—and it's kissing cousin, kitesurfing.

Reduit Beach, St. Lucia. This beach, at Rodney Bay, is the longest, broadest beach on St. Lucia; but the island's small beaches in quiet coves are equally appealing.

Diving and Snorkeling, St. Lucia. The best diving—wall, wreck, reef, and drift—is between The Pitons and Anse Cochon; beach-entry sites at Anse Chastanet and Anse Cochon appeal to divers and snorkelers alike.

Sea excursions, St. Lucia. A day sail along the coast between Rodney Bay or Vigie Cove and Soufrière is a perfect way to make your way to the island's distinctive natural and historic sites.

Sportfishing, St. Lucia. Fishing is generally catch-and-release, but the captain may let you bring a fish ashore for you (or the hotel chef) to prepare for your dinner.

Shopping

It's fun to bring home a memento for yourself and souvenirs for your friends and family. Here are some things you might like to take home:

Bajan souvenirs, Barbados. Best of Barbados sells products ranging from prints and housewares to arts and crafts—all made or designed on Barbados.

Rum, perfume, and more, Barbados. The departure lounge at Grantley Adams International Airport is a veritable shopping mall of duty-free goods.

Art, St. Lucia. Find original paintings and sculptures by St. Lucian artists, including world-renowned Llewellyn Xavier.

Sauces, spices, and more, St. Lucia. At Castries Market on Saturday morning, buy fresh fruit to enjoy during your stay and hot pepper sauce, vanilla extract, sticks of chocolate, bags of spices, straw mats, wood carvings, and a zillion other items to bring home.

WHEN TO GO

High season in Barbados and St. Lucia runs from mid-December through mid-April. If you wait until mid-May or June, prices may be 20% to 50% less, particularly in Barbados. The period from mid-August through late November is typically the least busy time in both Barbados and St. Lucia; however, some hotels on Barbados close for several weeks in September and/or October (the slowest months in the off-season) for annual maintenance and staff vacations. Some restaurants close during that time on both islands.

Temperatures are fairly consistent throughout the year in Barbados and St. Lucia. The "rainy season" (June–November), which coincides with the Atlantic hurricane season, seems hotter because there's more humidity. Major hurricanes are rare in Barbados because the island is 100 miles farther east than the rest of the Lesser Antilles chain, but they do happen.

Festivals and Events

In late April the popular **Barbados Reggae Festival** celebrates that infectious music with a week of live performances by both local and international bands. **Gospelfest** occurs in May, with performances by gospel headliners from around the world. Dating from the 19th century, **Crop Over**—a month-long festival similar to Carnival—begins in July and ends on **Kadooment Day** (a national holiday) to mark the end of the sugarcane harvest. In mid-November the annual **Food, Wine & Rum Festival** attracts international chefs, wine experts, and local rum ambassadors.

In April the **St. Lucia Golf Open** is an amateur tournament held at the St. Lucia Golf Resort & Country Club in Cap Estate. The **St. Lucia Jazz Festival,** featuring international stars, is held at various venues in early May; as it's the year's biggest event, finding accommodations during that week may be difficult. St. Lucia's summer **Carnival** is held in Castries beginning in late June, culminating in two days of music, dancing, and parading in mid-July. The **St. Lucia Billfishing Tournament,** which attracts anglers from far and wide, is held in late September or October.

October is Creole Heritage Month, which culminates in **Jounen Kwéyol Entenasyonnal** (International Creole Day)—featuring Creole food, music, games, and folklore performances in Castries and other locales—on the last Sunday of the month.

KIDS AND FAMILIES

Both islands have plenty of activities and attractions that will keep children of all ages (and their parents) busy and interested. Some resorts and hotels welcome children, others do not, and still others restrict kids to off-season visits. All but the very fancy (and most expensive) restaurants are kid-friendly.

In Barbados

Sandy Lane, the most fashionable of the island's resorts, welcomes children at any time with programs from all ages. Less pricey is **Tamarind,** a large resort hotel on Paynes Bay with children's programs and a great beach. On the south coast, **Casuarina Beach Resort, Turtle Beach Resort,** and **Bougainvillea Beach Resort** are all large properties with great beaches and lots of programs and activities for kids.

Dining out with the family is not an issue, as Barbados has more restaurants than you can count serving any type of cuisine you have in mind. The Friday night **Oistins Fish Fry** is definitely family-friendly.

The whole family will enjoy—and be amazed by—the tram ride through **Harrison's Cave.** At the **Barbados Wildlife Reserve** the green monkeys, parrots, and other exotica on the loose will thrill kids. **Folkestone Marine Park** has a playground, basketball court, picnic area, beach with lifeguards, and an underwater snorkeling trail.

In St. Lucia

While St. Lucia has earned its "most romantic" reputation, children are welcome at most St. Lucia resorts, hotels, and villa communities except for a handful of adults-only resorts. **Smugglers Cove Resort** is a huge, family-friendly property. **Cotton Bay Village** and **Windjammer Landing** are other good choices, although **Bay Gardens Beach Resort** may be the best bet. In the south, **Jalousie, Sugar Beach** has children's programs; **Coconut Bay Beach Resort,** near the airport in Vieux Fort, devotes half the property to families.

If your resort is not all-inclusive, Rodney Bay's family-friendly restaurants include **The Lime,** a casual bistro with all-day dining and reasonable prices.

Take a **catamaran cruise** to Soufrière from Rodney Bay for a wonderful day on the water. Be sure to visit **Our Planet Centre** at La Place Carenage in Castries, an interactive science center. Teens will be thrilled by a **zip-line** ride through the rain forest or **horseback riding** on the beach.

GREAT ITINERARIES

In Barbados

Barbados from Bottom to Top. You must visit Harrison's Cave—a unique natural wonder in the Caribbean. The underground tram ride through the cave will thrill the whole family. Afterward, visit Flower Forest and Orchid World, two beautiful gardens that are nearby and have snack bars where lunch is available. On your way home, stop at Gun Hill Signal Station for a panoramic view of the whole southern half of the island.

A Day in Barbados's Wild Wild East. From Speightstown, head east to Farley Hill and the Barbados Wildlife Reserve before continuing on to St. Nicholas Abbey, a beautifully restored and furnished greathouse that's definitely worth a stop. Nearby, the scenic overlook at Cherry Tree Hill provides a spectacular view of the whole Atlantic coast—definitely a photo op. Then, the ride along the coastal road, which hugs the Atlantic Ocean, is particularly scenic. You may glimpse some daredevil surfers at Bathsheba Soup Bowl! Stop for lunch—perhaps a Bajan buffet—at a cliff-side inn before heading back through the center of the island. From south-coast hotels, do the trip in reverse.

A Day at Sea Along the West Coast of Barbados. Catamaran party boats—*Tiami* and *Cool Run-nings*—depart from Bridgetown, near the cruise-ship terminal, for a full day of sailing, snorkeling, and swimming with turtles—a unique and fascinating experience. Lunch and drinks are included. Alternatively, explore wrecks and reefs 100 to 150 feet underwater without getting wet on an Atlantis Submarine cruise. Day trips on the submarine are fascinating; but on the evening cruise the sub's bright spotlights illuminate interesting sea creatures that only appear at night.

A Day (and Evening) on Barbados's South Coast. Escape the hot sun at the Barbados Museum in the Historic Garrison District, a World Heritage Site, and at the nearby George Washington House in Bush Hill—yes, he slept here. Then, head for busy St. Lawrence Gap and choose a place for lunch. If it's Friday night, stick around for the Oistins Fish Fry—a street party where you can buy an inexpensive meal of barbecued fish or chicken, sides, cold drinks, music, and see lots of people—locals and visitors alike.

A Day (and Evening) on Barbados's West Coast. At Mullins Beach, near Speightstown, you can rent watersports equipment and beach chairs and find all-day refreshments at Mullin's Restaurant. At night, head for First and Second streets

in Holetown. Pick any restaurant—they're all good—and end the evening at the lively Lexy's Piano Bar.

In St. Lucia

A Day in St. Lucia's South. Although many of the island's resorts are in the north, some of St. Lucia's most interesting natural attractions are in the south—specifically, in and around Soufrière. From Castries, take a sailing trip down the west coast and admire the eye-popping views of the Pitons as you come into Soufrière Harbour. Tour the sulfurous La Soufrière Drive-In Volcano, the spectacular Diamond Botanical Garden with its mineral-encrusted waterfall, and the historic Morne Coubaril agricultural estate (which also has a zip-line ride). Enjoy a creole lunch at Fond Doux Estate, where you can also walk along the garden pathways and learn how to turn cacao beans into delicious St. Lucian chocolate.

A Day in St. Lucia's Rain Forest. One of the island's best natural attractions is its vast rain forest. There are two ways to enjoy it—from above or below. Kids (and the young at heart) may prefer a thrilling zip-line trip through the forest canopy, while others may prefer the more sedate aerial tram that takes a slow, two-hour tour through the forest; both of these attractions are in the Castries Waterworks Rain Forest east of Rodney Bay. Those looking for a more down-to-earth experience may want to take a guided hike in the Edmund Forest Reserve in the central part of the island, but you'll need to hire a guide from the Forest & Lands Department.

A Day of Shopping in Castries, St. Lucia. St. Lucia's capital has one of the most extensive market complexes in the Caribbean. You'll find row upon picturesque row of tropical fruits and vegetables in the orange-roofed produce market, where vendors also sell spices, vanilla, and locally bottled sauces at bargain prices. Next door and across the street you'll find huge indoor markets with all kinds of souvenirs ranging from cheesy to handcrafted beauties. For duty-free shopping, try Place Carenage or Point Seraphine.

A Day at St. Lucia's Pigeon Island. Take a taxi, minibus, rental car, or ferry from Rodney Bay to Pigeon Island National Park—a historic site and natural playground at the island's northwestern tip. You'll find ruins of 18th-century batteries and garrisons scattered around the 44-acre grounds, along with a multimedia display of the islands ecology and history in the museum and two small beaches. Bring a picnic or buy refreshments at the snack bar.

WEDDINGS AND HONEYMOONS

There's no question that Barbados and St. Lucia (especially the latter) rank among the Caribbean's foremost honeymoon destinations. The picturesque beaches, turquoise water, swaying palm trees, balmy tropical breezes, and perpetual summer sunshine put people in the mood for love. St. Lucia may be the most popular wedding and honeymoon destination in the Caribbean; but at resorts on both islands you'll find wedding planners who can help you put together your perfect special day.

The Big Day

Choosing the Perfect Place. When choosing a location, remember that you really have two choices to make: the ceremony location and where to have the reception, if you're having one. For the former, there are beaches, bluffs overlooking beaches, gardens, private residences, resort lawns, and, of course, places of worship. As for the reception, there are these same choices, as well as restaurants. If you decide to go outdoors, remember the seasons—yes, the Caribbean has seasons. If you're planning a wedding outdoors, be sure you have a backup plan in case it rains. Also, if you're planning an outdoor wedding at sunset—which is very popular—be sure you match the time of your ceremony to the time the sun sets—which is at about 6 pm year-round.

Finding a Wedding Planner. If you and your loved one plan to invite more than a minister to your wedding ceremony, seriously consider an on-island wedding planner who can help select a location, coordinate the event, recommend a florist as well as a photographer, help plan the menu, and suggest any local traditions to incorporate into your ceremony. Alternatively, many resorts have their own on-site wedding planners and some, such as the three Sandals resorts on St. Lucia, offer free weddings with a honeymoon package.

Legal Requirements. There are no minimal residency requirements on both Barbados and St. Lucia, and no blood tests are required in either island. In Barbados you must appear in person to obtain a wedding license, but the formalities can often be completed in less than half an hour at the Ministry of Home Affairs in Bridgetown; the cost is less than $100. In St. Lucia you can either get married after being on the island for three days (for $125), or you can obtain a "special" license anytime after arrival—even the same day you land—for $200. Plan on $40 in additional fees on top of the license cost. On both islands you must provide valid pass-

ports for identification and a certified spousal death certificate or divorce decree if you were previously married. On Barbados an official marriage officer (or magistrate or minister) must perform the actual ceremony.

Wedding Attire. In the Caribbean basically anything goes, from long, formal dresses with trains to white bikinis. Floral sundresses are fine, too. Men can wear tuxedos or a simple pair of solid-color slacks with a nice white linen shirt. If you want formal dress and tuxedo, it's usually better to bring your formal attire with you.

Photographs. Deciding whether to use the photographer supplied by your resort or an independent photographer is an important choice. Resorts that host a lot of weddings usually have their own photographers, but you can also find independent, professional island-based photographers; an independent wedding planner will know the best in the area. Look at the portfolio (many photographers now have websites), and decide whether this person can give you the kind of memories you desire. If you're satisfied with the photographer that your resort uses, then make sure you see proofs and order prints before leaving the island.

The Honeymoon

Do you want champagne and strawberries delivered to your room each morning? A maze of a swimming pool in which to float? A five-star restaurant in which to dine? Then a resort is the way to go, and both Barbados and St. Lucia have options in different price ranges. Whether you want a luxurious experience or a more modest one, you'll certainly find a perfect romantic escape.

On Barbados, **Cobbler's Cove Hotel** is sophisticated and classy, particularly its splurge-worthy penthouse suites. The **Atlantis Hotel** blends historic atmosphere with modern amenities in a cliff-side location on the rugged east coast. While **The Crane** is huge and the resort remote, it is located high above the ocean and next to one of the island's loveliest beaches.

On St. Lucia, **Jade Mountain Club** is the crème de la crème; every "sanctuary" has its own extravagant infinity pool. **Jalousie Plantation, Sugar Beach** is a full-service, upscale resort right between the Pitons. Elegantly rustic, **Ladera** is a sophisticated small inn perched 1,100 feet above the sea between the Pitons.

DID YOU KNOW?

Covered with lush rain forest, St. Lucia has a good amount of biodiversity, including over 1,300 native plant species.

Barbados

WORD OF MOUTH

"Imagine an ideal day on a Caribbean island with beautiful beaches and as much sightseeing and activities as you desire. Add wonderful food! You're in Barbados."

—Knowing

By Jane E.
Zarem

BARBADOS STANDS APART from its neighbors in the Lesser Antilles archipelago, the chain of islands that stretches in a graceful arc from the Virgin Islands to Trinidad. Barbados is isolated in the Atlantic Ocean, 100 miles (160 km) due east of St. Lucia, its nearest neighbor.

Geologically, most of the Lesser Antilles are the peaks of a volcanic mountain range, whereas Barbados is the top of a single, relatively flat protuberance of coral and limestone—the source of building blocks for many a plantation manor. Several of those historic "great houses," in fact, have been carefully restored. Some are open to visitors.

Bridgetown, both capital city and commercial center, is on the southwest coast of pear-shape Barbados. Most of the 280,000 Bajans (*Bay*-juns, which derives from the phonetic British pronunciation of Barbadian) live and work in and around Bridgetown, elsewhere in St. Michael Parish, or along the idyllic west coast or busy south coast. Others reside in tiny villages that dot the interior landscape. Broad sandy beaches, craggy cliffs, and numerous coves make up the coastline, and the interior is consumed by forested hills and gullies and acre upon acre of sugarcane.

Without question, Barbados is the "most British" island in the Caribbean. In contrast to the turbulent colonial past experienced by neighboring islands, which included repeated conflicts between France and Britain for dominance and control, British rule in Barbados carried on uninterrupted for 340 years—from the first established British settlement in 1627 until independence was granted in 1966. That's not to say, of course, that there weren't significant struggles in Barbados, as elsewhere in the Caribbean, between the British landowners and their African-born slaves and other indentured servants.

With that unfortunate period of slavery relegated to the history books, the British influence on Barbados remains strong today in local manners, attitudes, customs, and politics—tempered, of course, by the characteristically warm nature of the Bajan people. In keeping with British-born traditions, many Bajans worship at the Anglican church, afternoon tea is a ritual, cricket is the national pastime (a passion, most admit), dressing for dinner is a firmly entrenched tradition, and patrons at some bars are as likely to order a Pimm's Cup or a shandy as a rum and Coke. And yet, Barbados is hardly stuffy—this is still the Caribbean, after all.

Tourist facilities are concentrated on the west coast in St. James and St. Peter parishes (appropriately dubbed the Platinum Coast) and on the south coast in Christ Church Parish. Traveling along the west coast to historic Holetown, the site of the first British settlement, and continuing north to the city of Speightstown, you can find posh beachfront resorts, luxurious private villas, and fine restaurants enveloped by lush gardens and tropical foliage. The trendier, more commercial south coast offers competitively priced hotels and beach resorts, and its St. Lawrence Gap area is jam-packed with shops, restaurants, and nightlife. The relatively wide-open spaces along the southeast coast are proving ripe for development, and some wonderful inns and hotels already take advantage of the intoxicatingly beautiful ocean vistas. For their own vacations, though, Bajans escape to the rugged east coast, where the Atlantic surf pounds the dramatic shoreline with unrelenting force.

All in all, Barbados is a sophisticated tropical island with a rich history, lodgings to suit every taste and pocketbook, and plenty to pique your interest both day and night—whether you're British or not!

PLANNING

WHEN TO GO

Barbados is busiest in the high season, which extends from December 15 through April 15. Off-season hotel rates can be half of those required during the busy period. During the high season, too, a few hotels may require you to buy a meal plan, which is usually not required in the low season. As noted in the listings, some hotels close in September and October, the slowest months of the off-season, for annual renovations. Some restaurants may close for brief periods within that time frame as well.

FESTIVALS AND EVENTS

In mid-January the **Barbados Jazz Festival** is a weeklong event jammed with performances by international artists, jazz legends, and local talent.

In February the weeklong **Holetown Festival** is held at the fairgrounds to commemorate the date in 1627 when the first European settlers arrived in Barbados.

Gospelfest occurs in May and hosts performances by gospel headliners from around the world.

LOGISTICS

Getting to Barbados: Several airlines fly nonstop to Barbados, or you may have to connect in Miami or San Juan. Grantley Adams International Airport (BGI) is in Christ Church Parish on the south coast; the airport is about 15 minutes from hotels situated along the south coast, 45 minutes from the west coast, and 30 minutes from Bridgetown.

Hassle Factor: Low.

On the Ground: Ground transportation is available immediately outside the customs area. Airport taxis aren't metered, but fares are regulated ($38–$40 to Speightstown, $30–$35 to west-coast hotels, $16–$22 to south-coast hotels). Be sure, however, to establish the fare before getting into the taxi and confirm whether the price quoted is in U.S. or Barbadian dollars.

Getting Around the Island: If you are staying in an isolated area, you may want or need to rent a car; but bus service is good, especially between Bridgetown and stops along the west and south coasts. Taxis, of course, are always an option.

Dating from the 19th century, **Crop Over,** a monthlong festival similar to Carnival that begins in July and ends on **Kadooment Day** (a national holiday), marks the end of the sugarcane harvest.

In mid-November, the annual **Food, Wine & Rum Festival** attracts international chefs, wine experts, and local rum ambassadors who provide demonstrations and tastings at some of the island's most exciting venues.

DO I NEED A CAR?

If you are staying in an isolated area, you may want or need to rent a car, but bus service is good, especially between Bridgetown and shops along the west and south coasts. Taxis may suffice (they operate 24 hours a day and charge fixed rates but must be called) for those travelers staying in busy resort areas. *For more information on car travel in Barbados and car rentals, see ⇨ Car Travel in Travel Smart.*

ACCOMMODATIONS

Most people stay either in luxurious enclaves on the fashionable west coast—north of Bridgetown—or on the action-packed south coast with easy access to small, independent restaurants, bars, and nightclubs. A few inns on the remote southeast and east coasts offer ocean views and tranquillity, but those on the east coast don't have good swimming beaches nearby. Prices in Barbados are sometimes twice as high in season as during the quieter months. Most hotels include no meals in their rates; some include breakfast, many offer a meal plan, some require you to purchase the meal plan in the high season, and a few offer all-inclusive packages.

Resorts: Great resorts run the gamut—from unpretentious to knock-your-socks-off—in terms of size, intimacy, amenities, and price. Many are well suited to families.

Small Inns: A few small, cozy inns may be found in the east and southeast regions of the island.

Villas and Condos: Families and long-term visitors may choose from a wide variety of condos (everything from busy time-share resorts to more sedate vacation complexes). Villas and villa complexes can be luxurious, simple, or something in between.

HOTEL AND RESTAURANT PRICES
Prices in the restaurant reviews are the average cost of a main course at dinner or, if dinner is not served, at lunch; taxes and service charges are generally included. Prices in the hotel reviews are the lowest cost of a standard double room in high season, excluding taxes, service charges, and meal plans (except at all-inclusives). Prices for rentals are the lowest per-night cost for a one-bedroom unit in high season.

SAFETY
Crime isn't a major problem in Barbados, but take normal precautions. Lock your room, and don't leave valuables—particularly passports, tickets, and wallets—in plain sight or unattended on the beach. Use your hotel safe. For personal safety, avoid walking on the beach or on unlighted streets at night. Lock your rental car, and don't pick up hitchhikers. Using or trafficking in illegal drugs is strictly prohibited in Barbados. Any offense is punishable by a hefty fine, imprisonment, or both.

WEDDINGS
There are no minimum residency requirements to get married; however, you need to obtain a marriage license from the Ministry of Home Affairs (☎246/228–8950). If either was divorced or widowed, appropriate paperwork must be presented to obtain the license.

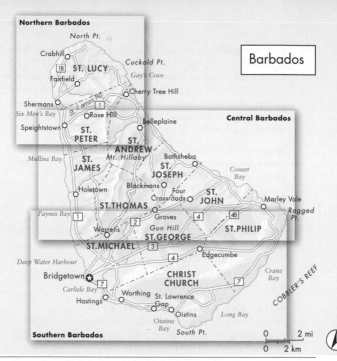

EXPLORING BARBADOS

The terrain changes dramatically from any one of the island's 11 parishes to the next, and so does the pace. Bridgetown, the capital, is a somewhat sophisticated city. West-coast resorts and private estates ooze luxury, whereas the small villages and vast sugar plantations found throughout central Barbados reflect the island's history. The relentless Atlantic surf shaped the cliffs of the dramatic east coast, and the northeast is called Scotland because of its hilly landscape and broad vistas. Along the lively south coast, the daytime hustle and bustle produce a palpable energy that continues well into the night at countless restaurants, dance clubs, and nightspots.

BRIDGETOWN

This bustling capital city is a major duty-free port with a compact shopping area. The principal thoroughfare is Broad Street, which leads west from National Heroes Square.

TOP REASONS TO GO

Great Resorts: They run the gamut—from unpretentious to over-the-top—in terms of size, intimacy, amenities, and price. Choose one on the lively south coast or on the ritzy west coast.

Great Golf: Golfers can choose from some of the best championship courses in the Caribbean—including a public course on the south coast with very reasonable greens fees.

Restaurants Galore: Great food includes everything from street-party barbecue to the finest dining.

Wide Range of Activities: With a broad assortment of land and water sports, sightseeing options, historic sites, cultural festivals, and nightlife, there's always plenty to do in Barbados.

Welcoming Locals: Bajans are friendly, welcoming, helpful, and hospitable. You'll like them; they'll like you.

WHAT TO SEE

The Careenage. In the early days, Bridgetown's natural harbor and gathering place is where schooners were turned on their sides (careened) to be scraped of barnacles and repainted. Today, the Careenage serves as a marina for pleasure yachts and excursion boats. A boardwalk skirts the north side of the Careenage; on the south side, a lovely esplanade has pathways and benches for pedestrians and a statue of Errol Barrow, the first prime minister of Barbados. The Chamberlain Bridge and the Charles Duncan O'Neal Bridge cross the Careenage. ⊠ *Bridgetown, St. Michael.*

National Heroes Square. Across Broad Street from the Parliament Buildings and bordered by High and Trafalgar streets, this triangular plaza marks the center of town. Its monument to Lord Horatio Nelson (who was in Barbados only briefly in 1777 as a 19-year-old navy lieutenant) predates Nelson's Column in London's Trafalgar Square by 36 years. Also here are a war memorial and a fountain that commemorates the advent of running water on Barbados in 1865. ⊠ *Broad St., across from Parliament, Bridgetown, St. Michael.*

Nidhe Israel Synagogue. Providing for the spiritual needs of one of the oldest Jewish congregations in the Western Hemisphere, this synagogue was formed by Jews who left Brazil in the 1620s and introduced sugarcane to Barbados. The adjoining cemetery has tombstones dating from

A steelpan band plays at the Cropover Festival

the 1630s. The original house of worship, built in 1654, was destroyed in an 1831 hurricane, rebuilt in 1833, and restored with the assistance of the Barbados National Trust in 1987. Friday-night services are held during the winter months, but the building is open to the public year-round. Shorts are not acceptable during services but may be worn at other times. ✉ *Synagogue La., Bridgetown, St. Michael* ☎ *246/436–6869* 💰 *Donation requested* ⊙ *Weekdays 9–4.*

Parliament Buildings. Overlooking National Heroes Square in the center of town, these Victorian buildings were constructed around 1870 to house the British Commonwealth's third-oldest parliament. A series of stained-glass windows depicts British monarchs from James I to Victoria. The National Heroes Gallery & Museum is located in the West Wing. ✉ *National Heroes Sq., Trafalgar St., Bridgetown, St. Michael* ☎ *246/427–2019* 💰 *Donations welcome* ⊙ *Tours weekdays at 11 and 2, when parliament isn't in session.*

Queen's Park. Northeast of Bridgetown, Queen's Park contains one of the island's two immense baobab trees. Brought to Barbados from Guinea, West Africa, around 1738, this tree has a girth of more than 60 feet. Queen's Park Art Gallery, managed by the National Culture Foundation, is the island's largest gallery; exhibits change monthly. Queen's Park House, built in 1783 and the historic home of the British troop commander, has been converted into a

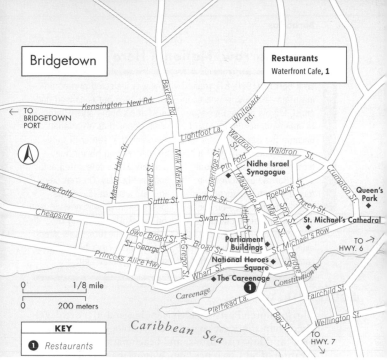

Bridgetown

Restaurants
Waterfront Cafe, **1**

TO ←
BRIDGETOWN
PORT

Kensington New Rd.

Baxters Rd.

Lightfoot La.

Whitepark Rd.

Waldron St.

Waldron St.

Pin Fold

Nidhe Israel Synagogue

Coleridge St.

Milk Market

Magazine La.

Roebuck St.

Crumpton St.

Queen's Park

Church St.

Mason Hall St.

Reed St.

Suttle St.

James St.

High St.

Spry St.

Marhill St.

St. Michael's Cathedral

Lakes Folly

Swan St.

Parliament Buildings

St. Michael's Row

TO →
HWY. 6

Cheapside

Lower Broad St.

St. George St.

McGregor St.

Broad St.

National Heroes Square

Bridge St.

Princess Alice Hwy.

Wharf St.

◆**The Careenage** **❶**

Constitution Rd.

Fairchild St.

Careenage

Pierhead La.

Bay St.

Wellington St.

Caribbean Sea

TO
HWY. 7

0   1/8 mile
0   200 meters

KEY
❶ *Restaurants*

theater, with an exhibition room on the lower floor and a restaurant. Originally called King's House, the name was changed upon Queen Victoria's accession to the throne. ✉ *Constitution Rd., Bridgetown, St. Michael* ☎ *246/427–2345 gallery* ⬚ *Free* ⊘ *Daily 9–5.*

St. Michael's Cathedral. Although no one has proved it, George Washington is said to have worshipped here in 1751 during his only trip outside the United States. By then the original structure was nearly a century old. Destroyed twice by hurricanes, it was rebuilt in 1784 and again in 1831. ✉ *Spry St., east of National Heroes Sq., Bridgetown, St. Michael.*

RENTING A CAR. If you're staying on the remote southeast or east coasts, you may want to rent a car for your entire stay. In more populated areas, where taxis and public transportation are readily available, you might rent a car for a day or two of exploring on your own. Rates start at about $55 per day during the high season.

CLOSE UP

Errol Barrow, National Hero

Errol Barrow (1920–87), trained in Britain as a lawyer and economist, led his native Barbados to independence in 1966 and became the island nation's first prime minister. During his initial tenure, which lasted through 1976, Barrow expanded the tourist industry, reduced the island's dependence on sugar, introduced national health insurance and social security, and extended free education to the community college level. Barrow was reelected prime minister in 1986 but collapsed and died at his home a year later. He is honored as a national hero and the "Father of Independence," and his birthday—January 21—is celebrated as a national holiday. On that day in 2007 a 9-foot-tall statue of Errol Barrow was erected on the esplanade along the Careenage, picturesquely sited between the city's two bridges and facing Parliament.

SOUTH COAST

Christ Church Parish, which is far busier and more developed than the west coast, is chockablock with condos, high- and low-rise hotels, and beach parks. It is also the location of St. Lawrence Gap, with its many places to eat, drink, shop, and party. As you move southeast, the broad, flat terrain comprises acre upon acre of cane fields, interrupted only by an occasional oil rig and a few tiny villages. Along the byways are colorful chattel houses, which were the traditional homes of tenant farmers. Historically, these typically Barbadian, ever-expandable small buildings were built so they could be dismantled and moved, as required.

WHAT TO SEE

C **Barbados Concorde Experience.** Opened to the public in April
★ 2007, the Concorde Experience focuses on the British Airways Concorde G-BOAE (Alpha Echo, for short) that for many years flew between London and Barbados and has made its permanent home here. Besides boarding the sleek supersonic aircraft itself, you'll learn about how the technology was developed and how this plane differed from other jets. You may or may not have been able to fly the Concorde when it was still plying the Atlantic, but this is your chance to experience some unique modern history—up close and personal. ⊠ *Grantley Adams International Airport, adjacent to the terminal building, Christ Church* ☎ *246/420–7738* ⊕ *www.barbadosconcorde.com* 🖃 *$20* ☉ *Daily 9–5.*

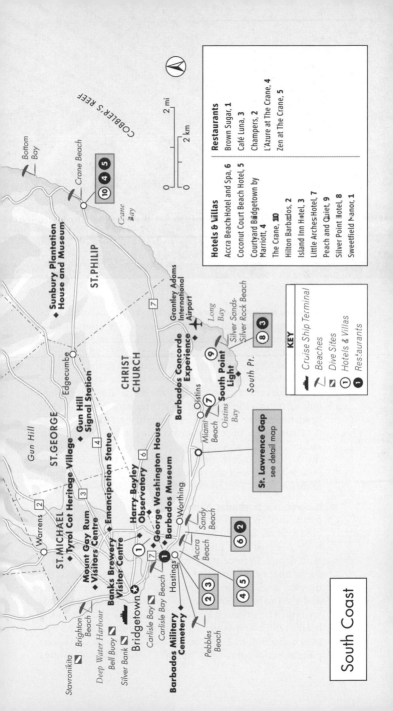

South Coast

COBBLER'S REEF

Bottom Bay

Crane Beach

10 4 5

Crane Bay

ST.PHILIP

◆ Sunbury Plantation House and Museum

Edgecumbe

ST.GEORGE

Gun Hill

◆ Gun Hill Signal Station

2

Warrens

ST.MICHAEL

◆ Tyrol Cot Heritage Village

3

◆ Mount Gay Rum Visitors Centre

Banks Brewery Visitor Centre

7

1

Bridgetown ★

Carlisle Bay

Carlisle Bay Beach

Hastings

Barbados Military Cemetery ◆

Pebbles Beach

◆ Emancipation Statue

◆ Harry Bayley Observatory

4

6

◆ George Washington House

◆ Barbados Museum

Worthing

Accra Beach

Sandy Beach

6 2

2 3

4 5

CHRIST CHURCH

St. Lawrence Gap see detail map

◆ Barbados Concorde Experience

6

Oistins

7

Miami Beach

Oistins Bay

Granley Adams International Airport

★

7

9

South Point Light

Long Bay

Silver Sands-Silver Rock Beach

South Pt.

8 3

Stavronikita ⬮

Brighton Beach ⬮

Deep Water Harbour ⚓

Bell Buoy ⬮

Silver Bank ⬮

2 mi

2 km

0

0

KEY

⚓ Cruise Ship Terminal

⬮ Beaches

⬮ Dive Sites

① Hotels & Villas

❶ Restaurants

Hotels & Villas

Accra Beach Hotel and Spa, **6**
Coconut Court Beach Hotel, **5**
Courtyard Bridgetown by Marriott, **4**
The Crane, **10**
Hilton Barbados, **2**
Island Inn Hotel, **3**
Little Arches Hotel, **7**
Peach and Quiet, **9**
Silver Point Hotel, **8**
Sweetfield Manor, **1**

Restaurants

Brown Sugar, **1**
Café Luna, **3**
Champers, **2**
L'Azure at The Crane, **4**
Zen at The Crane, **5**

A supersonic Concorde on display at the Concorde Experience

Barbados Military Cemetery. The cemetery, also referred to as the Garrison Military Cemetary, is near the shore behind historic St. Ann's Fort. First used in 1780, when the area was pretty much marshland, the dead were placed in shallow graves or simply left on top of the ground where, within a few short days, many were absorbed into the swamp. In the early 20th century, a number of the remaining graves were dug up to provide room for oil storage tanks; the salvaged headstones were placed on a cenotaph, erected in 1920–24. A "Cross of Sacrifice" was erected in 1982 to honor all the military dead; a second cenotaph, erected in 2003, honors the Barbadian merchant seamen who died in World War II. ⊠ *Graves End, near the Hilton Barbados, Needham's Point, St. Michael* ☎ *246/426–0982* ⊠ *Free* ⊘ *Daily 8–4.*

★ **Fodor'sChoice** **Barbados Museum.** This intriguing museum, ☾ established in 1933 in the former British Military Prison (1815) in the historic St. Ann's Garrison area, has artifacts from Arawak days (around 400 BC) along with galleries that depict 19th-century military history and everyday social history. You can see cane-harvesting tools, wedding dresses, ancient (and frightening) dentistry instruments, and slave sale accounts kept in spidery copperplate handwriting. The museum's Harewood Gallery showcases the island's flora and fauna, its Cunard Gallery has a permanent collection of 20th-century Barbadian and Caribbean paintings and engravings, and its Connell Gallery features

European decorative arts. Additional galleries include one with exhibits targeted to children. The Shilstone Memorial Library houses rare West Indian documentation—archival documents, genealogical records, photos, books, and maps—dating back to the 17th century. The museum also has a gift shop and a café. ✉ *St. Ann's Garrison, Hwy. 7, Garrison, St. Michael* ☎ *246/427–0201* ⊕ *www.barbmuse. org.bb* ☑ *$7.50* ⊙ *Mon.–Sat. 9–5, Sun. 2–6.*

Codrington Theological College. An impressive stand of royal palms lines the road leading to the coral-stone buildings and serene grounds of Codrington College, an Anglican theological seminary opened in 1745 on a cliff overlooking Conset Bay. The benefactor of the college was Christopher Codrington III (1668–1710), a former governor-general of the Leeward Islands whose antislavery views were unpopular in the plantocracy of the times. In an effort to "Christianize" the slaves and provide them with a general education, Codrington's will established that "300 negroes at least" would always be allowed to study at the institution; the planters who acted as trustees, however, were loath to teach the slaves how to read and write. You're welcome to tour the buildings, explore the grounds, and walk the nature trails. Keep in mind, though, that beach wear is not appropriate here. ✉ *Sargeant St., Conset Bay, St. John* ☎ *246/423–1140* ⊕ *www.codrington.org* ☑ *Donations welcome* ⊙ *Daily 10–4.*

Emancipation Statue. This powerful statue of a slave—whose raised hands, with broken chains hanging from each wrist, evoke both contempt and victory—is commonly referred to as the Bussa Statue. Bussa was the man who, in 1816, led the first slave rebellion on Barbados. The work of Barbadian sculptor Karl Brodhagen, the statue was erected in 1985 to commemorate the emancipation of the slaves in 1834. ✉ *St. Barnabas Roundabout, intersection of ABC Hwy. and Hwy. 5, Haggatt Hall, St. Michael.*

Ⓒ **George Washington House.** George Washington slept here!
★ This carefully restored and refurbished 18th-century plantation house in Bush Hill was the only place where the future first president of the United States actually slept outside North America. Teenage George and his older half-brother Lawrence, who was suffering from tuberculosis and seeking treatment on the island, rented this house overlooking Carlisle Bay for two months in 1751. Opened to the public in January 2007, the lower floor of the house and the kitchen

have period furnishings; the upper floor is a museum with both permanent and temporary exhibits that display artifacts of 18th-century Barbadian life. The site includes an original 1719 windmill and bathhouse, along with a stable added to the property in the 1800s. Guided tours begin with an informative 15-minute film appropriately called *George Washington in Barbados.* ⊠ *Bush Hill, Garrison, St. Michael* ☎ *246/228–5461* ⊕ *www.georgewashington-barbados.org* 🕮 *$10* ⊙ *Mon.–Sat. 9–4:30.*

🕒 **Harry Bayley Observatory.** The Barbados Astronomical Society headquarters since 1963, the observatory has a Celestron 14-inch reflector telescope—the only one in the eastern Caribbean. Visitors can view the moon, stars, planets, and other astronomical objects that may not be visible from North America or Europe. Call ahead to make sure it's open. ⊠ *Off Hwy. 6, Clapham, St. Michael* ☎ *246/426–1317, 246/422–2394* 🕮 *$5* ⊙ *Fri. 8:30 pm–11:30 pm.*

Ragged Point. The easternmost point of Barbados is the location of East Coast Light, one of four strategically placed lighthouses on the island. Although civilization in the form of new homes is encroaching on this once-remote location, the view of the entire Atlantic coastline of Barbados is still spectacular—and the cool ocean breeze is beautifully refreshing on a hot, sunny day. ⊠ *Marley Vale, St. Philip.*

South Point Light. This is the oldest of four lighthouses on Barbados. Assembled on the island in 1852, after being displayed at London's Great Exhibition the previous year, the landmark lighthouse is just east of Miami (Enterprise) Beach and marks the southernmost point of land on Barbados. The 89-foot tower, with its distinguishing red and white horizontal stripes, is closed to the public; but visitors may freely walk about the site, take photos, and enjoy the view. ⊠ *South Point, Atlantic Shores, Christ Church.*

★ **Fodor's**Choice **Sunbury Plantation House and Museum.** Lovingly rebuilt after a 1995 fire destroyed everything but the thick flint-and-stone walls, Sunbury offers an elegant glimpse of the 18th and 19th centuries on a Barbadian sugar estate. Period furniture, old prints, and a collection of horse-drawn carriages lend an air of authenticity. A buffet luncheon is served daily in the courtyard for $31 per person. A five-course candlelight dinner is served ($100 per person, reservations required) two nights a week at the 200-year-old mahogany dining table in the Sunbury dining room.

Sunbury Plantation House

✉ *Off Hwy. 5, Six Cross Roads, St. Philip* ☎ *246/423–6270*
🌐 *www.barbadosgreathouse.com* 🎟 *$7.50* 🕐 *Daily 9–4:30.*

Tyrol Cot Heritage Village. This coral-stone cottage just south of Bridgetown was constructed in 1854 and is preserved as an example of period architecture. In 1929 it became the home of Sir Grantley Adams, the first premier of Barbados and the namesake of its international airport. Part of the Barbados National Trust, the cottage is filled with antiques and memorabilia that belonged to the late Sir Grantley and Lady Adams. It's also the centerpiece of an outdoor "living museum," where artisans and craftsmen have their workshops in a cluster of traditional chattel houses. Workshops are open, crafts are for sale, and refreshments are available at the "rum shop" primarily during the winter season and when cruise ships are in port. ✉ *Rte. 2, Codrington Hill, St. Michael* ☎ *246/424–2074* 🎟 *$5.75* 🕐 *Weekdays 9–5.*

CENTRAL BARBADOS

On the west coast, in St. James Parish, Holetown marks the center of the Platinum Coast—so called for the vast number of luxurious resorts and mansions that face the sea. Holetown is also where Captain John Powell and the crew of the British ship *Olive Blossom* landed on May 14, 1625, to claim the island for King James I (who had actually died of a stroke seven weeks earlier). On the east coast, the crashing Atlantic surf has eroded the shoreline,

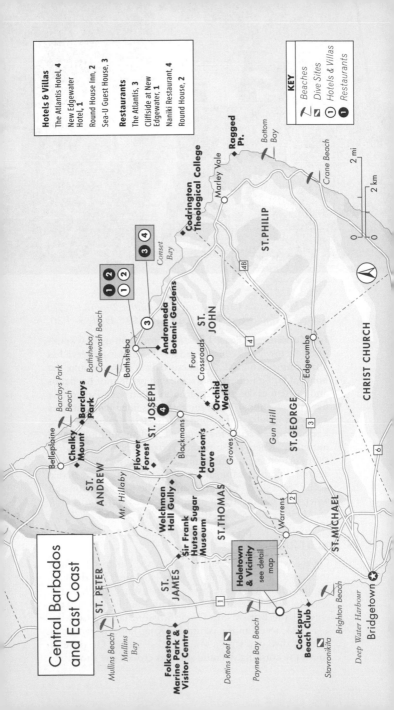

Central Barbados and East Coast

Hotels & Villas
The Atlantis Hotel, 4
New Edgewater Hotel, 1
Round House Inn, 2
Sea-U Guest House, 3

Restaurants
The Atlantis, 3
Cliffside at New Edgewater, 1
Naniki Restaurant, 4
Round House, 2

KEY
↗ Beaches
▨ Dive Sites
① Hotels & Villas
❶ Restaurants

ST. PETER

ST. JAMES

ST. ANDREW

ST. JOSEPH

ST. THOMAS

ST. JOHN

ST. PHILIP

ST. GEORGE

ST. MICHAEL

CHRIST CHURCH

Mullins Bay
Mullins Beach

Belleplaine

Chalky Mount

Mt. Hillaby

Barclays Park
Barclays Park Beach

Bathsheba/Cattlewash Beach

Bathsheba

Andromeda Botanic Gardens

Conset Bay

Codrington Theological College

Ragged Pt.

Bottom Bay

Crane Beach

Marley Vale

Four Crossroads

Orchid World

Flower Forest

Blackmans

Harrison's Cave

Welchman Hall Gully

Sir Frank Hutson Sugar Museum

Groves

Gun Hill

Edgecumbe

Folkestone Marine Park & Visitor Centre

Dottins Reef

Paynes Bay Beach

Holetown & Vicinity
see detail map

Cockspur Beach Club

Stavronikita

Brighton Beach

Bridgetown

Deep Water Harbour

Warrens

2 mi
2 km

forming steep cliffs and exposing prehistoric rocks that look like giant mushrooms. Bathsheba and Cattlewash are favorite seacoast destinations for local folks on weekends and holidays. In the interior, narrow roads weave through tiny villages and along and between the ridges. The landscape is covered with tropical vegetation and is rife with fascinating caves and gullies.

WHAT TO SEE

★ **Fodor's Choice Andromeda Botanic Gardens.** More than 600 beautiful and unusual plant specimens from around the world are cultivated in 6 acres of gardens nestled among streams, ponds, and rocky outcroppings overlooking the sea above the Bathsheba coastline. The gardens were created in 1954 with flowering plants collected by the late horticulturist Iris Bannochie. They're now administered by the Barbados National Trust. The Hibiscus Café serves snacks and drinks. ⊠ *Bathsheba, St. Joseph* ☎ *246/433–9384* ⊠ *$10* ☉ *Daily 9–5.*

Banks Brewery Visitor Centre. Since 1961, Banks has been the home brew of Barbados; and it's a very good brew at that. After a short audiovisual presentation in the "Brewseum," which is in the Old Brewhouse, see the original copper brewing kettles that have since been replaced by modern stainless-steel vats. Watch the computerized brewing, bottling, and crating process (10,000 bottles per day) as it occurs in the New Brewhouse and Bottling Hall, and then visit the adjacent Beer Garden for a sample or two. The souvenir shop sells Banks logo gear. Reservations are required for the half-hour tour. ⊠ *Wildey, St. Michael* ☎ *246/228–6782* ⊕ *www.banksbeer.com* ⊠ *$8; $18 including round-trip transportation* ☉ *Weekdays 10, noon, and 2.*

Barclays Park. Straddling the Ermy Bourne Highway on the east coast, just north of Bathsheba, this public park was donated by Barclays Bank (now First Caribbean International Bank). Pack a picnic lunch and enjoy the gorgeous ocean view. ⊠ *Ermy Bourne Hwy., Cattlewash, St. Andrew.*

Chalky Mount. This tiny east-coast village is perched high in the clay-yielding hills that have supplied local potters for about 300 years. A number of working potteries are open daily to visitors. You can watch as artisans create bowls, vases, candleholders, and decorative objects—which are for sale. ⊠ *Chalky Mount, St. Andrew.*

CLOSE UP

Holetown Landing

On May 14, 1625, British Captain John Powell anchored his ship off the west coast of Barbados and claimed the island on behalf of King James I. He named his landfall Jamestown. Nearly two years later, on February 17, 1627, Captain Henry Powell landed in Jamestown with a party of 80 settlers and 10 slaves. They used a small channel, or "hole," near the settlement to offload and clean ships, so Jamestown soon became known as Holetown. Today Holetown is a vibrant town with shopping centers, restaurants, nightspots, and, of course, hotels and resorts. It is also the site of the annual Holetown Festival—a week of parades, crafts, music, and partying—held in mid-February each year to commemorate the first settlement. The celebration begins at the Holetown Monument in the center of town.

⏾ **Cockspur Beach Club.** Just north of Bridgetown, the fun-loving folks at West Indies Rum Distillery, makers of Cockspur and Malibu rums, invite visitors to enjoy a day at the beach, a variety of water-sports options, and a complimentary rum punch. Changing rooms with lockers and showers are available for beachgoers to use, along with beach umbrellas and chairs. Snorkeling equipment can be rented for the day ($5). The beachside grill serves lunch and drinks. This is a very popular outing for cruise-ship passengers. ✉ *Brighton Beach, Black Rock, Brighton, St. Michael* ☎ *246/425–9393* 🖃 *$10* ⏲ *Daily 8:30–4:30.*

CUBAN MONUMENT. On October 6, 1976, Cubana Airlines Flight 455, a DC-8 aircraft en route to Cuba from Barbados, was brought down by a terrorist bombing attack, killing all 73 people on board. The aircraft crashed into the sea off Paynes Bay on the west coast of Barbados. Four anti-Castro Cuban exiles were arrested for the crime. Two were sentenced to 20-year prison terms; one was acquitted; the fourth was held for 8 years awaiting sentencing and later fled. A pyramid-shape granite monument dedicated to the victims was installed along Highway 1 at the approximate location where the wreckage was brought ashore; it was unveiled during a 1998 visit by Cuban president Fidel Castro.

★ Fodor'sChoice **Flower Forest.** It's a treat to meander among fragrant flowering bushes, canna and ginger lilies, puffball trees, and more than 100 other species of tropical flora in a cool, tranquil forest of flowers and other plants. A ½-mile-long (1-km-long) path winds through the 53.6-acre grounds, a former sugar plantation; it takes about 30 to 45 minutes to follow the path, or you can wander freely for as long as you wish. Benches throughout the forest give you places to pause and reflect. There's also a snack bar, a gift shop, and a beautiful view of Mt. Hillaby, at 1,100 feet the highest point of land on Barbados. ✉ *Hwy. 2, Richmond, St. Joseph* ☎ *246/433–8152* ⊕ *www.flowerforestbarbados. com* ✍ *$10* ☉ *Daily 9–5.*

☾ **Folkestone Marine Park and Visitor Centre.** The mission of family-oriented Folkestone Marine Park, a marine protected area just north of Holetown, is to provide high-quality recreational activities in a sustainable way that will educate and entertain Barbadians and visitors alike. Facilities include a playground, basketball court, picnic area, museum, and beach with lifeguards. The museum (two rooms with artifacts and photos of how the sea is used for various purposes) illuminates some of the island's marine life. For some firsthand viewing, there's an underwater snorkeling trail (equipment rental, $10 for the day) around Dottins Reef, just off the beach in the protected marine reserve area; nonswimmers can enjoy a glass-bottom boat tour. A barge sunk in shallow water is home to myriad fish, making it a popular dive site. The park is open around the clock, with full security; lifeguards are on duty at the beach from 9 to 5:30 every day. A canteen serves snacks and drinks. ✉ *Hwy. 1, Church Point, Holetown, St. James* ☎ *246/425–2871* ✍ *Free; 60 cents to view the exhibits* ☉ *Park daily 24 hrs; museum weekdays 9:30–5.*

★ Fodor'sChoice **Gun Hill Signal Station.** The 360-degree view
☾ from Gun Hill, 700 feet above sea level, gave this location strategic importance to the 18th-century British army. Using lanterns and semaphores, soldiers based here could communicate with their counterparts at the Garrison on the south coast and at Grenade Hill in the north. Time moved slowly in 1868, and Captain Henry Wilkinson whiled away his off-duty hours by carving a huge lion from a single rock—which is on the hillside just below the tower. Come for a short history lesson but mainly for the view; it's so gorgeous that military invalids were once sent here to convalesce. ✉ *Gun Hill, St. George* ☎ *246/429–1358* ✍ *$5* ☉ *Weekdays 9–5.*

The famous lion at Gun Hill Signal Station

★ **Fodor's Choice Harrison's Cave.** This limestone cavern, complete with stalactites, stalagmites, subterranean streams, and a 40-foot waterfall, is a rare find in the Caribbean—and one of Barbados's most popular attractions. Tours include a nine-minute video presentation and a 40-minute underground journey through the cavern via electric tram. The visitor center has interactive displays, life-size models and sculptures, a souvenir shop, restaurant facilities, and elevator access to the tram for people with disabilities. Tours fill up fast, so make a reservation. ⊠ *Hwy. 2, Welchman Hall, St. Thomas* ☎ 246/417–3700 ⊕ *www.harrisonscave.com* ⊒ *$30* ⊙ *Daily 8:30–4:30 (last tour 3:45).*

★ **Mount Gay Rum Visitors Centre.** On this popular tour you learn the colorful story behind the world's oldest rum—made in Barbados since 1703. Although the modern distillery is in the far north, in St. Lucy Parish, tour guides explain the rum-making procedure here in St. Michael. Equipment, both historic and modern, is on display, and rows and rows of barrels are stored in this location. The 45-minute tour runs hourly (last tour begins at 3:30 weekdays; 2:30 on Saturday) and concludes with a tasting and an opportunity to buy bottles of rum and gift items—and even have lunch or cocktails, depending on the time of day. ⊠ *Spring Garden Hwy., Brandons, St. Michael* ☎ 246/425–8757 ⊕ *www.mountgayrum.com* ⊒ *$7, $50 with lunch; $35 with cocktails* ⊙ *Weekdays 9–5.*

Orchid World. Follow meandering pathways through tropical gardens filled with thousands of colorful orchids. You'll see Vandaceous orchids attached to fences or wire frames, Schomburgkia and Oncidiums stuck on mahogany trees, Aranda and Spathoglottis orchids growing in a grotto, and Ascocendas suspended from netting in shady enclosures. You'll find seasonal orchids, scented orchids, multicolor Vanda orchids, and more. Benches are well placed to stop for a little rest, admire the flowers, or simply take in the expansive view of the surrounding cane fields and distant hills of Sweet Vale. Snacks, cold beverages, and other refreshments are served in the café. ⊠ *Hwy. 3B, Groves, St. George* ☎ *246/433–0306* ⊡ *$10* ⊘ *Daily 9–5.*

Welchman Hall Gully. This 1½-mile-long (2-km-long) natural gully is really a collapsed limestone cavern, once part of the same underground network as Harrison's Cave. The Barbados National Trust protects the peace and quiet here, making it a beautiful place to hike past acres of labeled flowers and stands of trees. You can see and hear some interesting birds—and, with luck, a native green monkey. The tour is self-guided (although a guide can be arranged with 24 hours' notice) and takes about 30 to 45 minutes; the last tour begins at 4 pm. ⊠ *Welchman Hall, St. Thomas* ☎ *246/438–6671* ⊕ *www.welchmanhallgullybarbados.com* ⊡ *$12* ⊘ *Daily 9–4:30.*

NORTHERN BARBADOS

Speightstown, the north's commercial center and once a thriving port city, now relies on its appealing local shops and informal restaurants. Many of Speightstown's 19th-century buildings, with traditional overhanging balconies, have been restored. The island's northernmost reaches, St. Peter and St. Lucy parishes, have a varied topography and are lovely to explore. Between the tiny fishing towns along the northwestern coast and the sweeping views out over the Atlantic to the east are forest and farm, moor and mountain. Most guides include a loop through this area on a daylong island tour—it's a beautiful drive.

WHAT TO SEE

ⓒ **Animal Flower Cave.** Small sea anemones, or sea worms (resembling flowers when they open their tiny tentacles), live in small pools in this sea cave at the island's very northern tip. The cave itself, discovered in 1780, has a coral floor that ranges from 126,000 to 500,000 years old, according

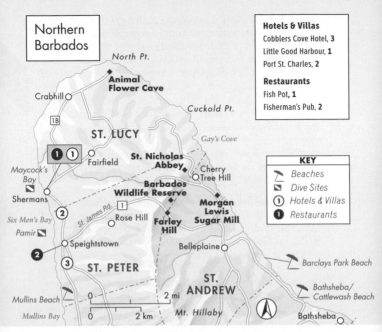

Northern Barbados

Hotels & Villas
Cobblers Cove Hotel, **3**
Little Good Harbour, **1**
Port St. Charles, **2**

Restaurants
Fish Pot, **1**
Fisherman's Pub, **2**

KEY
🏖 Beaches
◣ Dive Sites
① Hotels & Villas
❶ Restaurants

to geological estimates. The view of breaking waves from inside the cave is magnificent. ⊠ *North Point, St. Lucy* ☎ 246/439–8797 💰 $7.50 ⊙ Daily 9–4.

🄫 **Barbados Wildlife Reserve.** The reserve is the habitat of her-
★ ons, innumerable land turtles, screeching peacocks, shy deer, elusive green monkeys, brilliantly colored parrots (in a large walk-in aviary), a snake, and a caiman. Except for the snake and the caiman, the animals run or fly freely—so step carefully and keep your hands to yourself. Late afternoon is your best chance to catch a glimpse of a green monkey. ⊠ *Farley Hill, St. Peter* ☎ 246/422–8826 💰 $12 ⊙ Daily 10–5.

CHERRY TREE HILL. The cherry trees for which this spot was named have long since disappeared, but the view from Cherry Tree Hill, just east of St. Nicholas Abbey, is still one of the most spectacular in Barbados. Although only about 850 feet above sea level, it is one of the highest points on the island and affords a broad view of the rugged east coast and the entire Scotland District—so named because its rolling hills resemble the moors

CLOSE UP

Where de Rum Come From

For more than 300 years (from 1655 through "Black Tot Day, July 31, 1970"), a daily "tot" of rum (2 ounces) was duly administered to each sailor in the British Navy—as a health ration. At times rum has also played a less appetizing—but equally important—role. When Admiral Horatio Nelson died in 1805 aboard ship during the Battle of Trafalgar, his body was preserved in a cask of his favorite rum until he could be properly buried.

Hardly a Caribbean island doesn't have its own locally made rum, but Barbados is truly "where de rum come from." Mount Gay, the world's oldest rum distillery, has continuously operated on Barbados since 1703, according to the original deed for the Mount Gay Estate, which itemized two stone windmills, a boiling house, seven copper pots, and a still house. The presence of

rum-making equipment on the plantation at the time suggests that the previous owners were actually producing rum in Barbados long before 1703.

Today much of the island's interior is still planted with sugarcane—where the rum really does come from—and several great houses, on historic sugar plantations, have been restored with period furniture and are open to the public.

To really fathom rum, however, you need to delve a little deeper than the bottom of a glass of rum punch. Mount Gay offers an interesting 45-minute tour of its main plant, followed by a tasting. You can learn about the rum-making process from cane to cocktail, hear more rum-inspired anecdotes, and have an opportunity to buy bottles of its famous Eclipse or Extra Old rum at duty-free prices. Bottoms up!

---

of Scotland. Today, when approaching from the west, you drive through a majestic stand of mature, leafy mahogany trees.

Farley Hill. At this national park in northern St. Peter, across the road from the Barbados Wildlife Reserve, gardens and lawns, along with an avenue of towering royal palms and gigantic mahogany, whitewood, and casuarina trees, surround the imposing ruins of a plantation great house built by Sir Graham Briggs in 1861 to entertain royal visitors from England. Partially rebuilt for the filming of *Island in the Sun*, the classic 1957 film starring Harry Belafonte and Dorothy Dandridge, the structure was destroyed by fire in 1965. Behind the estate, there's a sweeping view of the

St. Nicholas Abbey, the island's oldest surviving plantation home

region called Scotland for its rugged landscape. ⊠ *Farley Hill, St. Peter* 🖃 *$2 per car, pedestrians free* ⊗ *Daily 8:30–6.*

Morgan Lewis Sugar Mill. Built in 1727, the mill was operational until 1945. Today it's the only remaining windmill in Barbados with its wheelhouse and sails intact. No longer used to grind sugarcane, except for occasional demonstrations, it was donated to the Barbados National Trust in 1962 and eventually restored to its original working specifications in 1998 by millwrights from the United Kingdom. The surrounding acres are now used for dairy farming. ⊠ *Southeast of Cherry Tree Hill, Morgan Lewis, St. Andrew* 🕾 *246/422–7429* 🖃 *$5* ⊗ *Weekdays 9–5.*

Sir Frank Hutson Sugar Museum. The Sugar Museum is in an old boiling house in the yard of the Portvale Sugar Factory, one of two sugar refineries in operation in Barbados. The museum has a collection of original machinery, old photographs, and other implements used to refine sugar and make molasses. A video presentation explains the production process from cutting the cane to sweetening your coffee to making rum. During the grinding season (February through May) you can also tour the modern factory to see how sugar is produced today. ⊠ *Hwy. 2A, Rock Hall, St. Thomas* 🕾 *246/432–0100* 🖃 *$4; $7.50 includes factory tour* ⊗ *Mon.–Sat. 9–5.*

CLOSE UP

Sugar: How Sweet It Is ...

Sugarcane was introduced to Barbados in the 1630s. Considered "white gold" by the original plantation owners, sugar production relied on forced labor (African slaves) and indentured servants (white civilians who wanted to emigrate overseas, kidnapped individuals, and convicted criminals dubbed "Red Legs," presumably because of the chafing marks that the chains made on their white legs). Slavery was abolished in 1834, yet records show that Barbados still had 491 active sugar plantations in 1846, along with 506 operating windmills. And until 1969, when the mechanical harvester was introduced in Barbados, cane was cut by manual labor. Nowadays, few people want the backbreaking job of cutting cane, so nearly all cane grown anywhere is cut mechanically. Today in Barbados some 1,500 small farms (about 200 acres each) produce about 60,000 tons of sugar annually, but only one operating windmill remains and just two companies refine sugar. Unfortunately, small farms and hilly terrain make mechanization inefficient. So while sugar remains an important agricultural product in Barbados, its value to the local economy has declined relative to tourism and other business interests.

★ Fodor's Choice **St. Nicholas Abbey.** The island's oldest great house (circa 1650) was named after the original British owner's hometown, St. Nicholas Parish near Bristol, and Bath Abbey nearby. Its stone-and-wood architecture makes it one of only three original Jacobean-style houses still standing in the Western Hemisphere. It has Dutch gables, finials of coral stone, and beautiful grounds that include an old sugar mill. The first floor, fully furnished with period furniture and portraits of family members, is open to the public. Fascinating home movies, shot by a previous owner's father, record Bajan life in the 1930s. Behind the great house is a rum distillery with a 19th-century steam press, which crushes cane the old-fashioned way each Wednesday and Thursday. Visitors can purchase artisanal plantation rum produced nearby (the Abbey's production will become fully aged about 2018) and enjoy light refreshments at the terrace café. ⊠ *Cherry Tree Hill, St. Peter* ☎ *246/422–5357* ⊕ *www.stnicholasabbey.com* ☎ *$17.50* ☉ *Sun.–Fri. 10–3:30.*

BEACHES

SOUTH COAST

A young, energetic crowd favors the south-coast beaches, which are broad and breezy, blessed with powdery white sand, and dotted with tall palms. The reef-protected areas with crystal-clear water are safe for swimming and snorkeling. The surf is medium to high, and the waves get bigger and the winds stronger (windsurfers take note) the farther southeast you go.

BEACH MASSAGE, LADY? The latest trend among beach vendors is offering massage services—sometimes including what they call reflexology—to sunbathers. While a beach massage sounds refreshing and may even feel good, these people are certainly not trained therapists. At best, you'll get a soothing back or foot rub. Be advised, though, that they use raw aloe vera as their massage oil, which can permanently stain clothing, towels, and chair cushions.

Accra Beach. This popular beach, also known as Rockley Beach, is next to the Accra Beach Hotel. You'll find gentle surf and a lifeguard, plenty of nearby restaurants for refreshments, a children's playground, and beach stalls for renting chairs and equipment for snorkeling and other water sports. Parking is available at an on-site lot. ⊠ *Hwy. 7, Rockley, Christ Church.*

★ **Bottom Bay Beach.** Popular for fashion and travel-industry photo shoots, Bottom Bay is the quintessential Caribbean beach. Secluded, surrounded by a coral cliff, studded with a stand of palms, and blessed with an endless ocean view, this dreamy enclave is near the southeasternmost point of the island. The Atlantic Ocean waves can be too strong for swimming, but it's the picture-perfect place for a day at the beach and a picnic lunch. Park at the top of the cliff and follow the steps down to the beach. ⊠ *Hwy. 5, Apple Hall, St. Philip.*

Pebbles Beach. On the southern side of Carlisle Bay, adjacent to the Hilton Barbados just south of Bridgetown, this broad half circle of white sand is one of the island's best beaches—but it can become crowded on weekends and holidays. Park at Harbour Lights or at the Boatyard Bar and Bayshore Complex, both on Bay Street, where you can also rent umbrellas and beach chairs and buy refreshments. ✉ *off Bay St., south of Bridgetown, Needham's Point, St. Michael.*

★ **Casuarina Beach.** Stretched in front of the Almond Casuarina Resort, where St. Lawrence Gap meets the Maxwell Coast Road, this broad strand of powdery white sand is great for both sunbathing and strolling, with the surf from low to medium. Find public access and parking on Maxwell Coast Road, near the Bougainvillea Resort. ✉ *Maxwell Coast Rd., Dover, Christ Church.*

★ Fodor's Choice **Crane Beach.** This exquisite crescent of pink sand on the southeast coast was named not for the elegant long-legged wading birds but for the crane used to haul and load cargo when this area was a busy port. Crane Beach usually has a steady breeze and lightly rolling surf that varies in color from aqua to turquoise to lapis and is great for bodysurfing. A lifeguard is on duty. Access to the beach is either down 98 steps or via a cliff-side, glass-walled elevator on The Crane resort property. ✉ *Crane Bay, St. Philip.*

★ Fodor's Choice **Miami Beach.** Also called Enterprise Beach, this isolated spot on the coast road, just east of Oistins, is an underrated slice of pure white sand with cliffs on either side and crystal-clear water. You can find a palm-shaded parking area, snack carts, and chair rentals. Bring a picnic. ✉ *Enterprise Beach Rd., Enterprise, Christ Church.*

Sandy Beach. This beach has shallow, calm waters and a picturesque lagoon, making it an ideal location for families with small kids. Park right on the main road. You can rent beach chairs and umbrellas, and plenty of places nearby sell food and drinks. ✉ *Hwy. 7, Worthing, Christ Church.*

Silver Sands–Silver Rock Beach. Nestled between South Point, the southernmost tip of the island, and Inch Marlow Point, Silver Sands–Silver Rock is a beautiful strand of white sand that always has a stiff breeze. That makes this beach the best in Barbados for intermediate and advanced windsurfers and, more recently, kiteboarders. ✉ *Off Hwy. 7, Christ Church.*

EAST COAST

Be cautioned: swimming at east-coast beaches is treacherous, even for strong swimmers, and is *not* recommended. Waves are high, the bottom tends to be rocky, the currents are unpredictable, and the undertow is dangerously strong.

Beware the Dreaded Manchineel Tree

Large, leafy manchineel trees grow along many of the west-coast beaches. Although they look like perfect shade trees, just touching a leaf or the bark can cause nasty blisters. And don't seek refuge under the tree during a rain shower, as even drips from its leaves can affect sensitive skin. The fruit of the tree, which looks like a tiny green apple, is toxic. Most of the manchineels are marked with signs or with red bands painted on the trunk. Why not just cut them all down? Their root systems are extremely important for preventing beach erosion.

Barclays Park Beach. Serious swimming is unwise at this beach, which follows the coastline in St. Andrew, but you can take a dip, wade, and play in the tide pools. A lovely shaded area with picnic tables is directly across the road. ⊠ *Ermy Bourne Hwy., Cattlewash, St. Andrew.*

★ **Bathsheba/Cattlewash Beaches.** Although not safe for swimming, the miles of untouched, windswept sand along the East Coast Road in St. Joseph Parish are great for beach-combing and wading. As you approach Bathsheba Soup Bowl, the southernmost stretch just below Tent Bay, the enormous mushroom-shaped boulders and rolling surf are uniquely impressive. This is also where expert surfers from around the world converge each November for the Independence Classic Surfing Championship. ⊠ *East Coast Rd., Bathsheba, St. Joseph.*

WEST COAST

Gentle Caribbean waves lap the west coast, and leafy mahogany trees shade its stunning coves and sandy beaches. The water is perfect for swimming and water sports. An almost unbroken chain of beaches runs between Bridgetown and Speightstown. Elegant homes and luxury hotels face much of the beachfront property in this area, dubbed Barbados's "Platinum Coast."

West-coast beaches are considerably smaller and narrower than those on the south coast. Also, prolonged stormy weather in September and October may cause sand erosion, temporarily making the beach even narrower. Even

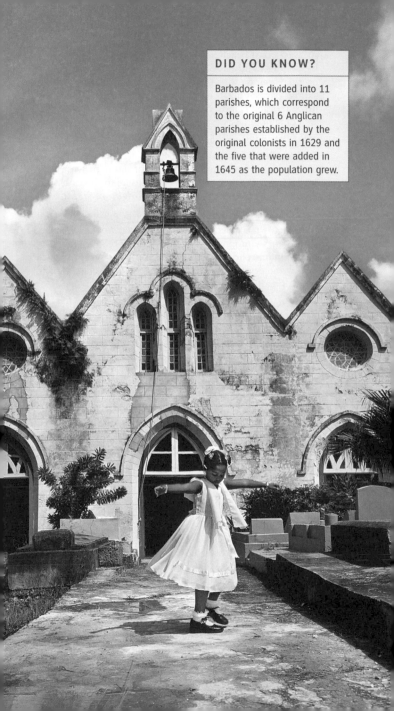

so, west-coast beaches are seldom crowded. Vendors stroll by, selling handmade baskets, hats, dolls, jewelry, even original watercolors; owners of private boats offer water-skiing, parasailing, and snorkeling excursions. There are no concession stands, but hotels and beachside restaurants welcome nonguests for terrace lunches (wear a cover-up), and you can buy picnic items at supermarkets in Holetown.

Brighton Beach. Calm as a lake, this is where you can find locals taking a quick dip on hot days. Just north of Bridgetown, Brighton Beach is also home to the Cockspur Beach Club. ⊠ *Spring Garden Hwy., Brighton, St. Michael.*

★ Fodor'sChoice **Mullins Beach.** This lovely beach just south of Speightstown is a perfect place to spend the day. The water is safe for swimming and snorkeling, there's easy parking on the main road, and Mullins Restaurant serves snacks, meals, and drinks—and rents chairs and umbrellas. ⊠ *Hwy. 1, Mullins Bay, St. Peter.*

Paynes Bay Beach. The stretch of beach just south of Sandy Lane is lined with luxury hotels. It's a very pretty area, with plenty of beach to go around and good snorkeling. Public access is available at several locations along Highway 1, though parking is limited. ⊠ *Hwy. 1, Paynes Bay, St. James.*

WHERE TO EAT

First-class restaurants and hotel dining rooms serve quite sophisticated cuisine—often prepared by chefs with international experience and rivaling that served in the world's best restaurants. Most menus include seafood: dolphin—the fish, not the mammal, and also called dorado or mahimahi—kingfish, snapper, and flying fish prepared every way imaginable. Flying fish is so popular that it has officially become a national symbol. Shellfish also abounds, as do steak, pork, and local black-belly lamb.

Local specialty dishes include *buljol* (a cold salad of pickled codfish, tomatoes, onions, sweet peppers, and celery) and *conkies* (cornmeal, coconut, pumpkin, raisins, sweet potatoes, and spices, mixed together, wrapped in a banana leaf, and steamed). *Cou-cou,* often served with steamed flying fish, is a mixture of cornmeal and okra, usually topped with a spicy creole sauce made from tomatoes, onions, and sweet peppers. Bajan-style pepper pot is a hearty stew of oxtail, beef chunks, and "any other meat" in a rich, spicy gravy and simmered overnight.

BEST BETS FOR DINING

With so many restaurants to choose from, how will you decide where to eat? Fodor's writers and editors have selected their favorite restaurants in the Best Bets lists below. The Fodor's Choice properties represent the "best of the best." Find the specific details about each restaurant in the reviews that follow.

Fodor'sChoice★

The Atlantis, Brown Sugar, Champers, The Cliff, Daphne's, Fish Pot, Pisces, The Tides, Waterfront Café

BEST VIEW
L'Azure at the Crane, Atlantis, Waterside

BEST FOR FAMILIES
Angry Annie's, Bellini's Trattoria

MOST ROMANTIC
The Mews, Lone Star

BEST FOR LOCAL BAJAN CUISINE
Cliffside at New Edgewater, Naniki, Waterfront Café

For lunch, restaurants often offer a traditional Bajan buffet of fried fish, baked chicken, salads, macaroni pie (macaroni and cheese), and a selection of steamed or stewed provisions (local roots and vegetables). Be cautious with the West Indian condiments—like the sun, they're hotter than you think. Typical Bajan drinks, besides Banks Beer and Mount Gay, Cockspur, or Malibu rum, are *falernum* (a liqueur concocted of rum, sugar, lime juice, and almond essence) and *mauby* (a nonalcoholic drink made by boiling bitter bark and spices, straining the mixture, and sweetening it). You're sure to enjoy the fresh fruit or rum punch.

What to Wear: The dress code for dinner in Barbados is conservative, casually elegant, and, on occasion, formal—a jacket and tie for gentlemen and a cocktail dress for ladies in the fanciest restaurants and hotel dining rooms, particularly during the winter holiday season. Jeans, shorts, and T-shirts (either sleeveless or with slogans) are always frowned upon at dinner. Beach attire is appropriate only at the beach.

BRIDGETOWN

★ Fodor'sChoice ✕ **Waterfront Café.** *Caribbean.* This friendly bis-
$$$ tro alongside the Careenage is the perfect place to enjoy a drink, snack, or meal—and to people-watch. Locals and tourists alike gather for all-day alfresco dining on sandwiches, salads, fish, pasta, pepper-pot stew, and tasty Bajan snacks such as buljol, fish cakes, or plantation pork (plantains stuffed with spicy minced pork). The panfried flying-

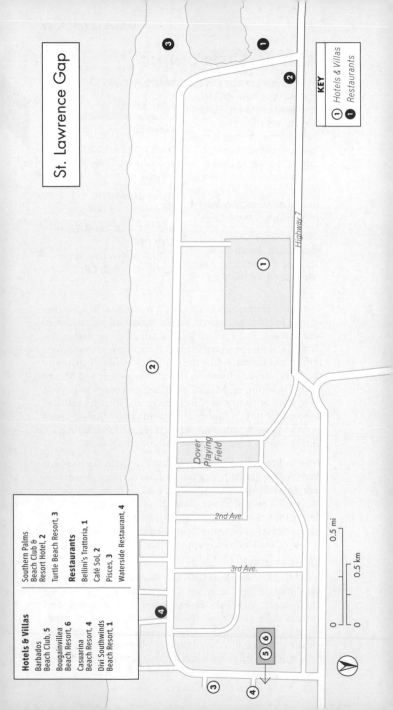

St. Lawrence Gap

Hotels & Villas
Barbados
Beach Club, **5**
Bougainvillea
Beach Resort, **6**
Casuarina
Beach Resort, **4**
Divi Southwinds
Beach Resort, **1**
Southern Palms
Beach Club &
Resort Hotel, **2**
Turtle Beach Resort, **3**

Restaurants
Bellini's Trattoria, **1**
Café Sol, **2**
Pisces, **3**
Waterside Restaurant, **4**

Dover
Playing
Field

2nd Ave.

3rd Ave.

Highway 7

KEY
① Hotels & Villas
❶ Restaurants

0   0.5 km
0   0.5 mi

fish sandwich is especially popular. In the evening you can gaze through the arched windows while savoring nouvelle Caribbean cuisine, enjoying cool trade winds, and listening to live jazz. There's a special Caribbean buffet and steel-pan music on Tuesday night from 7 to 9. ⑤ *Average main: $25* ✉ *The Careenage, Bridgetown, St. Michael* ☎ *246/427–0093* ⊕ *www.waterfrontcafe.com.bb* ۩ *Closed Sun.*

SOUTH COAST

$$$ ✕ **Bellini's Trattoria.** *Italian.* Classic northern Italian cuisine ۞ is the specialty at Bellini's, on the main floor of the Little Bay Hotel. The atmosphere here is smart-casual. Toast the evening with a Bellini cocktail (ice-cold sparkling wine with a splash of fruit nectar) and start your meal with bruschetta, an individual gourmet pizza, or perhaps a homemade pasta dish with fresh herbs and a rich sauce. Move on to the signature garlic shrimp entrée or the popular chicken parmigiana—then top it all off with chocolate mousse cake. On the other hand, the three-course daily special menu is the best deal. We recommend making your reservations early; request a table on the Mediterranean-style veranda to enjoy one of the most appealing dining settings on the south coast. ⑤ *Average main: $25* ✉ *Little Bay Hotel, St. Lawrence Gap, Dover, Christ Church* ☎ *246/420–7587* ⊕ *www.bellinisbarbados.com* ۩ *Reservations essential.*

★ **Fodor's** Choice ✕ **Brown Sugar.** *Caribbean.* Set back from the **$$$** road in a traditional Bajan home, the lattice-trimmed din- ۞ ing patios here are filled with ferns, flowers, and water features. Brown Sugar is a popular lunch spot for local businesspeople, who come for the nearly 30 delicious local and creole dishes spread out at the all-you-can-eat, four-course Bajan buffet. Here's your chance to try local specialties such as flying fish, cou-cou, buljol, *souse* (pickled pork, stewed for hours in broth), fish cakes, and pepper pot. In the evening, the à la carte menu has dishes such as fried flying fish, coconut shrimp, and plantain-crusted mahimahi; curried lamb, filet mignon, and broiled pepper chicken; and seafood or pesto pasta. Bring the kids—there's a special children's menu with fried chicken, fried flying-fish fingers, and pasta dishes. Save room for the warm pawpaw (papaya) pie or Bajan rum pudding with rum sauce. ⑤ *Average main: $26* ✉ *Bay St., Aquatic Gap, St. Michael* ☎ *246/426–7684* ⊕ *www.brownsugarbarbados.com* ۩ *No lunch Sat.*

$$$$ ✕ **Café Luna.** *Eclectic.* The sweeping view of pretty Miami (Enterprise) Beach from Café Luna, the alfresco dining deck on top of the Mediterranean-style Little Arches Hotel, is spectacular at lunchtime and magical in the moonlight. At lunch (for hotel guests only), sip on crisp white wine or a fruity cocktail while you await your freshly made salad, pasta, or sandwich. At dinner, co-owner and executive chef Mark de Gruchy prepares contemporary favorites from around the world, including fresh Scottish salmon grilled to perfection, oven-roasted New Zealand rack of lamb, fresh seafood bouillabaisse, and local chicken breast with mango chutney. Sushi is a specialty on Thursday and Friday nights; on Saturday night a champagne and lobster option enhances the regular menu. ⑤ *Average main: $33* ✉ *Little Arches Hotel, Enterprise Beach Rd., Oistins, Christ Church* ☎ *246/420–4689* ⊕ *www.littlearches.com* ⚍ *Reservations essential.*

$$ ✕ **Café Sol.** *Mexican.* Have a hankerin' for good Tex-Mex
☺ food? Enjoy nachos, tacos, burritos, empanadas, fajitas, and tostadas in this Mexican bar and grill at the entrance to busy St. Lawrence Gap. Or choose a burger, honey-barbecue chicken, or flame-grilled steak from the gringo menu. Helpings of rice and beans, a Corona, and plenty of jalapeño peppers, guacamole, and salsa give everything a Mexican feel. Some people come just for the margaritas— 15 fruity varieties rimmed with Bajan sugar instead of salt. Café Sol has two happy hours every night. This place gets really busy, and reservations are only accepted for parties of four or more. ⑤ *Average main: $18* ✉ *St. Lawrence Gap, Dover, Christ Church* ☎ *246/435–9531* ⊕ *www.cafesol-barbados.com* ⚍ *Reservations not accepted* ☉ *No lunch.*

★ **Fodor's**Choice ✕ **Champers.** *Eclectic.* Chiryl Newman's snazzy
$$$$ seaside restaurant and popular watering hole is in an old Bajan home on a quiet lane just off the main south-coast road in Rockley. Luncheon guests—about 75% local businesspeople—enjoy repasts such as char-grilled beef salad, Champers fish pie, grilled barracuda, or chicken-and-mushroom fettuccine in a creamy chardonnay sauce. Dinner guests swoon over dishes such as the roasted rack of lamb with spring vegetables and mint-infused jus, the sautéed sea scallops with stir-fried vegetables and noodles with red Thai curry sauce, and the Parmesan-crusted barracuda with whole-grain mustard sauce. But this isn't nouvelle cuisine. The portions are hearty and the food is well seasoned with Caribbean flavors, "just the way the locals like it," says Newman. The cliff-top setting overlooking the eastern end of Accra Beach offers diners a panoramic view of the sea and a relaxing atmosphere for daytime dining. At night, particularly at the bar, there's a definite buzz in the air.

Elegant Caribbean cuisine at Brown Sugar Restaurant

Nearly all the artwork gracing the walls is by Barbadian artists and may be purchased through the on-site gallery. ⑤ *Average main: $35* ⊠ *Skeetes Hill, off Hwy. 7, Rockley, Christ Church* ☎ *246/434–3463* ⊕ *www.champersbarbados. com* ⚑ *Reservations essential.*

$$$$ ✕ **L'Azure at the Crane.** *Seafood.* Perched on an oceanfront
☾ cliff, L'Azure is an informal breakfast and luncheon spot by day that becomes elegant after dark. Enjoy seafood chowder or a light salad or sandwich while absorbing the breathtaking panoramic view of Crane Beach and the sea beyond. At dinner, candlelight and a soft guitar enhance tamarind-glazed snapper or a fabulous Caribbean lobster seasoned with herbs, lime juice, and garlic butter and served in its shell; if you're not in the mood for seafood, try the crusted rack of lamb or herb-infused pork tenderloin. The dinner menu is prix fixe (two courses, $35; three courses and a glass of wine, $50). Sunday is really special, with a Gospel Brunch at 10 am and a Bajan Buffet at 12:30 pm. ⑤ *Average main: $38* ⊠ *The Crane, Crane Bay, St. Philip* ☎ *246/423–6220* ⊕ *www.thecrane.com* ⚑ *Reservations essential.*

★ **Fodor's** Choice ✕ **Pisces.** *Seafood.* For seafood lovers, this is nir-
$$$$ vana. Prepared in every way by chef-owner Larry Rogers— from charbroiled to gently sautéed—seafood specialties may include conch strips in tempura, rich fish chowder, panfried fillets of flying fish with a toasted-almond crust and a light mango-citrus sauce, and seared prawns in a fragrant curry sauce. Landlubbers in your party can select from the

chicken, beef, and pasta dishes on the menu. Whatever you choose, the herbs that flavor it and the accompanying vegetables will have come from the chef's own garden. Save room for the homemade bread pudding, yogurt-lime cheesecake, or rum-raisin ice cream. Twinkling white lights reflect on the water as you dine. ⓢ *Average main: $32* ⊠ *St. Lawrence Gap, Dover, Christ Church* ☎ *246/435–6564* ⊕ *www. piscesbarbados.com* ⚐ *Reservations essential* ⊘ *No lunch*.

$$$$ ✕ **Waterside Restaurant.** *Seafood.* You won't get much closer to dining on the water without being on a boat. Tables here are placed on a broad porch suspended over the beach and either gently rolling or crashing surf, depending on the weather. They're also spaced generously to allow for pleasant and private conversation. All the bustle of vibrant St. Lawrence Gap is left at the door. Once inside, the setting becomes sophisticated, tranquil, and definitely picturesque; the mood, quiet and intimate. And then there's the food. Chef Michael Hinds earned his stripes in world-class restaurants in New York, Miami, and London, as well as at Sandy Lane and Daphne's in Barbados. His truly elegant cuisine includes menu choices such as seared and crusted red snapper with tarragon emulsion, fire-roasted tiger prawns on bamboo and lemon-scented basmati rice with cashews, spice-rubbed loin of pork with sweet-potato gaufrettes, five-spice braised short rib with garlic mashed potatoes, molasses-glazed rack of lamb and minted couscous with sun-dried tomatoes, and more. For dessert, don't miss the spiced banana spring rolls with coconut ice cream and brandy caramel coulis. Hungry yet? ⓢ *Average main: $32* ⊠ *St. Lawrence Gap, Dover, Christ Church* ☎ *203/418– 9750* ⊕ *www.watersidebarbados.com* ⚐ *Reservations essential* ⊘ *Closed Mon. No lunch*.

$$$$ ✕ **Zen at the Crane.** *Asian.* Thai and Japanese specialties reign supreme in a magnificent setting overlooking Crane Beach. The centerpiece of the sophisticated, Asian-inspired decor is a 12-seat sushi bar, where chefs prepare exotic fare before your eyes. Try sizzling lobster kabayaki served in a cast-iron grill pan, teriyaki beef or chicken, tempura prawns, stir-fried meats and vegetables in oyster sauce, or a deluxe bento box. An extensive menu of Thai appetizers, soups, noodles, fried rice, and chef's specials and main courses from the wok are noted as being spicy, spicier, and spiciest. Choose to dine in the tatami room for a traditional Japanese dining experience. ⓢ *Average main: $30* ⊠ *The Crane, Crane Bay, St. Philip* ☎ *246/423–6220* ⊕ *www.thecrane. com* ⚐ *Reservations essential* ⊘ *Closed Tues*.

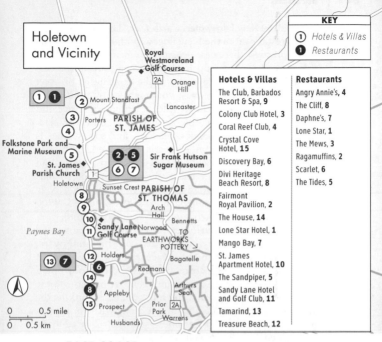

Holetown and Vicinity

KEY
① Hotels & Villas
❶ Restaurants

Hotels & Villas	Restaurants
The Club, Barbados Resort & Spa, 9	Angry Annie's, 4
Colony Club Hotel, 3	The Cliff, 8
Coral Reef Club, 4	Daphne's, 7
Crystal Cove Hotel, 15	Lone Star, 1
Discovery Bay, 6	The Mews, 3
Divi Heritage Beach Resort, 8	Ragamuffins, 2
Fairmont Royal Pavilion, 2	Scarlet, 6
The House, 14	The Tides, 5
Lone Star Hotel, 1	
Mango Bay, 7	
St. James Apartment Hotel, 10	
The Sandpiper, 5	
Sandy Lane Hotel and Golf Club, 11	
Tamarind, 13	
Treasure Beach, 12	

0   0.5 mile
0   0.5 km

EAST COAST

★ **Fodor's** Choice ✕ **The Atlantis.** *Caribbean.* For decades, an
$$$ alfresco lunch on the Atlantis deck overlooking the ocean
has been a favorite of visitors touring the east coast and
Bajans alike. Totally renovated and reopened in 2009 by
the owners of Little Good Harbour and the Fishpot on the
west coast, the revived restaurant effectively combines the
atmosphere and good food that have always been the draw
with an up-to-date, rather elegant dining room and a top-
notch menu that focuses on local produce, seafood, and
meats. The Bajan buffet lunch on Wednesday and Sunday is
particularly popular; it's also well used for special occasions
for local folks. At dinner, entrées include fresh fish, lobster
(sometimes), roasted black-belly lamb or free-range chicken,
fricassee of rabbit, and more. Or choose more traditional
pepper pot, saltfish, or chicken stew with peas and rice,
cou-cou, yam pie, or breadfruit mash, all of which are avail-
able at the Bajan buffet. Rotis and cutters (sandwiches) are
always available, along with pasta specials, salads, soups,
and fried flying fish. ⑤ *Average main: $30* ✉ *Tent Bay, St.
Joseph* ☎ *246/433–9445* ⊕ *www.atlantishotelbarbados.com*
⌁ *Reservations essential* ⊗ *No dinner Sun.*

$$$ ✕ **Cliffside at New Edgewater.** *Caribbean.* The outdoor deck
☾ of this restaurant in the New Edgewater hotel provides one
of the prettiest, breeziest ocean views in all Barbados, and
therefore is a good stop for lunch when touring the east
coast. From noon to 3 pm, choose the Bajan buffet or select
from the menu. Either way, you might enjoy fried flying
fish, roast or stewed chicken, local lamb chops, rice and
peas, steamed root vegetables, sautéed plantains, and salad.
Afternoon tea with scones, pastries, and sandwiches is
served from 3:30 to 6 pm. Dinner is also served, but mostly
to hotel guests and local residents, who are able to find
their way home in the dark on the neighborhood's wind-
ing, often unmarked roads. ⑤ *Average main: $25* ✉ *New
Edgewater Hotel, Bathsheba, St. Joseph* ☎ *246/433–9900*
⊕ *www.newedgewater.com* ⚑ *Reservations essential.*

$$ ✕ **Naniki Restaurant.** *Caribbean.* Rich wooden beams and
stone tiles, clay pottery, straw mats, colorful dinnerware,
and fresh flowers from the adjacent anthurium farm set
the style here. Huge picture windows and outdoor porch
seating allow you to enjoy the exhilarating panoramic
view of surrounding fields and hills and, when making the
alfresco choice, a refreshing breeze along with your lunch
of exquisitely prepared Caribbean standards. Seared flying
fish, grilled dorado, stewed lambi (conch), curried chicken,
and jerk chicken or pork are accompanied by cou-cou, peas
and rice, or salad. For dinner (by special request only),
start with conch fritters or Caribbean fish soup; then try
roasted Bajan black-belly lamb, grilled snapper, or shrimp
garnished with tarragon. Sunday brunch is a Caribbean
buffet often featuring great jazz music by some of the
Caribbean's best musicians. Vegetarian dishes are always
available. ⑤ *Average main: $28* ✉ *Lush Life Nature Resort,
Suriname, St. Joseph* ☎ *246/433–1300* ⊕ *www.lushlife.bb*
⚑ *Reservations essential.*

$$ ✕ **Round House.** *Seafood.* Owners Robert and Gail Manley
☾ oversee the menu for guests staying in their inn, tour-
ists enjoying the east coast, and Bajans dining out. The
lunch menu—served on the deck overlooking the Atlan-
tic Ocean—includes homemade soups and quiches, sand-
wiches, salads, and pasta. Dinner choices—served in the
moonlight—extend from shrimp scampi, oven-baked dol-
phin steak, or grilled flying-fish fillet to baked ham, sirloin
steak, or homemade pasta specials. Some people come
just for the flying-fish pâté. Rolls and breads (whether for
sandwiches or dessert), along with apple and coconut pies,
are personally made by the owners. The Round House is

an ocean-facing manse-turned-inn built in 1832. From the outdoor dining deck, the view of ocean waves smashing on the rugged coastline is mesmerizing. ⑤ *Average main: $25* ✉ *Bathsheba, St. Joseph* ☎ *246/433–9678* ⊕ *www.round-housebarbados.com* ⚄ *Reservations essential* ⊘ *No dinner Sun. (except for inn guests).*

WEST COAST

$$ ✕ **Angry Annie's.** *Caribbean.* You can't miss this place. Outside and inside, everything's painted in cheerful Caribbean pinks, blues, greens, and yellows—and it's just steps from the main road. The food is just as lively: barbecued "jump-up" ribs and chicken (as tasty as the roadside barbecue sold at street parties), grilled fresh fish or juicy steaks, "Rasta pasta" for vegetarians, and several spicy curries. Eat inside on gaily colored furniture, outside under the stars, or take it away with you. ⑤ *Average main: $24* ✉ *1st St., Holetown, St. James* ☎ *246/432–2119* ⊘ *No lunch.*

★ **Fodor's** Choice ✕ **The Cliff.** *Eclectic.* Chef Paul Owens's mastery
$$$$ is the foundation of one of the finest dining experiences in the Caribbean, with prices to match. Steep steps hug the cliff on which the restaurant sits to accommodate those arriving by yacht, and every candlelit table has a sea view. Starter suggestions include smoked salmon ravioli with garlic sauce or grilled portobello mushroom on greens with truffle vinaigrette; for the main course, try char-grilled swordfish with Thai yellow curry sauce, roasted duck breast with wild mushroom fumée, seared tuna with saffron caper sauce and tomato coulis, or Cajun salmon with pesto cream sauce. Dessert falls into the sinful category, and service is impeccable. The prix-fixe menu will set you back $105 per person for a two-course meal (starter–main course or main course–dessert) or $125 per person for a three-course meal. Reserve days or even weeks in advance to snag a table at the front of the terrace for the best view. ⑤ *Average main: $105* ✉ *Hwy. 1, Derricks, St. James* ☎ *246/432–1922* ⊕ *www.thecliffbarbados.com* ⚄ *Reservations essential* ⊘ *Closed Sun. Apr. 15–Dec. 15. No lunch.*

★ **Fodor's** Choice ✕ **Daphne's.** *Italian.* The beachfront restaurant
$$$$ of The House, Daphne's is the chic Caribbean outpost of the famed London eatery Daphne's of Chelsea. Chef Marco Festini Cromer whips up contemporary Italian cuisine. Grilled mahimahi, for example, becomes "modern Italian" when combined with Marsala wine, *peperonata* (stewed peppers, tomatoes, onions, and garlic), and zucchini. Perfectly prepared *melanzane* (eggplant) and zucchini

Dessert at Daphne's Restaurant in The House

alla parmigiana is a delicious starter, and a half portion of risotto with porcini mushrooms, green beans, and Parma ham is fabulously rich. Pappardelle with braised duck, red wine, and oregano is a sublime pasta choice. The extensive wine list features both regional Italian and fine French selections. $ *Average main: $45* ⊠ *The House, Hwy. 1, Paynes Bay, St. James* ☎ *246/432–2731* ⊕ *www.daphnes-barbados.com* ⌕ *Reservations essential* ⊘ *No lunch. Closed Mon. June–Nov.*

★ **Fodor's** Choice ✕ **Fish Pot.** *Mediterranean.* Just north of the
$$$$ little fishing village of Six Men's Bay, toward the northern end of the west coast of Barbados, this attractive seaside restaurant serves excellent Mediterranean cuisine and some of the island's freshest fish. Gaze seaward through windows framed with pale-green louvered shutters while lunching on a seafood crepe, a grilled panino, snow-crab salad, or perhaps pasta with seafood or roasted-pepper-and-chili tomato sauce; in the evening, the menu may include seafood bouillabaisse; seared, herb-crusted tuna on garlic-and-spinach polenta; sun-dried-tomato risotto tossed with vegetables; or cracker-crusted rack of lamb with thyme jus on roasted ratatouille. Bright and cheery by day and relaxed and cozy by night, the Fish Pot offers a tasty dining experience in a setting that's classier than its name might suggest. $ *Average main: $35* ⊠ *Little Good Harbour Hotel, Shermans, St. Peter* ☎ *246/439–3000* ⊕ *www.littlegoodharbourbarbados. com* ⌕ *Reservations essential.*

$$ ✕ **Fisherman's Pub.** *Caribbean.* This is as local as local gets. Fisherman's Pub is an open-air, waterfront restaurant built on stilts just a stone's throw from the Speightstown fish market. For years fishermen and other locals have come here daily for the inexpensive, authentic Creole buffet served at lunchtime. For $10 or less you can soak up the atmosphere and fill your plate with fried flying fish, stewed chicken or pork, curried goat or lamb, macaroni pie, fried plantain, cou-cou, and crisp green salad. On Wednesday nights, fill your plate from the buffet and dance—or simply listen—to catchy steel pan or calypso music. (Whether dinner is served varies from season to season, so call ahead.) ⑤ *Average main: $20* ✉ *Queen's St., Speightstown, St. Peter* ☎ *246/422–2703* ⌔ *Reservations not accepted.*

$$$$ ✕ **Lone Star.** *European.* In the 1940s this was the only commercial garage on the west coast; today, it's a snazzy restaurant in the tiny but chic Lone Star Hotel, where top chefs in the open-plan kitchen turn the finest local ingredients into gastronomic delights. The menu is extensive but pricey, even for lunch. All day, such tasty dishes as fish soup with rouille, Caesar or Thai chicken salad, tuna tartare, rotisserie chicken, and linguine with tomato-basil sauce and feta cheese are served in the oceanfront beach bar. At sunset the casual daytime atmosphere turns trendy. You might start with tuna tartare with mango or Thai crab cakes with peppers and lemongrass dip, followed by crispy Peking duckling, grilled fish of the day, or lamb shank with basil mashed potatoes—or choose from dozens of other tasty land, sea, and vegetarian dishes. ⑤ *Average main: $32* ✉ *Lone Star Hotel, Hwy. 1, Mount Standfast, St. James* ☎ *246/419–0599* ⊕ *www.thelonestar.com.*

$$$$ ✕ **The Mews.** *European.* Dining at the Mews is like being invited to a friend's very chic home for dinner. This restaurant once was, in fact, a private home. The front room is now an inviting bar, and an interior courtyard is an intimate, open-air dining area. The second floor is a maze of small dining rooms and dining balconies, but you've come for the food, after all. The international cuisine is presented with contemporary flair. A plump chicken breast, for example, will be stuffed with cream cheese, smoked salmon, and herb pâté and served on a garlic-and-chive sauce. A braised lamb shank is presented on a bed of cabbage with a port-thyme jus and creamed potatoes, and fillet of mahimahi is poached in a lemongrass, ginger, and cilantro broth. The warm molten chocolate cake is a must for dessert. Some call the atmosphere avant-garde; others

call it quaint. Everyone calls the food delicious. But don't stop at dinner; by about 10 pm the bar begins to bustle. On weekends the fun spills out into the street. ⑤ *Average main: $38* ✉ *2nd St., Holetown, St. James* ☎ *246/432–1122* ⚑ *Reservations essential* ⊘ *Closed Sun. No lunch*.

$$$ ✕ **Ragamuffins.** *Caribbean.* The only restaurant on Barbados in an authentic chattel house, Ragamuffins is tiny, funky, lively, and informal. The menu offers seafood, perfectly broiled T-bone steaks, West Indian curries, and vegetarian dishes such as Bajan stir-fried vegetables with noodles. Dine inside or out. The kitchen is within sight of the bar—which is a popular meeting spot most evenings for vacationers and locals alike. ⑤ *Average main: $22* ✉ *1st St., Holetown, St. James* ☎ *246/432–1295* ⊕ *www.ragamuffinsbarbados. com* ⚑ *Reservations essential* ⊘ *No lunch*.

$$$ ✕ **Scarlet.** *Eclectic.* When you see a bright-red building on the side of the road, you'll know you've found Scarlet. Movers and groovers come here in the evening to chill over a martini and share nibbles, such as a plate of flying-fish lollipops, or to settle in after cocktails for a burger with sophisticated toppings, Bajan ham with corn pancakes, or perhaps Baxter's Road chicken. Enjoy your meal sitting at the large bar—the centerpiece of this casual but stylish watering hole—or at a nearby table. Specialty of the house: Scarlet Rocks (vodka, raspberry schnapps, strawberries, cranberry juice, basil, and black pepper!). ⑤ *Average main: $28* ✉ *Hwy. 1, Paynes Bay, St. James* ☎ *246/432–3663* ⊕ *www.scarletbarbados.com* ⚑ *Reservations essential* ⊘ *Closed Sun. and Mon. No lunch*.

★ **Fodor's** Choice ✕ **The Tides.** *European.* Local residents and repeat
$$$$ visitors agree that the Tides is one of the island's best restaurants. Enter into a pretty courtyard and have a cocktail at the cozy bar or the coral-stone lounge in what was once a private mansion (or visit the on-site art gallery), then proceed to your seaside table. Perhaps the most intriguing feature of this stunning setting—besides the sound of waves crashing onto the shore just feet away—is the row of huge tree trunks growing right through the dining room. The food is equally dramatic. Chef Guy Beasley and his team give a contemporary twist to fresh seafood, fillet of beef, rack of lamb, and other top-of-the-line main courses by adding inspired sauces and delicate vegetables and garnishes. Save room for the sticky toffee pudding—definitely worth the calories. ⑤ *Average main: $40* ✉ *Balmore House, Hwy. 1, Holetown, St. James* ☎ *246/432–8356* ⊕ *www.tidesbarbados.com* ⚑ *Reservations essential* ⊘ *No lunch weekends*.

WHERE TO STAY

Most visitors stay on either the fashionable west coast, north of Bridgetown, or on the action-packed south coast. On the west coast the beachfront resorts in St. Peter and St. James parishes are mostly luxurious, self-contained enclaves. Highway 1, a two-lane road with considerable traffic, runs past these resorts, which can make strolling to a nearby bar or restaurant a bit difficult. Along the south coast in Christ Church Parish many hotels are clustered near the busy strip known as St. Lawrence Gap, convenient to dozens of small restaurants, bars, and nightclubs. On the much more remote east coast a few small inns offer oceanfront views and get-away-from-it-all tranquillity.

In keeping with the smoke-free policy enforced throughout Barbados, smoking is restricted to open outdoor areas such as the beach. It is not permitted in hotels (neither rooms nor public areas) or in restaurants.

Prices in Barbados may be twice as high in season (December 15–April 15) compared with the quieter months. Most hotels include no meals in their rates, but some include breakfast, and many offer a meal plan. Some require you to purchase a meal plan in the high season, and a few offer all-inclusive packages.

Resorts run the gamut—from unpretentious to exceedingly formal—in terms of size, intimacy, amenities, and price. Families and long-term visitors may choose from a wide variety of villas and condos. A few small, cozy inns are found along the east and southeast coasts, as well as the northwest. They can be ultra-luxurious, fairly simple, or something in between.

Villa and condo complexes, which are continually cropping up along the south and west coasts of Barbados, may be the most economical option for families, other groups, or couples vacationing together. Non-owner vacationers rent individual units directly from the property managers, the same as reserving hotel accommodations. Units with fully equipped kitchens, two to six bedrooms, and as many baths run $200 to $2,500 per night in the off-season—double that in winter.

For expanded reviews, facilities, and current deals, visit Fodors.com.

BEST BETS FOR LODGING

Fodor's offers a selective listing of quality lodging experiences, from the island's best boutique hotel to its most luxurious beach resort. Here, we've compiled our top recommendations based on the different types of lodging found on the island. The very best properties—in other words, those that provide a particularly remarkable experience—are designated in the listings with the Fodor's Choice logo.

Fodor's Choice★

Accra Beach Hotel, Almond Beach Club, Atlantis Hotel, Coral Reef Club, Hilton Barbados, Little Arches Hotel, Peach and Quiet, Sandy Lane, The Sandpiper, Sweetfield Manor

BEST FOR HONEYMOONERS

Cobblers Cove, Fairmont Royal Pavilion, The House, Treasure Beach

BEST FOR FAMILIES

Almond Casuarina, Bougainvillea, Royal Westmoreland, Tamarind, Turtle Beach

PRIVATE VILLAS AND CONDOS

Local real-estate agencies will arrange vacation rentals of privately owned villas and condos along the west coast in St. James and St. Peter. All villas and condos are fully furnished and equipped, including appropriate staff depending on the size of the villa or unit—which can range from one to eight bedrooms; the staff usually works six days a week. Most villas have TVs, DVDs and/or VCRs, and CD players; all properties have telephones, and some have Internet access. International telephone calls are usually blocked; plan on using your own mobile phone or a phone card or calling card. Vehicles generally are not included in the rates, but rental cars can be arranged for and delivered to the villa upon request. Linens and basic supplies (such as bath soap, toilet tissue, and dishwashing detergent) are normally included.

Units with one to six bedrooms and as many baths run $200 to $2,500 per night in summer, and double that in winter. Rates include utilities and government taxes. The only additional cost is for groceries and staff gratuities. A security deposit is required upon booking and refunded seven days after departure less any damages or unpaid miscellaneous charges.

2

CLOSE UP

Turtle Time

Along Casuarina Beach, which stretches in front of both Almond Casuarina Resort and the aptly named Turtle Beach Resort, mother hawksbill turtles dig a pit in the sand, lay 100 or more eggs, cover the nest with sand, and then return to the sea. The eggs, which look just like Ping-Pong balls, are usually deposited between May and November and take about 60 days to hatch. If you happen to be strolling along the beach at the time they emerge, you'll see a mass of newborn turtles scrambling out of the sand and making a dash (at turtle speed, of course) for the sea. While the journey takes only a few minutes, this can be a very dangerous time for the tiny turtles. They are easy prey for gulls and large crabs. Meantime, the folks involved in the Barbados Sea Turtle Project (☎ 246/230–0142) at the University of the West Indies are working hard to protect and conserve the marine turtle populations in Barbados through educational workshops, tagging programs, and other research efforts.

Apartments are available for vacation rentals in buildings or complexes that can have as few as three or four units or as many as 30 to 40 units—or even more. Prices range from $30 to $300 per night.

Villa Rental Contacts Altman Real Estate. ⊠ Hwy. 1, Derricks, St. James ☎ 246/432–0840, 866/360–5292 in the U.S. ⊕ www.aaaltman.com. **Bajan Services.** ⊠ Newton House, Battaleys, St. Peter ☎ 246/422–2618, 866/978–5239 in the U.S. ⊕ www.bajanservices. com. **Island Villas.** ⊠ Trents Bldg., Holetown, St. James ☎ 246/432–4627, 866/978–8499 in the U.S. ⊕ www.island-villas.com.

Apartment Rental Contacts Barbados Tourism Authority. The Barbados Tourism Authority on Harbour Road in Bridgetown has a listing of apartments in prime resort areas on both the south and west coasts, complete with facilities offered and current rates. ⊠ Harbour Rd., Bridgetown, St. Michael ☎ 246/427–2623 ⊕ www.visitbarbados. org ▭ No credit cards.

SOUTH COAST

★ **Fodor's**Choice ▥ **Accra Beach Hotel and Spa.** *Hotel.* An excel-
$ lent choice if you prefer a full-service resort in the middle of the busy south coast, the Accra is large, it's modern, it faces a great beach, and it's competitively priced. **Pros:** right on a great beach and, on the street side, near shopping, restaurants, and nightspots; terrific value; pleasant staff.

Cons: standard rooms are fairly ordinary—at least opt for accommodations with a pool or ocean view. ⑤ *Rooms from: $218* ⊠ *Hwy. 7, Rockley, Christ Church* ☎ *246/435–8920, 888/712–2272 in the U.S.* ⊕ *www.accrabeachhotel.com* ➷ *188 rooms, 36 suites* ⦿*Multiple meal plans.*

$$$$ 🖾 **Almond Casuarina Beach Resort.** *All-inclusive.* One of two all-inclusive Almond properties in Barbados—and the only one on the south coast—Almond Casuarina Beach Resort offers guests countless opportunities for dining, socializing, and water and land sports. **Pros:** great beach and beautiful garden; every amenity you could imagine; wonderful for kids. **Cons:** lots of good restaurants to try in nearby St. Lawrence Gap, but you've paid for an all-inclusive. ⑤ *Rooms from: $465* ⊠ *St. Lawrence Gap, at Maxwell Coast Rd., Dover, Christ Church* ☎ *246/428–3600* ⊕ *www. almondresorts.com* ➷ *280 rooms* ⦿*All-inclusive.*

$ 🖾 **Barbados Beach Club.** *All-inclusive.* Designed with families in mind, this four-story hotel (with elevators) sits on a beautiful stretch of south-coast beach—and offers tremendous value. **Pros:** great beach; good value; wonderful for kids; golf package. **Cons:** rooms need updating; limited access to fine-dining restaurants. ⑤ *Rooms from: $266* ⊠ *Maxwell Coast Rd., Maxwell, Christ Church* ☎ *246/428–9900* ⊕ *www.barbadosbeachclub.com* ➷ *105 rooms, 2 penthouse suites* ⦿*All-inclusive.*

$ 🖾 **Bougainvillea Beach Resort.** *Resort.* Attractive seaside townhouses, each with a separate entrance, wrap around the pool or face the beachfront; the suites are huge compared with hotel suites elsewhere in this price range, are decorated in appealing Caribbean pastels, and have full kitchens. **Pros:** great for families but also appeals to honeymooners; popular wedding venue; easy stroll to St. Lawrence Gap or to Oistins. **Cons:** rooms are on four levels with no elevator; sea can be rough for swimming. ⑤ *Rooms from: $271* ⊠ *Maxwell Coast Rd., Maxwell, Christ Church* ☎ *246/418–0990, 800/495–1858 in the U.S.* ⊕ *www.bougainvillearesort.com* ➷ *138 suites* ⦿*Multiple meal plans.*

$ 🖾 **Coconut Court Beach Hotel.** *Hotel.* This beachfront hotel is popular among families, particularly British families, who especially love the welcoming atmosphere, the activities room for kids, the kitchenettes, and the fact that children under 12 stay free (although there is also a maximum of three people to a room). **Pros:** beautiful beachfront; cooking facilities handy for snacks and light meals; Room 21 has the best ocean view. **Cons:** nothing luxurious here; rooms are rather simply decorated; restricted views of the beach in "west wing" rooms. ⑤ *Rooms from: $205* ✉ *Main Rd., The Garrison Historic Area, Hastings, Christ Church* ☎ *246/427–1655* ⊕ *www.coconut-court.com* ⇨ *120* ❢◉❢ *Multiple meal plans.*

$ ☷ **Courtyard Bridgetown by Marriott.** *Hotel.* Comfortable, contemporary, convenient, and economical, this place is pleasant and the rooms are well appointed. **Pros:** Good value; especially suited to business travelers; modern, attractive accommodations. **Cons:** Walk to beach and restaurants; comparatively little "Caribbean" atmosphere; minimum on-site dining options. ⑤ *Rooms from: $199* ✉ *The Garrison, Hastings, Christ Church* ☎ *246/625–0000* ⊕ *www. marriott.com* ⇨ *118* ❢◉❢ *No meals.*

$ ☷ **The Crane.** *Rental.* Hugging a seaside bluff on the southeast coast, the Crane is the island's oldest hotel in continuing operation; today the original coral-stone hotel building (1887) is the centerpiece of a luxurious, 40-acre villa complex. **Pros:** enchanting view; lovely beach; fabulous suites; great restaurants. **Cons:** remote location; rental car recommended; not all villas have laundry facilities. ⑤ *Rooms from: $264* ✉ *Crane Bay, St. Philip* ☎ *246/423–6220* ⊕ *www.thecrane. com* ⇨ *4 rooms, 14 suites, 202 villas* ❢◉❢ *Multiple meal plans.*

$ ☷ **Divi Southwinds Beach Resort.** *Resort.* The all-suites Divi
ᐲ Southwinds is on 20 acres of lawn and gardens bisected by action-packed St. Lawrence Gap. **Pros:** beautiful beach; beach villas are the best value; close to shopping, restaurants, and nightspots. **Cons:** few water sports available and none included; some rooms aching for renovations; comparatively pricey for the value received. ⑤ *Rooms from: $218* ✉ *St. Lawrence Main Rd., Dover, Christ Church* ☎ *246/428–7181* ⊕ *www.divisouthwinds.com* ⇨ *121 1-bedroom suites, 12 2-bedroom suites* ❢◉❢ *Multiple meal plans.*

★ Fodor'sChoice ☷ **Hilton Barbados.** *Hotel.* Beautifully situated on
$$ the sandy Needham's Point peninsula, all 350 rooms and
ᐲ suites in the high-rise Hilton Barbados have private balconies overlooking either the ocean or Carlisle Bay; 77 rooms are on executive floors, with a private lounge and concierge services. **Pros:** great location near town and on a beautiful beach; excellent accommodations; lots of services and amenities; frequent promotional deals provide real value. **Cons:** huge convention hotel; attracts groups; lacks "island" ambience. ⑤ *Rooms from: $299* ✉ *Needham's Point, St. Michael* ☎ *246/426–0200* ⊕ *www.hiltonbarbadoshotel.com* ⇨ *317 rooms, 33 suites* ❢◉❢ *Multiple meal plans.*

$$ ☷ **Island Inn Hotel.** *All-inclusive.* Originally constructed in 1804 as a rum storage facility for the British regiment, this

quaint, all-inclusive boutique hotel—less than a mile from Bridgetown and steps away from beautiful Pebbles Beach on Carlisle Bay—appeals to singles, couples, and families. **Pros:** friendly, accommodating atmosphere; smartly decorated rooms; excellent value. **Cons:** small pool; request a room near the pool, as rooms near the front (the restaurant and entertainment) can be noisy and don't have a patio. ⑤ *Rooms from: $350* ✉ *Garrison Historic Area, Aquatic Gap, St. Michael* ☎ *246/436–6393* ⊕ *www.islandinnbarbados.com* ⌒ *20 rooms, 4 suites* ⑩ *All-inclusive.*

$$ ⑪ **Little Arches Hotel.** *Hotel.* Just east of the fishing village of
★ Oistins, this classy boutique hotel has a distinctly Mediterranean ambience and a perfect vantage point overlooking the sea. **Pros:** stylish accommodations; good restaurant; across from fabulous Miami Beach; on-site car rental. **Cons:** fairly remote; rental car advised. ⑤ *Rooms from: $295* ✉ *Enterprise Beach Rd., Enterprise, Christ Church* ☎ *246/420–4689* ⊕ *www.littlearches.com* ⌒ *8 rooms, 2 suites* ⑩ *Multiple meal plans.*

★ **Fodor's**Choice ⑪ **Peach and Quiet.** *Hotel.* Forgo the flashy accou-
$ trements of a resort and, instead, claim one of the stylish suites in this small seaside inn just east of Oistins. **Pros:** the rates alone make this inn a great choice; peace and quiet; adults-only environment; engaging owners; stargazing and nature walks are special treats. **Cons:** inn is closed half the year; remote location requires a rental car. ⑤ *Rooms from: $119* ✉ *Inch Marlow Main Rd., Inch Marlow, Christ Church* ☎ *246/428–5682* ⊕ *www.peachandquiet.com* ⌒ *22 suites* ⊘ *Closed May–Oct.* ⑩ *No meals.*

$$ ⑪ **Silver Point Hotel.** *Hotel.* This gated community of modern condos at Silver Sands–Silver Rock Beach is operated as a trendy boutique hotel that appeals to singles, couples, and families—but especially to windsurfers. **Pros:** stylish suites; perfect location for windsurfers; gated community. **Cons:** very remote; not within walking distance of anything except the beach; sea can be rough for swimming; rental car recommended. ⑤ *Rooms from: $343* ✉ *Silver Sands, Christ Church* ☎ *246/420–4416* ⊕ *www.silverpointhotel.com* ⌒ *60 suites* ⑩ *Multiple meal plans.*

$$ ⑪ **Southern Palms Beach Club & Resort Hotel.** *Resort.* This resort
☺ is pretty in pink, you might say. The pink, plantation-style main building opens onto an inviting pool area and 1,000 feet of white sandy beach. **Pros:** friendly and accommodating staff; close to lots of restaurants and entertainment; nice beach. **Cons:** rooms are large and clean but dated; beach vendors can be a nuisance (not the hotel's fault). ⑤ *Rooms*

Coral Reef Club, luxury cottage

Sweetfield Manor

Peach and Quiet

Hilton Barbados Executive Lounge

Sandy Lane Hotel

from: $325 ✉ *St. Lawrence Gap, Dover, Christ Church* ☎ *246/428–7171* ⊕ *www.southernpalms.net* ⤷ *72 rooms, 20 suites* ⦿ *Multiple meal plans.*

★ FodorśChoice ⬚ **Sweetfield Manor.** *B&B/Inn.* George and Ann
$ Clarke transformed a decrepit manse (circa 1900) perched on a ridge about a mile from Bridgetown—the former residence of the Dutch ambassador to Barbados—into the island's most delightful bed-and-breakfast inn. **Pros:** peaceful enclave primarily suitable for adults; inviting pool and gardens; gracious and friendly innkeepers; delicious gourmet breakfast; perfect wedding venue. **Cons:** long walk to beach; rental car advised; not the best choice for kids. ⑤ *Rooms from: $175* ✉ *Britton New Road, St. Michael* ☎ *246/429–8356* ⊕ *www.sweetfieldmanor.com* ⤷ *6 rooms, 4 with bath, 1 suite* ⦿ *Breakfast.*

$$$ ⬚ **Turtle Beach Resort.** *All-inclusive.* Families flock to Turtle
☾ Beach because it offers large, bright suites and enough all-included activities for everyone to enjoy. **Pros:** perfect for family vacations; nice pools; roomy accommodations; lots of services and amenities. **Cons:** beach is fairly narrow and congested compared with other south-coast resorts; open vent between room and hallway can be noisy at night. ⑤ *Rooms from: $729* ✉ *St. Lawrence Gap, Dover, Christ Church* ☎ *246/428–7131* ⊕ *www.turtlebeachresortbarbados.com* ⤷ *164 suites* ⦿ *All-inclusive.*

DID YOU KNOW? Portuguese explorer Pedro a Campos is credited with naming Barbados. In 1536, when he stopped by the island en route to Brazil, he and his crew were intrigued by the bearded appearance of the indigenous fig trees. "Os Barbados," or "the bearded ones," he proclaimed—and the name stuck.

EASTERN BARBADOS

★ FodorśChoice ⬚ **The Atlantis Hotel.** *B&B/Inn.* The legendary
$ Atlantis Hotel, a fixture on the rugged east coast for more than a century and renowned for its spectacular oceanfront location, was completely renovated and reopened in 2009 by the owners of Little Good Harbour. **Pros:** historical and modern blend works wonderfully; spectacular oceanfront location; excellent restaurant. **Cons:** oceanfront rooms have fabulous views, but the smashing waves can be noisy at night; remote location, so rental car advised; no beach for swimming. ⑤ *Rooms from: $255* ✉ *Tent Bay, St. Joseph* ☎ *246/433–9445* ⊕ *www.atlantishotelbarbados.com* ⤷ *5 rooms, 3 suites, 2 apartments* ⊘ *Closed Sept.* ⦿ *Breakfast.*

2

$ ⊞ **New Edgewater Hotel.** *B&B/Inn.* This seaside outpost overlooking a 9-mile stretch of the stunning east coast has been a cliffside retreat since the 1700s. Today the hotel is comparatively rustic and attracts guests who are content with taking a walk or curling up with a good book, as well as surfers who like the location near Bathsheba Beach and its famous Soup Bowl. **Pros:** spectacular setting; surfers' paradise; quiet and peaceful; nice pool area. **Cons:** remote location; no nearby beach for swimming; don't expect luxury; public bathroom needs some attention. ⑤ *Rooms from: $133* ⊠ *Bathsheba, St. Joseph* ☎ *246/433–9900* ⊕ *www.newedgewater.com* ⇆ *20 rooms, 4 suites* ⑩ *Breakfast.*

$ ⊞ **Round House Inn.** *B&B/Inn.* It's hard to tell which is more appealing: the view of the rugged coastline or the magnificent historic (1832) manse strategically perched on the cliff to take advantage of the view. **Pros:** beautiful east-coast views; waterfront; small and intimate. **Cons:** remote location; simply furnished rooms; no TV (if you care); nearby beach not good for swimming. ⑤ *Rooms from: $85* ⊠ *Bathsheba, St. Joseph* ☎ *246/433–9678* ⊕ *www.roundhousebarbados.com* ⇆ *4 rooms* ⑩ *No meals.*

$ ⊞ **Sea-U Guest House.** *B&B/Inn.* Uschi Wetzels, a German travel writer in an earlier life, became smitten with the wild and woolly east coast of Barbados while on assignment and returned in 1999 to build this tiny guesthouse. **Pros:** peaceful and relaxing; couldn't be friendlier; there's Wi-Fi. **Cons:** remote location; few on-site activities. ⑤ *Rooms from: $159* ⊠ *Tent Bay, St. Joseph* ☎ *246/433–9450* ⊕ *www.seaubarbados.com* ⇆ *8 rooms* ⑩ *Breakfast.*

WEST COAST

$$$ ⊞ **The Club, Barbados Resort & Spa.** *All-inclusive.* Among several similar beachfront resorts south of Holetown, The Club distinguishes itself as an adults-only environment with all-inclusive rates (only spa and salon services are extra). **Pros:** adults only; intimate atmosphere; short walk to Holetown; next door to Sandy Lane Beach. **Cons:** beach erodes to almost nothing at certain times of the year—usually the result of fall storms; rooms could use updating. ⑤ *Rooms from: $450* ⊠ *Hwy. 1, Vauxhall, St. James* ☎ *246/432–7840 or 866/317–8009* ⊕ *www.theclubbarbados.com* ⇆ *133 rooms, 28 suites* ⑩ *All-inclusive.*

$$$$ ⊞ **Cobblers Cove Hotel.** *Hotel.* "English Country" best describes the style of this lovely resort favored by British sophisticates. **Pros:** very classy establishment; lovely

grounds; the penthouse suites are amazing; very quiet. **Cons:** too quiet for some; only bedrooms have a/c. ⑤ *Rooms from: $870* ⊠ *Road View, Speightstown, St. Peter* ☎ *246/422–2291* ⊕ *www.cobblerscove.com* ⌖ *40 suites* ⦿ *Multiple meal plans.*

$$$$ ⛨ **Colony Club Hotel.** *Resort.* As the signature hotel of five Ele-
★ gant Hotel properties on Barbados, the Colony Club is certainly elegant—but with a quiet, friendly, understated style.
Pros: clubby atmosphere; some rooms open directly onto
the lagoon pool. **Cons:** relatively pricey; beach comes and
goes, depending on storms. ⑤ *Rooms from: $719* ⊠ *Hwy. 1,*
Porters, St. James ☎ *246/422–2335* ⊕ *www.colonyclubho-*
tel.com ⌖ *64 rooms, 32 junior suites* ⦿ *Multiple meal plans.*

★ **Fodor's**Choice ⛨ **Coral Reef Club.** *Resort.* The upscale Coral
$$$$ Reef Club offers the epitome of elegance and style, along
with a welcoming, informal atmosphere. **Pros:** absolutely
delightful; elegant yet informal; beautiful suites with huge
verandas; delicious dining; six computers with free Internet access available to guests. **Cons:** few room TVs (if that
matters); narrow beach sometimes disappears, depending
on the seasonal weather; no kids mid-January to mid-
March. ⑤ *Rooms from: $805* ⊠ *Hwy. 1, Porters, St. James*
☎ *246/422–2372* ⊕ *www.coralreefbarbados.com* ⌖ *29*
rooms, 57 suites, 2 villas ⊘ *Closed mid-May–mid-July,*
September. ⦿ *Multiple meal plans.*

$$$$ ⛨ **Crystal Cove Hotel.** *All-inclusive.* Crystal Cove, a colony
of attached duplex cottages that are whitewashed and
trimmed in the perky pastels typical of the Caribbean,
appeals to both couples and families. **Pros:** rooms are large
and comfortable; good food; nice beach; exchange dining
program with sister resorts. **Cons:** not much available
immediately outside the resort, although it's not too far
from Bridgetown. ⑤ *Rooms from: $719* ⊠ *Hwy. 1, Appleby,*
St. James ☎ *246/432–2683* ⊕ *www.crystalcovehotelbarba-*
dos.com ⌖ *62 rooms, 26 suites* ⦿ *All-inclusive.*

$ ⛨ **Discovery Bay.** *Resort.* The price is right at this resort just
off the roadside in Holetown, considering the beachfront
location and convenience to the shopping, restaurants,
and nightlife opportunities—a five-minute walk from your
room. **Pros:** great Holetown location; good beach; good
value. **Cons:** rooms and service still relatively "rustic" ver-
sus top-of-the-line—but, again, the location is great and
the price is very affordable. ⑤ *Rooms from: $258* ⊠ *Hwy.*
1, Holetown, St. James ☎ *246/432–1301* ⊕ *www.rexresorts.*
com ⌖ *79 rooms, 9 suites* ⦿ *Multiple meal plans.*

$ ▦ **Divi Heritage Beach Resort.** *Resort.* This small, quiet, adults-only oceanfront enclave is simple, with few amenities—but it's a good option if you want to stay on the west coast at a good price. **Pros:** affordable; great location—walk to shopping and restaurants; access to pool and activities next door. **Cons:** tiny beach; no on-site dining facilities; rooms are due for an overhaul. Ⓢ *Rooms from: $145* ⌧ *Hwy. 1, Sunset Crest, St. James* ☎ *246/432–2968* ⊕ *www.diviresorts. com* ☞ *22 suites* ⓘ *No meals.*

★ **Fodor's** Choice ▦ **Fairmont Royal Pavilion.** *Resort.* Every guest room and suite in this luxurious adults-oriented resort (kids welcome April to October) has immediate access to 11 acres of lush tropical gardens and an uninterrupted view of the sea from its broad balcony or patio. **Pros:** beautiful resort; excellent service—everyone remembers your name; dining is excellent. **Cons:** dining is expensive; in fact, everything here is expensive. Ⓢ *Rooms from: $975* ⌧ *Hwy. 1, Porters, St. James* ☎ *246/422–5555* ⊕ *www.fairmont.com* ☞ *48 rooms, 24 suites, 1 3-bedroom villa* ⓘ *Multiple meal plans.*
$$$$

$$$$ ▦ **The House.** *Resort.* Privacy, luxury, and service are hall-
★ marks of this intimate adult sanctuary next door to sister resort Tamarind. **Pros:** trendy and stylish; striking public areas; privacy assured; pure relaxation. **Cons:** suites due for updating; atmosphere can be a little stuffy, but you can always head next door to Tamarind for a reality check. Ⓢ *Rooms from: $749* ⌧ *Hwy. 1, Paynes Bay, St. James* ☎ *246/432–5525, 888/996–9948 in the U.S.* ⊕ *www.the-housebarbados.com* ☞ *34 suites* ⓘ *Breakfast.*

$$$ ▦ **Little Good Harbour.** *Resort.* This cluster of modern, spa-
☺ cious, self-catering cottages with one-, two-, and three-bedroom duplex suites overlooks a narrow strip of beach in the far north of Barbados—just beyond the fishing village of Six Men's Bay. **Pros:** laid-back atmosphere; good for families; individualized experience. **Cons:** busy road; tiny beach; remote location. Ⓢ *Rooms from: $399* ⌧ *Hwy. 1B, Shermans, St. Peter* ☎ *246/439–3000* ⊕ *www.littlegoodhar-bourbarbados.com* ☞ *21 suites* ☾ *Closed Sept.* ⓘ *No meals.*

$$$$ ▦ **Lone Star Hotel.** *Hotel.* British owners transformed this 1940s-era service station into a sleek four-suite boutique hotel that—fortunately or unfortunately—has been discovered by celebrities. **Pros:** rub shoulders and chill with celebs (perhaps); enjoy great cuisine; you'll love the decor. **Cons:** not a good choice for kids; rubbing shoulders and chilling with celebs can get very expensive. Ⓢ *Rooms from: $850* ⌧ *Hwy. 1, Holetown, St. James* ☎ *246/419–0599* ⊕ *www. thelonestar.com* ☞ *4 rooms, 1 beach house* ⓘ *No meals.*

$$$ 🏨 **Mango Bay.** *All-inclusive.* In the heart of Holetown, this convenient boutique resort is within walking distance of shops, restaurants, nightspots, historic sites, and the public bus to either Bridgetown or Speightstown. **Pros:** nice rooms; great food; friendly staff; walk to Holetown shopping and entertainment. **Cons:** small pool; narrow beach; although heroic measures continue to be taken to address the problem, a natural drainage stream on the north side of the property can become odoriferous when it floods. $ *Rooms from: $400* ✉ *2nd St., Holetown, St. James* ☎ *246/432–1384* ⊕ *www.mangobaybarbados.com* ⬎ *64 rooms, 10 suites, 2 penthouse suites* ⫯⊙⫯ *All-inclusive.*

$$$$ 🏨 **Port St. Charles.** *Rental.* A luxury residential marina development near historic Speightstown on the northwest tip of Barbados, Port St. Charles is a perfect choice for boating enthusiasts who either arrive on their own yacht or plan to charter one during their stay. **Pros:** a boater's dream; well-appointed units with beautiful views; friendly and safe; great restaurant. **Cons:** not the best spot for little kids; minimum 14-night stay for some units in high season; noise is a problem for villas adjacent to the main road. $ *Rooms from: $507* ✉ *Hwy. 1B, Heywoods, St. Peter* ☎ *246/419–1000* ⊕ *www.portstcharles.com* ⬎ *25 villas* ⫯⊙⫯ *No meals.*

★ **Fodor'sChoice** 🏨 **The Sandpiper.** *Resort.* This little gem just
$$$$ north of Holetown is every bit as elegant as its sister hotel, Coral Reef Club, yet the atmosphere is more like a private hideaway. **Pros:** chic and sophisticated, the Tree Top Suites are fabulous; the bathrooms are amazing. **Cons:** beach is small—typical of west-coast beaches; hotel is small and many guests return year after year, so reservations can be hard to get. $ *Rooms from: $805* ✉ *Hwy. 1, Holetown, St. James* ☎ *246/422–2251* ⊕ *www.sandpiperbarbados.com* ⬎ *22 rooms, 25 suites* ⊙ *Closed Sept.* ⫯⊙⫯ *Multiple meal plans.*

★ **Fodor'sChoice** 🏨 **Sandy Lane Hotel and Golf Club.** *Hotel.* Few
$$$$ places on Earth can compare to Sandy Lane's luxurious
⟳ facilities and ultrapampering service—or to its astronomical prices. **Pros:** top of the line, cream of the crop—no debate about that; excellent dining; lovely beach; amazing spa; great golf courses. **Cons:** over the top for most mortals; very formal—you'll feel like dressing up just to walk through the lobby. $ *Rooms from: $2,355* ✉ *Hwy. 1, Paynes Bay, St. James* ☎ *246/444–2000* ⊕ *www.sandylane.com* ⬎ *96 rooms, 16 suites, 1 5-bedroom villa* ⫯⊙⫯ *Breakfast.*

$$ 🏨 **St. James Apartment Hotel.** *Hotel.* These apartments are perfectly situated right on Paynes Bay Beach, one of the best on the west coast. **Pros:** save money by cooking some

Port Charles Marina in Bridgetown, the island's capital

meals yourself; great quarters for independent travelers and long stays; great beach and sundeck; convenient to shopping and restaurants. **Cons:** no pool; no organized activities. Ⓢ *Rooms from: $280* ✉ *Hwy. 1, Paynes Bay, St. James* ☎ *246/432–0489* ⊕ *www.the-stjames.com* ➭ *11 apartments* ⦿ *No meals.*

$$$$ 🏨 **Tamarind.** *Resort.* This sleek Mediterranean-style resort, ☾ completely renovated and modernized in 2010, sprawls ★ along 750 feet of prime west-coast beachfront and is large enough to cater to sophisticated couples and active families while, at the same time, offering cozy privacy to honeymooners. **Pros:** very big resort, yet layout still affords privacy; central location right on Paynes Bay beach; lots of free water sports. **Cons:** even after the renovations, some rooms need a little TLC; uninspired buffet breakfast. Ⓢ *Rooms from: $535* ✉ *Hwy. 1, Paynes Bay, St. James* ☎ *246/432– 1332* ⊕ *www.tamarindbarbados.com* ➭ *57 rooms, 47 suites* ⦿ *Multiple meal plans.*

$$$$ 🏨 **Treasure Beach.** *Hotel.* Quiet, upscale, and intimate, this boutique all-suites hotel has a residential quality. **Pros:** cozy retreat; congenial crowd; swimming with the turtles just offshore. **Cons:** narrow beach; only bedrooms are air-conditioned; offshore turtles attract boatloads of tourists. Ⓢ *Rooms from: $575* ✉ *Hwy. 1, Paynes Bay, St. James* ☎ *246/432–1346, 800/355–6161 in the U.S.* ⊕ *www.trea-surebeachhotel.com* ➭ *35 suites* ⊙ *Closed Sept.–mid-Oct.* ⦿ *Multiple meal plans.*

NIGHTLIFE

When the sun goes down, the people come out to "lime" (which may be anything from a chat to a full-blown "jump-up" or street party). Performances by world-renowned stars and regional groups are major events, and tickets can be hard to come by—but give it a try. Most resorts have nightly entertainment in season, and nightclubs often have live bands for listening and dancing. The busiest bars and dance clubs rage until 3 am. On Saturday nights some clubs—especially those with live music—charge a cover of about $15.

Barbados supports the rum industry with more than 1,600 "rum shops," simple bars where (mostly) men congregate to discuss the world or life in general, drink rum, and eat a cutter (sandwich). In more sophisticated establishments you can find upscale rum cocktails made with the island's renowned Mount Gay and Cockspur brands—and no shortage of Barbados's own Banks Beer.

BRIDGETOWN

Boatyard. There's never a dull moment at The Boatyard, a popular pub with both a DJ and live bands. From happy hour until the wee hours the patrons are mostly local and visiting professionals. ✉ *Bay St., south of town, Carlisle Bay, Bridgetown, St. Michael* ☎ *246/436–2622* ⊕ *www. theboatyard.com.*

Harbour Lights. This open-air, beachfront club claims to be the "home of the party animal," and has dancing under the stars most nights to live reggae and soca music. ✉ *Upper Bay St., Bridgetown, St. Michael* ☎ *246/436–7225* ⊕ *www. harbourlightsbarbados.com.*

Waterfront Café. There's live jazz in the evening at Waterfront Cafe, which also has a small dance floor. The location alongside the wharf is also a draw. ✉ *The Careenage, Bridgetown, St. Michael* ☎ *246/427–0093.*

SOUTH COAST

Bubba's Sports Bar. On the south coast, Bubba's offers merrymakers and sports lovers live sports on three 10-foot video screens and a dozen TVs, along with a Bajan à la carte menu and drinks at the bar. ✉ *Main Rd., Rockley, Christ Church* ☎ *246/435–6217* ⊕ *bubbassportsbar.net.*

CLOSE UP

Nightspots A-Plenty

St. Lawrence Gap, the narrow waterfront byway with restaurants, bars, and nightclubs one right after another, is where the action is on the south coast. In Holetown, on the west coast, the restaurants and clubs on 1st and 2nd streets are giving "the Gap" a run for its money. Along with a half dozen or so restaurants that offer fare ranging from ribs or pizza to elegant cuisine, a handful of nightspots and night "experiences" have cropped up recently. After-dinner drinks at the Mews or at Lexy Piano Bar are popular any evening, but on Sunday evenings locals and tourists alike descend on One Love Rum Shop for the karaoke and to Ragamuffin's restaurant, next door, for the after-dinner drag show.

McBride's Pub. McBride's is, as you night have guessed, a popular Irish pub with Irish beer on tap, pub grub from the kitchen, and Irish music, karaoke, reggae, rock, Latin, or techno music every night. Happy hour(s) run from 11 pm to 1 am every night. ⊠ *St. Lawrence Gap, Dover, Christ Church* ☎ *246/436–6352.*

★ Fodor'sChoice **Oistins Fish Fry.** Oistins is the place to be on Friday evenings, when the south-coast fishing village becomes a convivial outdoor street party. Barbecued chicken and a variety of fish are served right from the grill, along with all the traditional sides (rice and peas, yams, fries, salad, etc.), and consumed at roadside picnic tables; servings are huge, and prices are inexpensive—about $10 per plate. Drinks, music, and dancing add to the fun. ⊠ *Oistins, Christ Church.*

DID YOU KNOW? Baxter's Road is sometimes called "The Street that Never Sleeps." Night owls head for Baxter's Road, in Bridgetown, any night of the week for after-hours fun and food. The strip of rum shops begins to hit its stride at 11 pm, but locals usually show up around 3 am. Street vendors sell freshly made "Baxter's Road" fried chicken and other snacks all night long, but Enid's is the place to see and be seen.

★ Fodor'sChoice **Plantation Restaurant and Garden Theater.** On Wednesday and Friday evenings the Tropical Spectacular calypso cabaret presents *Bajan Roots and Rhythms*, a delightful extravaganza representing West Indian culture that the whole family will enjoy. The show includes steel-

The Oistins Fish Fry, held every night in the south coast fishing village

band music, fire eating, limbo, and dancing to the reggae, soca, and pop music sounds of popular Barbadian singer John King and the Plantation House Band. The fun begins at 8 pm. A Barbadian buffet dinner, unlimited drinks, transportation, and the show cost $85; for the show and drinks only, it's $50. ⊠ *Plantation Complex, St. Lawrence Main Rd., Dover, Christ Church* ☎ *246/621–5048* ⊕ *www. plantationtheatre.com.*

★ **Reggae Lounge.** This is a popular nightspot in the Gap, where live bands or DJs play the latest Jamaican hits and old reggae favorites. ⊠ *St. Lawrence Gap, Dover, Christ Church* ☎ *246/435–6462.*

WEST COAST

★ **Lexy Piano Bar.** Lexy's is a cool, trendy club named for owner Alex Santoriello, a transplanted Broadway singer and actor. A changing roster of singer-pianists play sing-along standards, classic rock, R&B, and Broadway tunes—and you can also enjoy a treat from the sushi bar. Most any night you'll find Santoriello there. ⊠ *2nd St., Holetown, St. James* ☎ *246/432–5399* ⊕ *www.lexypianobar.com* ⊙ *Closed Mon.*

Bajan Roots and Rhythms at the Plantation Restaurant and Garden Theatre

SHOPPING

WHAT TO BUY

One of the most long-lasting souvenirs to bring home from Barbados is a piece of authentic Caribbean art. The colorful flowers, quaint villages, mesmerizing seascapes, and fascinating cultural experiences and activities that are endemic to the region and familiar to visitors have been translated by local artists onto canvas and into photographs, sculpture, and other mediums. Gift shops and even some restaurants display local artwork for sale, but the broadest array of artwork will be found in a gallery. Typical crafts include pottery, shell and glass art, wood carvings, handmade dolls, watercolors, and other artwork (both originals and prints).

Although many of the private homes, great houses, and museums in Barbados are filled with priceless antiques, you'll find few for sale—mainly British antiques and some local pieces, particularly mahogany furniture. Look especially for planters' chairs and the classic Barbadian rocking chair, as well as old prints and paintings.

DUTY-FREE SHOPPING

Duty-free luxury goods—china, crystal, cameras, porcelain, leather items, electronics, jewelry, perfume, and clothing—are found in Bridgetown's Broad Street department stores and their branches, at the high-end Limegrove Lifestyle Centre in Holetown, at the Bridgetown Cruise Terminal shops (for passengers only), and in the departure-lounge shops at Grantley Adams International Airport. Prices are often 30% to 40% less than at home. To buy goods at duty-free prices, you must produce your passport, immigration form, or driver's license, along with departure information (such as flight number and date) at the time of purchase—or you can have your purchases delivered free to the airport or harbor for pickup. Duty-free alcohol, tobacco products, and some electronic equipment *must* be delivered to you at the airport or harbor.

BRIDGETOWN

Bridgetown's **Broad Street** is the primary downtown shopping area. **DaCosta Manning Mall,** in the historic Colonnade Building on Broad Street, has more than 25 shops that sell everything from Piaget watches to postcards; across the street, **Mall 34** has 22 shops where you can buy duty-free goods, souvenirs, and snacks. At the **cruise-ship terminal** shopping arcade, passengers can buy both duty-free goods and Barbadian-made crafts at more than 30 boutiques and a dozen vendor carts and stalls.

BRIDGETOWN SHOPPING SHUTTLE. A free Bridgetown shuttle serves hotels on the south and west coasts, so guests can visit downtown shops, see the sites, and perhaps have lunch. The shuttle operates Monday through Saturday, departing from the hotels at 9:30 and 11 am and returning from Bridgetown at 1:30 and 3 pm. Reserve your seat with your hotel concierge a day ahead.

CLOTHING

Dingolay. Dingolay sells tropical clothing designed and made in Barbados for women and girls, as well as shoes, handbags, and accessories from around the world. ⊠ *Da-Costa–Mannings Mall, Broad St., Bridgetown, St. Michael* ☎ *246/437–4107* ⊠ *Chattel House Village, Hwy. 1, Holetown, St. James* ☎ *246/432–8709.*

Irie Blue. Check out the colorful T-shirts from this company, which designs and makes its products in Barbados. You can also find them in many gift shops. ⊠ *DaCosta–Mannings Mall, Broad St., Bridgetown, St. Michael* ☎ *246/431–0017.*

DEPARTMENT STORES

Cave Shepherd. Cave Shepherd offers a wide selection of clothing and luxury goods; branch stores are in Holetown, at the airport, and at the cruise-ship terminal. ⊠ *Broad St., Bridgetown, St. Michael* ☎ *246/431–2121.*

Harrison's. Harrison's is a department store with several locations, including two large stores on Broad Street and branches at the airport and cruise-ship terminal. ⊠ *Broad St., Bridgetown, St. Michael* ☎ *246/431–5500.*

DUTY-FREE GOODS

Little Switzerland. This mini-chain's anchor shop is at DaCosta-Mannings Mall, with branches at the cruise-ship terminal and in Holetown. Here you can find perfume, jewelry, cameras, audio equipment, Swarovski and Waterford crystal, and Wedgwood china. ⊠ *DaCosta-Mannings Mall, Broad St., Bridgetown, St. Michael* ☎ *246/431–0030.*

Royal Shop. The Royal Shop carries fine watches and jewelry fashioned in Italian gold, Caribbean silver, diamonds, and other gems. ⊠ *32 Broad St., Bridgetown, St. Michael* ☎ *246/429–7072.*

★ **Pelican Craft Centre.** Pelican is made up of a cluster of workshops halfway between the cruise-ship terminal and downtown Bridgetown, where craftspeople create and sell locally made leather goods, batik, basketry, carvings, jewelry, glass art, paintings, pottery, and other items. It's open weekdays 9 to 5 and Saturday 9 to 2; things here are most active when cruise ships are in port. ⊠ *Princess Alice Hwy., Bridgetown, St. Michael* ☎ *246/427–5350.*

SOUTH COAST

The St. Lawrence Gap, like Holetown, has a **Chattel House Village,** where you can buy locally made crafts and other souvenirs. In Rockley, Christ Church, **Quayside Shopping Center** houses a small group of boutiques, restaurants, and services.

Best of Barbados. Best of Barbados was the brainchild of architect Jimmy Walker as a place to showcase the works of his artist wife. Now with five locations, the shops offer products that range from Jill Walker's frameable prints, housewares, and textiles to arts and crafts in both "native" style and modern designs. Everything is made or designed on Barbados. ⊠ *Quayside Centre, Main Rd., Rockley, Christ Church* ☎ *246/435–6820* ⊕ *www.best-of-barbados.com.*

Tyrol Cot Heritage Village. In the chattel houses at Tyrol Cot Heritage Village, you can watch local artisans make hand-painted figurines, straw baskets, clothing, paintings, and pottery—and buy their wares. The workshops are open primarily during the winter season and when cruise ships are in port. ✉ *Codrington Hill, St. Michael* ☎ *246/424–2074.*

WEST COAST

Holetown has the upscale **Limegrove Lifestyle Centre,** a stylish shopping mall with high-end designer boutiques, as well as **Chattel House Village,** a cluster of shops selling local products, fashions, beachwear, and souvenirs. Also in Holetown, **Sunset Crest Mall** has two branches of the Cave Shepherd department store, a bank, a pharmacy, and several small shops; at **West Coast Mall** you can buy duty-free goods, island wear, and groceries.

Dingolay. Dingolay sells tropical clothing designed and made in Barbados for women and girls, as well as shoes, handbags, and accessories from around the world. ✉ *Chattel House Village, Hwy. 1, Holetown, St. James* ☎ *246/432–8709.*

★ **Fodor's Choice Earthworks Pottery.** Earthworks is a family-owned and -operated pottery workshop, where you can purchase anything from a dish or knickknack to a complete dinner service or one-of-a-kind art piece. You can find the characteristically blue or green pottery—and, more recently, peach and brown hues—decorating hotel rooms and for sale in gift shops throughout the island; but the biggest selection (including some "seconds") is at Earthworks, where you also can watch the potters at work. ✉ *Edgehill Heights, St. Thomas* ☎ *246/425–0223* ⊕ *www.earthworks-pottery. com* ⊘ *Closed Sun.*

Gallery of Caribbean Art. This gallery is committed to promoting Caribbean art from Cuba to Curaçao, including a number of pieces by Barbadian artists. A branch gallery is at the Hilton Barbados hotel, Needham's Point. ✉ *Northern Business Centre, Queen St., Speightstown, St. Peter* ☎ *246/419–0858* ⊕ *www.artgallerycaribbean.com* ⊘ *Closed Sun.*

Greenwich House Antiques. Greenwich House Antiques fills an entire plantation house with vintage Barbadian mahogany furniture, art deco pieces, crystal, silver, china, books, and pictures; it's open daily from 10:30 to 5:30. ✉ *Greenwich Village, Trents Hill, St. James* ☎ *246/432–1169.*

On the Wall Art Gallery. This gallery, adjacent to Earthworks Pottery, has an array of original paintings by Barbadian artists, along with arts and crafts products. An additional gallery is in dedicated space at Champers restaurant on the south coast. ⊠ *Earthworks Pottery, Edgehill Heights, St. Thomas* ☎ *246/425–0223* ⊕ *www.onthewallartgallery. com* ⊘ *Closed Sun.*

Red Clay Pottery and Fairfield Gallery. This gallery has been operated by potter Denis Bell all his life, "save a little time spent doing some engineering and raising a family." Visitors are welcome to watch the potters at work in the studio, which is in an old sugar-boiling house, and, in the adjacent shop, purchase plates, platters, bowls, place settings, and fine decorative items designed by Bell's daughter, Maggie. ⊠ *Fairfield House, Fairfield Cross Rd., Fairfield, St. Michael* ☎ *246/424–3800.*

SPORTS AND ACTIVITIES

Cricket, football (soccer), polo, and rugby are extremely popular sports in Barbados among participants and spectators alike, with local, regional, and international matches held throughout the year. Contact the Barbados Tourism Authority or check local newspapers for information about schedules and tickets.

DIVING AND SNORKELING

More than two dozen dive sites lie along the west coast between Maycocks Bay and Bridgetown and off the south coast as far as the St. Lawrence Gap. Certified divers can explore flat coral reefs and see dramatic sea fans, huge barrel sponges, and more than 50 varieties of fish. Nine sunken wrecks are dived regularly, and at least 10 more are accessible to experts. Underwater visibility is generally 80 to 90 feet. The calm waters along the west coast are also ideal for snorkeling. The marine reserve, a stretch of protected reef between Sandy Lane and the Colony Club, contains beautiful coral formations accessible from the beach.

On the west coast, **Bell Buoy** is a large, dome-shape reef where huge brown coral tree forests and schools of fish delight all categories of divers at depths ranging from 20 to 60 feet. At **Dottins Reef,** off Holetown, you can see schooling fish, barracudas, and turtles at depths of 40 to 60 feet. **Maycocks Bay,** on the northwest coast, is a particularly enticing

Cricket, a popular sport because of the island's British heritage

site; large coral reefs are separated by corridors of white sand, and visibility is often 100 feet or more. The 165-foot freighter *Pamir* lies in 60 feet of water off Six Men's Bay; it's still intact, and you can peer through its portholes and view dozens of varieties of tropical fish. **Silver Bank** is a healthy coral reef with beautiful fish and sea fans; you may get a glimpse of the *Atlantis* submarine at 60 to 80 feet. Not to be missed is the *Stavronikita*, a scuttled Greek freighter at about 135 feet; hundreds of butterfly fish hang out around its mast, and the thin rays of sunlight filtering down through the water make fully exploring the huge ship a wonderfully eerie experience.

Farther south, **Carlisle Bay** is a natural harbor and marine park just below Bridgetown. Here you can retrieve empty bottles thrown overboard by generations of sailors and see cannons and cannonballs, anchors, and six unique ship-wrecks (*Berwyn*, *Fox*, *CTrek*, *Eilon*, the barge *Cornwallis*, and *Bajan Queen*) lying in 25 to 60 feet of water, all close enough to visit on the same dive. The *Bajan Queen*, a cruise vessel that sank in 2002, is the island's newest wreck.

Dive shops provide a two-hour beginner's "resort" course ($85 to $100) followed by a shallow dive, or a weeklong certification course (about $425). Once you're certified, a one-tank dive runs about $60 to $75; a two-tank dive is $90 to $100. All equipment is supplied, and you can purchase multidive packages. Gear for snorkeling is available (free or for a small rental fee) from most hotels. Snorkelers can usually accompany dive trips for $25 for a one- or two-hour trip. Most dive shops have relationships with several hotels and offer special dive packages, with transportation, to hotel guests.

Dive Shop, Ltd. Near the Carlisle Bay marine park just south of Bridgetown, the Dive Shop, Ltd—the island's oldest dive shop—offers daily reef and wreck dives, plus beginner classes, certification courses, and underwater photography instruction. Underwater cameras are available for rent. Free transfers are provided between your hotel and the dive shop. ⊠ *Amey's Alley, Upper Bay St., Bridgetown, St. Michael* ☎ *246/426–9947, 888/898–3483 in the U.S.* ⊕ *www.divebds.com.*

Hightide Watersports. On the west coast, Hightide Watersports offers three dive trips—one- and two-tank dives and night reef–wreck–drift dives—daily for up to eight divers, along with PADI instruction, equipment rental, and free transportation. ⊠ *Coral Reef Club, Hwy. 1, Holetown, St. James* ☎ *246/432–0931, 800/970–0016, 800/513–5763* ⊕ *www.divehightide.com.*

Reefers & Wreckers Dive Shop. In Speightstown, the most northerly dive shop allows easy access to the unspoiled reefs in the north but also offers regular trips to the dive sites and wrecks along the west coast and in Carlisle Bay. ⊠ *Queen St., Speightstown, St. Peter* ☎ *246/422–5420* ⊕ *www.scubadiving.bb.*

FISHING

Fishing is a year-round activity in Barbados, but its prime time is January through April, when game fish are in season. Whether you're a serious deep-sea fisher looking for marlin, sailfish, tuna, and other billfish or you prefer angling in calm coastal waters where wahoo, barracuda, and other small fish reside, you can choose from a variety of half- or full-day charter trips departing from the Careenage in Bridgetown. Expect to pay $175 per person for a shared half-day charter; for a private charter, expect to pay $500 to $600 per boat for a four-hour half-day or $950 to $1,000 for an eight-hour full-day charter. Spectators who don't fish are welcome for $50 per person.

Billfisher II. *Billfisher II*, a 40-foot Pacemaker, accommodates up to six passengers with three fishing chairs and five rods.

CLOSE UP

Sports Legend: Sir Garfield Sobers

Cricket is more than a national pastime in Barbados. It's a passion. And no one is more revered than Sir Garfield Sobers, the greatest sportsman ever to come from Barbados and globally acknowledged as the greatest all-round cricketer the game has ever seen. Sobers played his first test match in 1953 at the age of 17 and continually set and broke records until his last test match in 1973. He was an equally accomplished batsman and bowler. He was knighted by Queen Elizabeth II in 1974 for his contributions to the sport and honored as a national hero of Barbados in 1999.

2

Captain Winston ("The Colonel") White has been fishing these waters since 1975. His full-day charters include a full lunch and guaranteed fish (or a 25% refund); all trips include drinks and transportation to and from the boat. ⊠ *Bridge House Wharf, The Careenage, Bridgetown, St. Michael* ☎ *246/431–0741.*

Blue Jay & Blue Marlin. *Blue Jay* is a spacious, fully equipped, 45-foot Sport Fisherman; *Blue Marlin* is a 36-foot Sport Fisherman. Each has a crew that knows the water's denizens—blue marlin, sailfish, barracuda, and kingfish. Most fishing is done by trolling. Drinks, snacks, bait, tackle, and transfers are provided. ⊠ *Fishing Charters Barbados, Inc., 50 Ridge Ave., Durants, Christ Church* ☎ *246/234–1688* ⊕ *www.bluemarlinbarbados.com.*

Cannon II. *Cannon II*, a 42-foot Hatteras Sport Fisherman, has three chairs and five rods and accommodates six passengers; drinks and snacks are complimentary, and lunch is served on full-day charters. ⊠ *Cannon Charters, Prior Park, St. James* ☎ *246/424–6107.*

GOLF

Barbadians love golf, and golfers love Barbados.

Barbados Golf Club. Barbados Golf Club, the first public golf course on Barbados, is an 18-hole championship course (6,805 yards, par 72) redesigned in 2000 by golf course architect Ron Kirby. Greens fees with a cart are $125 for 18 holes; $80 for 9 holes. Unlimited three-day and seven-day

golf passes are available. Several hotels offer preferential tee-time reservations and reduced rates. Club and shoe rentals are available. ✉ *Hwy. 7, Durants, Christ Church* ☎ *246/428–8463* ⊕ *www.barbadosgolfclub.com.*

★ Fodor'sChoice **Country Club at Sandy Lane.** At the prestigious Country Club at Sandy Lane, golfers can play on the Old Nine or on either of two 18-hole championship courses: the Tom Fazio–designed Country Club Course or the spectacular Green Monkey Course, reserved for hotel guests and club members only. Golfers have complimentary use of the club's driving range. The Country Club Restaurant and Bar, which overlooks the 18th hole, is open to the public. Greens fees in high season are $155 for 9 holes ($135 for hotel guests) or $240 for 18 holes ($205 for hotel guests). Golf carts, caddies, or trolleys are available for hire, as are clubs and shoes. Carts are equipped with GPS, which alerts you to upcoming traps and hazards, provides tips on how to play the hole, and allows you to order refreshments! ✉ *Sandy Lane, Hwy. 1, Paynes Bay, St. James* ☎ *246/444–2500* ⊕ *www.sandylane.com/golf.*

Rockley Golf and Country Club. Rockley Golf and Country Club, on the south coast, has a challenging 9-hole course (2,800 yards, par 35) that can be played as 18 from varying tee positions. Club and cart rentals are available. Greens fees are $61.50 for 18 holes and $51 for 9 holes. Weekly rates are available. ✉ *Golf Club Rd., Rockley, Christ Church* ☎ *246/435–7873* ⊕ *www.rockleygolfclub.com.*

★ **Royal Westmoreland Golf Club.** The Royal Westmoreland Golf Club has a well-regarded Robert Trent Jones Jr.–designed, 18-hole championship course (6,870 yards, par 72) that meanders through the 500-acre property. This challenging course is primarily for villa renters, with a few midmorning tee times for visitors subject to availability. Greens fees for villa renters or guests at hotels with golf privileges at the club are $300 for tee times before 10 am or $250 after 10 am for 18 holes and $125 after 2 pm for 9 holes. Greens fees for visitors (10 am to 11 am tee times only) are $375. Greens fees include use of an electric cart (required); club rental is available. ✉ *Royal Westmoreland Resort, Westmoreland, St. James* ☎ *246/419–0394* ⊕ *www. royal-westmoreland.com.*

GUIDED TOURS

Taxi drivers will give you a personalized tour of Barbados for about $35 to $40 per hour for up to three people. Or you can choose an overland mountain-bike journey, a 4x4 safari expedition, or a full-day bus excursion. The prices vary according to the mode of travel and the number and kind of attractions included. Ask guest services at your hotel to help you make arrangements.

Highland Adventure Centre. Highland Adventure Centre offers mountain-bike tours for $60 per person, including transportation, guides, and refreshments. The trip is an exhilarating 7½-mile (12-km) ride (15% uphill) through the heart of northern Barbados, ending up at Barclays Park on the east coast. ✉ *Cane Field, St. Thomas* ☎ *246/438–8069.*

Island Safari. Island Safari will take you to all the popular spots via a 4x4 Land Rover—including some gullies, forests, and remote areas that are inaccessible by conventional cars and buses. The cost for half-day or full-day tours ranges from $50 to $92.50 per person, including snacks or lunch. ✉ *CWTS Complex, Salters Rd., Lower Estate, St. George* ☎ *246/429–5337* ⊕ *www.islandsafari.bb.*

HIKING

Hilly but not mountainous, the northern interior and the east coast are ideal for hiking.

Arbib Heritage and Nature Trail. The Arbib Heritage and Nature Trail, maintained by the Barbados National Trust, is actually two trails—one offers a rigorous hike through gullies and plantations to old ruins and remote north-country areas; the other is a shorter, easier walk through Speightstown's side streets and past an ancient church and chattel houses. Three-hour guided hikes take place daily at 9:30 and 2:30 and cost $50 for one or two people; group rates are available. Book ahead, preferably four days in advance. Not recommended for children under 5. ✉ *Speightstown, St. Peter* ☎ *246/426–2421* ⊕ *trust.funbarbados.com.*

Hike Barbados. A program of free walks sponsored by the Barbados National Trust, Hike Barbados treks take place year-round on Sunday from 6 am to about 9 am and from 3:30 pm to 6 pm; once a month a moonlight hike substitutes for the afternoon hike and begins at 5:30 pm (bring a flashlight). Experienced guides group you with others of similar levels of ability. Stop and Stare hikes go 5 to 6 miles

(8 to 10 km); Here and There, 8 to 10 miles (13 to 16 km); and Grin and Bear, 12 to 14 miles (19 to 23 km). Wear loose clothes, sensible shoes, sunscreen, and a hat, and bring your camera and a bottle of water. Routes and locations change, but each hike is a loop, finishing in the same spot where it began. Check local newspapers, call the Trust, or check online for the full hike schedule or the scheduled meeting place on a particular Sunday. ⊠ *Wildey House, Wildey, St. Michael* ☎ *246/436–9033, 246/426–2421* ⊕ *www.trust. funbarbados.com.*

HORSE RACING

Barbados Turf Club. Horse racing is administered by the Barbados Turf Club; races take place on alternate Saturdays throughout the year at the Garrison Savannah, a 6-furlong grass oval in Christ Church, about 3 miles (5 km) south of Bridgetown. The important races are the Sandy Lane Barbados Gold Cup, held in late February or early March, and the United Insurance Barbados Derby Day in August. Post time is 1:30 pm. General admission is $7.50; it's $15 for grandstand seats and $25 for the clubhouse. (Prices are higher on Gold Cup day.) ⊠ *Garrison, St. Michael* ☎ *246/426–3980* ⊕ *www.barbadosturfclub.org.*

SEA EXCURSIONS

Mini-submarine voyages are enormously popular with families and those who enjoy watching fish but don't wish to snorkel or dive. Party boats depart from Bridgetown's Deep Water Harbour for sightseeing and snorkeling or romantic sunset cruises. Prices are $75 to $90 per person for daytime cruises and $60 to $85 for three-hour sunset cruises, depending on the type of refreshments and entertainment included; transportation to and from the dock is provided. For an excursion that may be less splashy in terms of a party atmosphere—but is definitely splashier in terms of the actual experience—turtle tours allow participants to feed and swim with a resident group of hawksbill and leatherback sea turtles.

⟲ *Atlantis* **Submarine.** The 48-passenger *Atlantis* Submarine turns the Caribbean into a giant aquarium. The 45-minute underwater voyage aboard the 50-foot submarine ($104 per person, including transportation) takes you to wrecks and reefs as deep as 150 feet. Children love the adventure, but they must be at least 3 feet tall to go on board. ⊠ *Shal-*

The Sandy Lane Gold Cup at the Barbados Turf Club

low Draught, Bridgetown, St. Michael ☎ 246/436–8929 ⊕ *barbados.atlantissubmarines.com.*

Cool Runnings. On the catamaran *Cool Runnings*, owner Captain Povey skippers a five-hour lunch cruise with stops to swim with the fishes, snorkel with sea turtles, and explore a shallow shipwreck. A four-hour sunset cruise includes swimming, snorkeling, and exploring underwater as the sun sinks below the horizon. Delicious meals with wine, along with an open bar, are part of all cruises. ✉ *Carlisle House, Carlisle Wharf, Hincks St., Bridgetown, St. Michael* ☎ 246/436–0911 ⊕ *www.coolrunningsbarbados.com.*

Jolly Roger 1. The whole family will get a kick out of a "pirate" ship sailing adventure on *Jolly Roger 1*. The four-hour day and sunset cruises along the island's west coast include a barbecue lunch or dinner, free-flowing drinks, lively music, swimming with turtles, and "pirate" activities such as walking the plank and rope swinging. ✉ *Shallow Draught, Bridgetown, St. Michael* ☎ 246/436–2885, 246/826–7245 ⊕ *www.barbadosblackpearl-jollyroger1.com.*

☾ **MV *Harbour Master*.** Five-hour daytime cruises along the west coast on the 100-foot MV *Harbour Master* party boat (four decks of fun) stop in Holetown and land at beaches along the way; evening cruises are shorter but add a buffet dinner and entertainment. Day or night you can view the briny deep from the ship's onboard 34-seat semi-

submersible. ✉ *Shallow Draught, Bridgetown, St. Michael* ☎ *246/430–0900* ⊕ *www.tallshipscruises.com.*

Tiami. The 53-foot catamaran *Tiami* offers a luncheon cruise to a secluded bay or a romantic sunset and moonlight cruise with special catering and live music. ✉ *Shallow Draught, Bridgetown, St. Michael* ☎ *246/430–0900* ⊕ *www.tallshipscruises.com.*

SURFING

The best surfing is at Bathsheba Soup Bowl on the east coast, but the water here, on the windward (Atlantic Ocean) side of the island, is safe only for the most experienced surfers. Surfers also congregate at Surfer's Point, at the southern tip of Barbados near Inch Marlow, where the Atlantic Ocean meets the Caribbean Sea.

Barbados Surfing Association. The Independence Classic Surfing Championship (an international competition) is held at Bathsheba Soup Bowl every November—when the surf is at its peak. For information, contact the Barbados Surfing Association. ✉ *Olympic Centre, Garfield Sobers Sports Complex, Wildey, St. Michael* ☎ *246/826–7661* ⊕ *www.barbadossurfingassociation.org.*

Dread or Dead Surf Shop. Dread or Dead Surf Shop promises to get beginners from "zero to standing up and surfing" in a single afternoon. The four-hour course—"or until you stand up or give up"—costs $75 per person and includes a board, wax, a rash guard (if necessary), a ride to and from the surf break, and an instructor; additional lessons cost $37.50. Intermediate or experienced surfers can get all the equipment and the instructor for a full day of surfing for $150. ✉ *Hastings Main Rd., Hastings, Christ Church* ☎ *246/228–4785* ⊕ *www.dreadordead.com.*

Zed's Surfing Adventures. Zed's Surfing Adventures rents surfboards, provides lessons, and offers surf tours—which include equipment, a guide, and transportation to surf breaks appropriate for your experience. ✉ *Surfer's Point, Inch Marlow, Christ Church* ☎ *246/428–7873* ⊕ *www.barbadossurfholidays.com.*

CLOSE UP

Sea Urchin Alert

Black spiny sea urchins lurk in the sand on the shallow sea bottom and near reefs. Should you step on one, its sharp venom-filled spines will cause a painful wound. They've even been known to pierce wet suits, so divers should be careful when brushing up against submerged rock walls. Getting several stings at once can cause muscle spasms and breathing difficulties for some people, so victims need to get help immediately. Clean the wound before carefully removing the stinger(s). Some say ammonia (aka urine) is the best remedy. We say it's lime and alcohol. So should the worst happen, find the nearest bartender.

2

WINDSURFING AND KITEBOARDING

Barbados is on the World Cup Windsurfing Circuit and is one of the prime locations in the world for windsurfing—and, increasingly, for kiteboarding. Winds are strongest November through April at the island's southern tip, at Silver Sands–Silver Rock Beach, which is where the Barbados Windsurfing Championships are held in mid-January. Use of windsurfing boards and equipment, as well as instruction, is often among the amenities included at larger hotels, and some also rent to nonguests. Kiteboarding is a more difficult sport that requires several hours of instruction to reach proficiency; Silver Sands is about the only location where you'll find kiteboarding equipment and instruction.

deAction Surf Shop. At his shop directly on Silver Sands–Silver Rock Beach, Brian "Irie Man" Talma stocks a range of rental surfing equipment and offers beginner windsurfing, kiteboarding, and surfing lessons taught by a professional team of instructors. The conditions here are ideal, with waves off the outer reef and flat water in the inner lagoon. Kiteboarding, which isn't easy, generally involves six hours of instruction broken up into two or three sessions: from flying a small kite to getting the body dragged with a big kite to finally getting up on the board. All equipment is provided. ⊠ *Silver Sands–Silver Rock Beach, Silver Sands, Christ Church* ☎ *246/428–2027* ⊕ *www.briantalma.com.*

3

St. Lucia

WORD OF MOUTH

"St. Lucia is very lush, with mountains, flora, fauna, plantations, and waterfalls. Reminded us of Jamaica and Hawaii. Driving can be a little difficult, and everything is quite spread out. The beaches are made up of coarse brownish/beige sand and the water is a dark blue. There are a few black sand beaches also."

—KVR

By Jane E.
Zarem

A LUSH, MOUNTAINOUS ISLAND between Martinique and St. Vincent, St. Lucia has evolved into one of the Caribbean's most popular vacation destinations—particularly for honeymooners and other romantics enticed by the island's striking natural beauty, its many splendid resorts and appealing inns, and its welcoming atmosphere.

The capital city of Castries and nearby villages in the northwest are home to 40% of the population. This area, along with Rodney Bay farther north and Marigot Bay just south of the capital, are the destinations of most vacationers. In the central and southwestern parts of the island dense rain forest, jungle-covered mountains, and vast banana plantations dominate the landscape. A tortuous road follows most of the coastline, bisecting small villages, cutting through mountains, and passing by fertile valleys. On the southwest coast, Petit Piton and Gros Piton, the island's unusual twin peaks that rise out of the sea to more than 2,600 feet, are familiar landmarks for sailors and aviators alike. Divers are attracted to the reefs found just north of Soufrière, which was the capital during French colonial times. Most of the natural tourist attractions are in this area, along with several more fine resorts and inns.

The pirate François Le Clerc, nicknamed Jambe de Bois (Wooden Leg) for obvious reasons, was the first European "settler" in St. Lucia. In the late 16th century Le Clerc holed up on Pigeon Island, just off the island's northernmost point, and used it as a staging ground for attacking passing ships. Now Pigeon Island is a national park, connected by a causeway to the mainland; today Sandals Grande St. Lucian Spa & Beach Resort, one of the largest resorts in St. Lucia, and The Landings, a luxury villa community, sprawl along that causeway.

Like most of its Caribbean neighbors, St. Lucia was first inhabited by Arawaks and then the Carib Indians. British settlers attempted to colonize the island twice in the early 1600s, but it wasn't until 1651, after the French West India Company suppressed the local Caribs, that Europeans gained a foothold. For 150 years battles over possession of the island were frequent between the French and the British, with a dizzying 14 changes in power before the British finally took possession in 1814. The Europeans established sugar plantations, using slaves from West Africa to work the fields. By 1838, when the slaves were emancipated, more than 90% of the population was of

African descent—roughly the same proportion of today's 170,000 St. Lucians.

On February 22, 1979, St. Lucia became an independent state within the British Commonwealth of Nations, with a resident governor-general appointed by the queen. Still, the island appears to have retained more relics of French influence—notably the island patois, cuisine, village names, and surnames—than of the British. Most likely, that's because the British contribution primarily involved the English language, the educational and legal systems, and the political structure, whereas the French culture historically had more influence on the arts—culinary, dance, and music.

The island becomes especially tuneful for 10 days every May, when the St. Lucia Jazz Festival welcomes renowned international musicians who perform for enthusiastic fans at Pigeon Island National Park and other island venues. St. Lucians themselves love jazz—and the beat of Caribbean music resonates throughout the island.

PLANNING

WHEN TO GO
The high season runs from mid-December through mid-April and during the annual St. Lucia Jazz Festival and Carnival events; at other times of the year hotel rates can be significantly cheaper. December and January are the coolest months, and June through August are the hottest. Substantial rain (more than just a tropical spritz) is more likely from June through November.

FESTIVALS AND EVENTS
In April the **St. Lucia Golf Open** is an amateur tournament at the St. Lucia Golf Resort & Country Club in Cap Estate.

The **St. Lucia Jazz Festival** in early May is the year's big event; during that week you may have trouble finding a hotel room at any price.

St. Lucia's summer **Carnival** is held in Castries beginning in late June and continuing into July.

The **St. Lucia Billfishing Tournament**, which attracts anglers from far and wide, is held in late September or early October.

October is Creole Heritage Month, which culminates in **Jounen Kwéyòl Entenasyonnal** (International Creole Day) on the last Sunday of the month.

LOGISTICS

Getting to St. Lucia: St. Lucia's primary gateway is Hewanorra International Airport (UVF) in Vieux Fort, on the island's southern tip. Regional airlines fly into George F. L. Charles Airport (SLU) in Castries, commonly called Vigie Airport and more convenient to resorts in the north. The drive between Hewanorra and resorts in the north takes 90 minutes; the trip between Hewanorra and Soufrière takes about 45 minutes.

Hassle Factor: Medium to high, because of the long drive from Hewanorra International Airport.

On the Ground: Taxis are available at both airports, although transfers may be included in your travel package. It's an expensive ride to the north from Hewanorra—at least $75—and about $65 to Soufrière. A helicopter shuttle cuts the transfer time to about 10 minutes, but the cost doubles.

Getting Around the Island: A car is more important if you are staying at a small inn or hotel away from the beach. If you're staying at an all-inclusive beach resort and you don't plan to leave for meals, taxis may be the better bet.

In late November or early December the finish of the **Atlantic Rally for Cruisers,** the world's largest ocean-crossing race, is marked by a week of festivities at Rodney Bay.

DO I NEED A CAR?

A car is more important if you are staying at a small inn or hotel away from the beach. Just keep in mind that driving is on the left, British-style. If you're staying at an all-inclusive beach resort and you don't plan to leave for meals, taxis may be the better bet. However, privately owned and operated minivans constitute St. Lucia's bus system, an inexpensive and efficient means of transportation used primarily by locals. Buses are a good way to travel between Castries and the Rodney Bay area. Water taxis are also available in some places and can save time.

SAFETY

Although crime isn't a significant problem in St. Lucia, take the same precautions you would at home—lock your door, secure your valuables, and don't carry too much money or flaunt expensive jewelry on the street. It's safe (not to mention convenient) to ride local buses in the Rodney Bay area. The Rapid Response Unit is a special police brigade dedicated to visitor security in and around Rodney Bay.

ACCOMMODATIONS

Nearly all of St. Lucia's resorts and small inns are tucked into lush surroundings on secluded coves, unspoiled beaches, or forested hillsides in three locations along the calm Caribbean (western) coast. They're in the greater Castries area between Marigot Bay, a few miles south of the city, and Labrelotte Bay in the north; in and around Rodney Bay and north to Cap Estate; and in and around Soufrière on the southwest coast near the Pitons. There's only one resort in Vieux Fort, near Hewanorra. The advantage of being in the north is that you have access to a wider range of restaurants and nightlife; in the south you may be limited to your hotel's offerings and a few other dining options—albeit some of the best—in and around Soufrière.

Beach Resorts: Most people choose to stay in one of St. Lucia's many beach resorts, the majority of which are upscale and fairly pricey. Several are all-inclusive, including three Sandals resorts, two Sunswept resorts (The Body Holiday and Rendezvous), Morgan Bay Beach Resort, East Winds Inn, and Smugglers Cove Resort & Spa. Others may offer an all-inclusive option.

Small Inns: If you are looking for something more intimate and perhaps less expensive, a locally owned inn or small hotel is a good option; it may or may not be directly on the beach.

Villas: Luxury villa communities that operate like hotels are a good alternative for families. Several are in the north in or near Cap Estate.

HOTEL AND RESTAURANT PRICES

Prices in the restaurant reviews are the average cost of a main course at dinner or, if dinner is not served, at lunch; taxes and service charges are generally included. Prices in the hotel reviews are the lowest cost of a standard double room in high season, excluding taxes, service charges, and meal plans (except at all-inclusives). Prices for rentals are the lowest per-night cost for a one-bedroom unit in high season.

WEDDINGS

Wedding licenses that cost $125 require a three-day waiting period; those that cost $200 don't require a waiting period. Some resorts offer free weddings.

EXPLORING ST. LUCIA

Except for a small area in the extreme northeast, one main route circles all of St. Lucia. The road snakes along the coast, cuts across mountains, makes hairpin turns and sheer drops, and reaches dizzying heights. It takes at least four hours to drive the whole loop. Even at a leisurely pace with frequent sightseeing stops, and whether you're driving or being driven, the curvy roads make it a tiring drive in a single outing.

The West Coast Road between Castries and Soufrière (a 1½- to 2-hour journey) has steep hills and sharp turns, but it's well marked and incredibly scenic. South of Castries the road tunnels through Morne Fortune, skirts the island's largest banana plantation (more than 127 varieties of bananas, called "figs" in this part of the Caribbean, grow on the island), and passes through tiny fishing villages. Just north of Soufrière the road negotiates the island's fruit basket, where most of the mangoes, breadfruit, tomatoes, limes, and oranges are grown. In the mountainous region that forms a backdrop for Soufrière, you will notice 3,118-foot Mt. Gimie (pronounced Jimmy), St. Lucia's highest peak. Approaching Soufrière, you'll have spectacular views of the Pitons, and that spume of smoke wafting out of the thickly forested mountainside just east of Soufrière emanates from the so-called "drive-in" volcano.

The landscape changes dramatically between the Pitons and Vieux Fort on the island's southeastern tip. Along the South Coast Road traveling southeasterly from Soufrière, the terrain starts as steep mountainside with dense vegetation, progresses to undulating hills, and finally becomes rather flat and comparatively arid. Anyone arriving at Hewanorra International Airport, which is in Vieux Fort, and staying at a resort near Soufrière will travel along this route, a journey of about 30 minutes.

From Vieux Fort north to Castries, a 1½-hour drive, the East Coast Road twists through Micoud, Dennery, and other coastal villages. It then winds up, down, and around mountains, crosses Barre de l'Isle Ridge, and slices through the rain forest. Much of the scenery is breathtaking. The Atlantic Ocean pounds against rocky cliffs, and acres and acres of bananas and coconut palms blanket the hillsides. If you arrive at Hewanorra and stay at a resort near Castries or Rodney Bay, you'll travel along the East Coast Road.

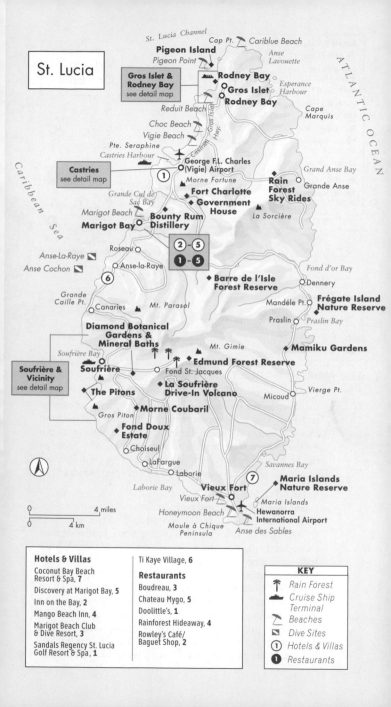

St. Lucia

St. Lucia Channel

Cap Pt. • Cariblue Beach
Pigeon Island
Pigeon Point
Anse Lavouette

Gros Islet & Rodney Bay see detail map

Rodney Bay
Gros Islet
Rodney Bay
Esperance Harbour

ATLANTIC OCEAN

Reduit Beach

Cape Marquis

Choc Beach
Vigie Beach
Pte. Seraphine
Castries Harbour

Castries see detail map

George F.L. Charles (Vigie) Airport
Morne Fortune

Rain Forest Sky Rides
Grande Anse
Grand Anse Bay

Grande Cul de Sac Bay
Marigot Beach
Marigot Bay
Fort Charlotte
Government House
Bounty Rum Distillery
La Sorcière

Caribbean Sea

Roseau

② - ⑤
① - ⑤

Anse-la-Raye
Anse Cochon
⑥
Anse-la-Raye

Fond d'or Bay

Barre de l'Isle Forest Reserve
Dennery

Grande Caille Pt.
Canaries
Mt. Parasol
Mandéle Pt.
Frégate Island Nature Reserve
Praslin
Praslin Bay

Diamond Botanical Gardens & Mineral Baths

Soufrière Bay
Mt. Gimie
Mamiku Gardens

Soufrière & Vicinity see detail map

Soufrière
Fond St. Jacques
Edmund Forest Reserve

The Pitons
La Soufrière Drive-In Volcano
Micoud
Vierge Pt.

Morne Coubaril
Gros Piton
Fond Doux Estate
Choiseul
LaFargue
Laborie
Savannes Bay

Laborie Bay
⑦
Maria Islands Nature Reserve

Vieux Fort
Vieux Fort
Maria Islands
Hewanorra International Airport

Honeymoon Beach
Moule à Chique Peninsula
Anse des Sables

Ⓝ

0 ___ 4 miles
0 ___ 4 km

Hotels & Villas

Coconut Bay Beach Resort & Spa, **7**

Discovery at Marigot Bay, **5**

Inn on the Bay, **2**

Mango Beach Inn, **4**

Marigot Beach Club & Dive Resort, **3**

Sandals Regency St. Lucia Golf Resort & Spa, **1**

Ti Kaye Village, **6**

Restaurants

Boudreau, **3**

Chateau Mygo, **5**

Doolittle's, **1**

Rainforest Hideaway, **4**

Rowley's Café/ Baguet Shop, **2**

KEY

🌴 Rain Forest

⚓ Cruise Ship Terminal

◤ Beaches

◪ Dive Sites

① Hotels & Villas

❶ Restaurants

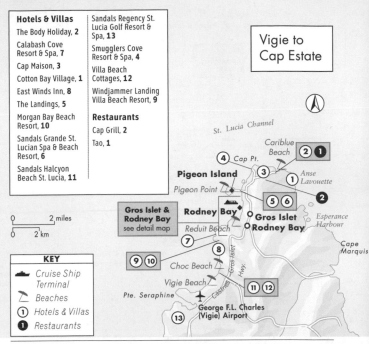

Hotels & Villas

The Body Holiday, **2**

Calabash Cove Resort & Spa, **7**

Cap Maison, **3**

Cotton Bay Village, **1**

East Winds Inn, **8**

The Landings, **5**

Morgan Bay Beach Resort, **10**

Sandals Grande St. Lucian Spa & Beach Resort, **6**

Sandals Halcyon Beach St. Lucia, **11**

Sandals Regency St. Lucia Golf Resort & Spa, **13**

Smugglers Cove Resort & Spa, **4**

Villa Beach Cottages, **12**

Windjammer Landing Villa Beach Resort, **9**

Restaurants

Cap Grill, **2**

Tao, **1**

Gros Islet & Rodney Bay
see detail map

0   2 miles
0   2 km

KEY

⚓ Cruise Ship Terminal

≈ Beaches

① Hotels & Villas

❶ Restaurants

St. Lucia Channel

Cap Pt.

Cariblue Beach

Anse Lavouette

Pigeon Island

Pigeon Point

Rodney Bay

Reduit Beach

Gros Islet
Rodney Bay

Esperance Harbour

Cape Marquis

Choc Beach

Vigie Beach

Pte. Seraphine

George F.L. Charles (Vigie) Airport

Castries/Gros Islet Hwy.

THE NORTH: RODNEY BAY TO CAP ESTATE

From Castries north toward Rodney Bay, Gros Islet, and Cap Estate, the roads are straight, mostly flat, and easy to navigate. This is the most developed part of the island, and many of St. Lucia's resorts, restaurants, and nightspots can be found here. The beaches in the north are also some of the St. Lucia's best. Pigeon Island, one of the island's most important historical sites, is at the island's northwestern tip.

WHAT TO SEE

Pigeon Island National Landmark. Jutting out from the northwest coast, Pigeon Island is connected to the mainland by a causeway. Tales are told of the pirate Jambe de Bois (Wooden Leg), who once hid out on this 44-acre hilltop islet—a strategic point during the French and British struggles for control of St. Lucia. Now it's a national park and a venue for concerts, festivals, and family gatherings. There are two small beaches with calm waters for swimming and snorkeling, a restaurant, and picnic areas. Scattered around the grounds are ruins of barracks, batteries, and garrisons that date from 18th-century French and English battles. In the Museum and Interpretative Centre, housed

TOP REASONS TO GO

The Beauty: Magnificent, lush scenery makes St. Lucia one of the most beautiful Caribbean islands.

The Romance: A popular honeymoon spot, St. Lucia is filled with romantic retreats.

Indulgent Accommodations: Sybaritic lodging options include an all-inclusive spa resort with daily pampering, a posh dive resort sandwiched between a mountain and the beach, and two picturesque resorts with prime locations between the Pitons.

The St. Lucia Jazz Festival: Performers and fans come from all over the world for this musical event.

The Welcome: The friendly St. Lucians love sharing their island and their cultural heritage with visitors.

in the restored British officers' mess, a multimedia display explains the island's ecological and historical significance. Pigeon Island National Landmark is administered by the St. Lucia National Trust. ⊠ *Pigeon Island, Rodney Bay* ☎ *758/452–5005* ⊕ *www.slunatrust.org* ☎ *$5* ⊘ *Daily 9–5.*

RODNEY BAY, THEN AND NOW. A mosquito-infested swamp near beautiful Reduit Beach was drained and opened up to the sea in the 1970s, creating a beautiful lagoon and ensuring the value of the surrounding real estate for tourism development. Today Rodney Bay Village is a hive of tourist activity, with hotels, restaurants, much of the island's nightlife, and, of course, Rodney Bay Marina.

Rodney Bay. This natural bay and an 80-acre man-made lagoon are now surrounded by a huge complex of hotels, popular restaurants, a big mall, and the island's only casino. It's named for Admiral George Rodney, who sailed the British Navy out of Gros Islet Bay in 1780 to attack and ultimately destroy the French fleet. With 232 slips, Rodney Bay Marina is one of the Caribbean's premier yachting centers and the destination of the Atlantic Rally for Cruisers (a transatlantic yacht crossing) each December. Yacht charters and sightseeing day trips can be arranged at the marina. Rodney Bay is about 15 minutes north of Castries; the Rodney Bay Ferry makes hourly crossings between the marina and the mall, as well as daily excursions to Pigeon Island. ⊠ *Rodney Bay.*

dors' **Arcade**, across Peynier Street from the Craft Market, you'll find still more handicrafts and souvenirs. ⊠ *Corner of Jeremie and Peynier Sts., Castries* ⊘ *Closed Sun.*

Cathedral of the Immaculate Conception. Directly across Laborie Street from Derek Walcott Square stands Castries's Roman Catholic cathedral, which was built in 1897. Though it appears rather somber on the outside, the interior walls are decorated with colorful murals reworked by St. Lucian artist Dunstan St. Omer just prior to Pope John Paul II's visit in 1985. This church has an active parish and is open daily for both public viewing and religious services. ⊠ *Laborie St., Castries* ⊘ *Daily.*

Derek Walcott Square. The city's green oasis is bordered by Brazil, Laborie, Micoud, and Bourbon streets. Formerly Columbus Square, it was renamed to honor the hometown poet who won the 1992 Nobel prize for literature—one of two Nobel laureates from St. Lucia (the late Sir W. Arthur Lewis won the 1979 Nobel prize in economics). Some of the 19th-century buildings that have survived fire, wind, and rain can be seen on Brazil Street, the square's southern border. On the Laborie Street side there's a huge, 400-year-old samaan (monkey pod) tree with leafy branches that shade a good portion of the square. ⊠ *Bordered by Brazil, Laborie, Micoud, and Bourbon Sts., Castries.*

La Place Carenage. On the south side of the harbor near the pier and markets is a duty-free shopping complex with a dozen shops and a café. ⊠ *Jeremie St., Castries* ☎ *758/453–2451* ⊘ *Weekdays 9–4, Sat. 9–1.*

★ **Fodor'sChoice Our Planet Centre.** The only such attraction of its kind, at least to date, Our Planet Centre is devoted to the many facets of the Earth's environment. It's a fascinating, educational stop for the entire family, and an especially good option on a rainy day. Using cutting-edge technology, the exhibits include an Immersion Tunnel, where you can see how the planet was created and grew into its current state; Hurricane Island, where touch screens allow you to manipulate weather patterns to create a hurricane; Mirrorsphere, which gives a kaleidoscopic view of Earth's plants and animals; Science on a Sphere, installed by NOAA/NASA, which views the Earth from space complete with hurricanes, earthquakes, volcanoes, and tsunamis; and—the best part—a laser show in the Special Effects Theatre, where the lighting, shaking seats, wind, and mist mimic extreme weather events. The personalized guided tour takes

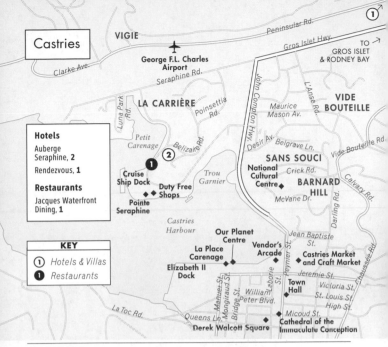

Castries

VIGIE

Peninsular Rd.

Gros Islet Hwy.

TO GROS ISLET & RODNEY BAY

Clarke Ave.

George F.L. Charles Airport

Seraphine Rd.

LA CARRIÈRE

Poinsettia Rd.

VIDE BOUTEILLE

Maurice Mason Av.

Luna Park Rd.

Petit Carenage

Belzaire Rd.

Desir Av. Belgrave Ln.

Vide Boutelle Rd.

SANS SOUCI

Crick Rd.

National Cultural Centre

BARNARD HILL

McVane Dr.

Darling Rd.

Calvary Rd.

Trou Garnier

Cruise Ship Dock

Duty Free Shops

Pointe Seraphine

Castries Harbour

Our Planet Centre

La Place Carenage

Vendor's Arcade

Jean Baptiste St.

Castries Market and Craft Market

Elizabeth II Dock

Peymer St.

Jeremie St.

Town Hall

Victoria St.

St. Louis St.

High St.

La Toc Rd.

Queens Ln.

Manuel St.

Mongiraud St.

Bridge St.

William Peter Blvd.

Laborie St.

Micoud St.

Cathedral of the Immaculate Conception

Derek Walcott Square

Hotels
Auberge Seraphine, **2**
Rendezvous, **1**

Restaurants
Jacques Waterfront Dining, **1**

KEY
① Hotels & Villas
❶ Restaurants

CASTRIES

Castries, the capital city, and the area north and just south of it are the island's most developed areas. About 15 minutes south of Castries, lovely Marigot Bay is both a yacht haven and a picture-pretty destination for landlubbers.

The capital, a busy commercial city of some 65,000 people, wraps around a sheltered bay. Morne Fortune rises sharply to the south of town, creating a dramatic green backdrop. The charm of Castries lies almost entirely in its liveliness, since four fires that occurred between 1796 and 1948 destroyed most of the colonial buildings. Freighters (exporting bananas, coconut, cocoa, mace, nutmeg, and citrus fruits) and cruise ships come and go frequently, making Castries Harbour one of the Caribbean's busiest ports.

WHAT TO SEE

Castries Market. Under a brilliant orange roof, the bustling **Castries Market** is at its liveliest on Saturday morning, when farmers bring their produce and spices to town—as they have for more than a century. Next door to the produce market is the **Craft Market,** where you can buy pottery, wood carvings, and handwoven straw articles. At the Ven-

Dunstan St. Omer

The murals of Dunstan St. Omer, one of St. Lucia's leading artists—if not *the* leading artist—adorn many walls and churches throughout the island, and his paintings and portraits are prized both locally and internationally. St. Omer is best known locally for frescoing the walls of the **Cathedral of the Immaculate Conception**, in Castries, with the images of black saints just prior to a visit by Pope John Paul II in 1985. He also designed St. Lucia's national flag. A 2004 recipient of the St. Lucia Cross, the nation's highest award, he inspired generations of youngsters for more than 30 years as an art instructor in the public schools. St. Omer is also the father of nine children, two of whom—Luigi and Julio—inherited their father's talent and have followed in his footsteps.

about 90 minutes, but you'll probably want to linger longer at some of the exhibits and interactive games—which is fine. A gift shop features locally made recycled, reused, natural products. ⊠ *La Place Carenage, Jeremie St., Castries* ☎ *758/453–0107* ⊕ *www.ourplanetcentre.org* ⊠ *$35* ⊙ *Mon.–Sat. 9–4:30 (last booking at 3:30), Sun. by reservation or when a cruise ship is in port.*

Pointe Seraphine. This duty-free shopping complex is on the north side of the harbor, about a 20-minute walk or 2-minute cab ride from the city center; a launch ferries passengers across the harbor when cruise ships are in port. Pointe Seraphine's attractive Spanish-style architecture houses more than 20 upscale duty-free shops, a tourist information kiosk, a taxi stand, and car-rental agencies. The shopping center is adjacent to the cruise-ship pier. ⊠ *Castries Harbour, Castries* ☎ *758/452–3036* ⊙ *Weekdays 9–4, Sat. 9–1.*

Vendor's Arcade. Across Peynier Street from the craft market you'll find a maze of handicraft and souvenir vendors. ⊠ *Corner of Jeremie and Peynier Sts., Castries* ⊙ *Mon.–Sat. 6–5.*

SOUTH OF CASTRIES

Just south and east of Castries are several of the island's popular sights.

Barre de l'Isle Forest Reserve. St. Lucia is divided into eastern and western halves by Barre de l'Isle ridge. A mile-long (1½-km-long) trail cuts through the reserve, and four lookout points provide panoramic views. Visible in the distance are Mt. Gimie, immense green valleys, both the Caribbean Sea and the Atlantic Ocean, and coastal communities. The trailhead is about a half-hour drive from Castries; it takes about an hour to walk the trail—an easy hike—and another hour to climb Mt. La Combe Ridge. Permission from the St. Lucia Forest & Lands Department is required to access the trail in Barre de l'Isle; a naturalist or forest officer guide will accompany you. ⊠ *East Coast Rd., midway between Castries and Dennery, Ravine Poisson* ☎ *758/450–2231, 758/450–2078* ☜ *Guide services $10* ⊗ *Daily, by appointment only.*

Bounty Rum Distillery. St. Lucia Distillers, which produces the island's own Bounty and Chairman's Reserve rums, offers 90-minute Rhythm and Rum tours of its distillery, including information on the history of sugar, the background of rum, a detailed description of the distillation process, colorful displays of local architecture, a glimpse at a typical rum shop, Caribbean music, and a chance to sample the company's rums and liqueurs. The distillery is at the Roseau Sugar Factory in the Roseau Valley, on the island's largest banana plantation, a few miles south of Castries and not far from Marigot. Reservations for the tour are essential. ⊠ *Roseau Sugar Factory, West Coast Rd., Roseau* ☎ *758/451–4528* ⊕ *www.saintluciarums.com* ☜ *$10* ⊗ *Weekdays 9–3.*

Ft. Charlotte. Begun in 1764 by the French as the Citadelle du Morne Fortune, Ft. Charlotte was completed after 20 years of battling and changing hands. Its old barracks and batteries are now government buildings and local educational facilities, but you can drive around and look at the remains, which include redoubts, a guardroom, stables, and cells. You can also walk up to the Inniskilling Monument, a tribute to the 1796 battle in which the 27th Foot Royal Inniskilling Fusiliers wrested the Morne from the French. At the military cemetery, which was first used in 1782, faint inscriptions on the tombstones tell the tales of French and English soldiers who died here. Six former governors of the island are buried here, as well. From this point atop Morne Fortune, you have a beautiful view of Castries Harbour, Martinique farther north, and the twin peaks of the Pitons to the south. ⊠ *Morne Fortune, Castries.*

Government House. The official residence of the governor-general of St. Lucia, one of the island's few remaining examples of Victorian architecture, is perched high above

Plas Kassav

As you're traveling south to Soufrière, watch for Plas Kassav Bread Bakery in Anse La Verdure, a blink-and-you'll-miss-it spot on the West Coast Road between Anse La Raye and Canaries. If you're there early enough, you can see the cassava roots being grated and processed into flour using traditional methods, and the cassava bread dough being mixed in huge copper caldrons. Cinnamon, cherries and raisins, coconut, and other flavorings are added, then the dough—13 varieties in all—is formed into small buns, placed on banana leaves, and baked over hot coals. Plas Kassav (Creole for Cassava Place) began as a small family bakery in 1998 and has grown into a popular local enterprise simply by word of mouth. There is a large sign, but taxi drivers all know where it is and will not hesitate to stop so you can try a warm, mouthwatering treat that is a staple of St. Lucia's traditional cuisine.

Castries, halfway up Morne Fortune—the "Hill of Good Fortune"—which forms a backdrop for the capital city. Morne Fortune has also overlooked more than its share of *bad* luck over the years, including devastating hurricanes and four fires that leveled Castries. Within Government House itself is **Le Pavillon Royal Museum,** which houses important historical photographs and documents, artifacts, crockery, silverware, medals, and awards; original architectural drawings of Government House are displayed on the walls. However, you must make an appointment to visit. ⊠ *Morne Fortune, Castries* ☎ *758/452–2481* ⊠ *Free* ☉ *Tues. and Thurs. 10–noon and 2–4, by appointment only.*

★ Fodor'sChoice **Marigot Bay.** This is one of the prettiest natural harbors in the Caribbean. In 1778 British admiral Samuel Barrington sailed into this secluded bay-within-a-bay and, the story goes, covered his ships with palm fronds to hide them from the French. Today this small community is a favorite anchorage for boaters and a peaceful destination for landlubbers. **Discovery at Marigot Bay**—a luxury resort, marina, and marina village with restaurants, bars, grocery store, bakery, and boutiques—has revitalized the area without marring the beauty or the ecology of Marigot Bay. A 24-hour ferry ($2 round-trip) connects the bay's two shores—a voyage that takes about a minute each way. ⊠ *Marigot Bay.*

Rain Forest Sky Rides. Ever wish you could get a bird's-eye view of the rain forest? Or at least experience it without hiking up and down miles of mountain trails? Here's your chance. Depending on your athleticism and spirit of adventure, choose a two-hour aerial tram ride, a zip-line experience, or both. Either guarantees a magnificent view as you peacefully slip above or actively zip through the canopy of the 3,442-acre Castries Waterworks Rain Forest in Babonneau, 30 minutes east of Rodney Bay. On the tram ride, eight-passenger gondolas glide slowly among the giant trees, twisting vines, and dense thickets of vegetation accented by colorful flowers as a tour guide explains and shares anecdotes about the various trees, plants, birds, and other wonders of nature found in the area. The zip line, on the other hand, is a thrilling experience in which you're rigged with a harness, helmet, and clamps that attach to cables strategically strung through the forest. Short trails connect the 10 lines, so riders come down to earth briefly and hike to the next station before speeding through the forest canopy to the next stop. Bring binoculars and a camera. ⊠ *Chassin, Babonneau* ☎ *758/458–5151* ⊕ *www.rainforestadventure.com* 🚋 *Tram $72, zip line $69, combo $85* ☉ *Tues.–Sun. 9–4.*

THE "SNAKE MAN." Driving along the West Coast Road just north of Canaries, don't be surprised if you see a man selling coconuts on the northbound side of the road with a boa constrictor wrapped around his neck. The "snake man" has been a fixture here for years—usually from mid-morning to mid-afternoon—and we're sure the startled looks on tourists' faces give him a kick. Taxi drivers will stop if you want some coconut water or just a closer look. For a small tip, the "snake man" will let you take his picture—wearing his boa, of course.

SOUFRIÈRE

The oldest town in St. Lucia and the former French colonial capital, Soufrière was founded by the French in 1746 and named for its proximity to the volcano of the same name. The wharf is the center of activity in this sleepy town (which currently has a population of about 9,000), particularly when a cruise ship anchors in pretty Soufrière Bay. French colonial influences are evident in the second-story verandas, gingerbread trim, and other appointments of the wooden buildings that surround the market square. The market building itself is decorated with colorful murals.

The site of much of St. Lucia's renowned natural beauty, Soufrière is also the destination of most sightseeing trips. This is where you can get up close to the landmark Pitons and explore the French colonial capital of St. Lucia, with its "drive-in" volcano, botanical gardens, working plantations, waterfalls, and countless other examples of the natural beauty for which St. Lucia is deservedly famous.

WHAT TO SEE

★ Fodor'sChoice **Diamond Falls Botanical Gardens and Mineral Baths.** These splendid gardens are part of Soufrière Estate, a 2,000-acre land grant presented by King Louis XIV in 1713 to three Devaux brothers from Normandy in recognition of their services to France. The estate is still owned by their descendants; Joan DuBouley Devaux maintains the gardens. Bushes and shrubs bursting with brilliant flowers grow beneath towering trees and line pathways that lead to a natural gorge. Water bubbling to the surface from underground sulfur springs streams downhill in rivulets to become Diamond Waterfall, deep within the botanical gardens. Through the centuries, the rocks over which the cascade spills have become encrusted with minerals and tinted yellow, green, and purple. Near the falls, mineral baths are fed by the underground springs. King Louis XVI of France provided funds in 1784 for the construction of a building with a dozen large stone baths to fortify his troops against the St. Lucian climate. It's claimed that Joséphine Bonaparte bathed here as a young girl while visiting her father's plantation nearby. During the Brigand's War, just after the French Revolution, the bathhouse was destroyed. In 1930 André DuBoulay had the site excavated, and two of the original stone baths were restored for his use. Outside baths were added later. For a small fee, you can slip into your swimsuit and soak for 30 minutes in one of the outside pools; a private bath costs slightly more. ⊠ *Soufrière Estate, Diamond Rd.* ☎ *758/459–7155* ⊕ *www.diamondstlucia. com* ☞ *$5, public bath $4, private bath $6* ⊙ *Mon.–Sat. 10–5, Sun. 10–3.*

Edmund Forest Reserve. Dense tropical rain forest stretches from one side of the island to the other, sprawling over 19,000 acres of mountains and valleys. It's home to a multitude of exotic flowers and plants, as well as rare birds—including the brightly feathered Jacquot parrot. The Edmund Forest Reserve, on the island's western side, is most easily accessible from the road to Fond St. Jacques, which is just east of Soufrière. A trek through the lush

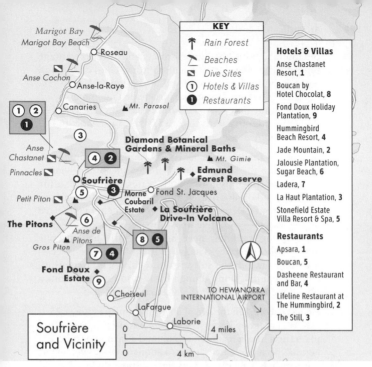

KEY

✝ Rain Forest
⟍ Beaches
◢ Dive Sites
① Hotels & Villas
❶ Restaurants

Hotels & Villas

Anse Chastanet Resort, **1**

Boucan by Hotel Chocolat, **8**

Fond Doux Holiday Plantation, **9**

Hummingbird Beach Resort, **4**

Jade Mountain, **2**

Jalousie Plantation, Sugar Beach, **6**

Ladera, **7**

La Haut Plantation, **3**

Stonefield Estate Villa Resort & Spa, **5**

Restaurants

Apsara, **1**

Boucan, **5**

Dasheene Restaurant and Bar, **4**

Lifeline Restaurant at The Hummingbird, **2**

The Still, **3**

Soufrière and Vicinity

landscape, with spectacular views of mountains, valleys, and the sea beyond, can take three or more hours. It takes about 30 minutes from Soufrière and 90 minutes or more from the north end of St. Lucia to reach the reserve by car. It's a strenuous hike, so you need plenty of stamina and sturdy hiking shoes. Permission from the Forest & Lands Department is required to access reserve trails, and the department requires that a naturalist or forest officer guide you because the vegetation is so dense. ☎ 758/450–2231, 758/450–2078 for Forest & Lands Department ⊕ www. malff.com ⚌ Guide for nature trails $10; hiking trails $25; bird-watching $30; guided tours including hotel transfers $55–$85 ⊙ Daily by appointment only.

Fond Doux Estate. One of the earliest French estates established by land grants (1745 and 1763), this plantation still produces cocoa, citrus, bananas, coconut, and vegetables on 135 hilly acres; the restored 1864 plantation house is still in use, as well. A 30-minute walking tour begins at the cocoa fermentary, where you can see the drying process under way. You then follow a trail through the lush cultivated area, where a guide points out various fruit- or spice-bearing trees and tropical flowers. Additional trails lead to

old military ruins, a religious shrine, and another vantage point for viewing the spectacular Pitons. Cool drinks and a creole buffet lunch are served at the Jardin Cacao restaurant. Souvenirs, including just-made chocolate sticks, are sold at the boutique. ☒ *Chateaubelair* ☎ *758/459-7545* ⊕ *www.fonddouxestate.com* ☜ *$10; $25 includes buffet lunch* ⊙ *Daily 8–4.*

La Soufrière Drive-In Volcano. As you approach, your nose will pick up the strong scent of the sulfur springs—more than 20 belching pools of muddy water, multicolor sulfur deposits, and other assorted minerals baking and steaming on the surface. Despite the name, you don't actually drive all the way in—you drive up within a few hundred feet of the gurgling, steaming mass and then walk behind your guide—whose service is included in the admission price—around a fault in the substratum rock. It's a fascinating, educational half hour, though it can also be pretty stinky on a hot day. ☎ *758/459-5500* ☜ *$2* ⊙ *Daily 9–5.*

Morne Coubaril. On the site of an 18th-century estate, a 250-acre land grant by Louis XIV of France in 1713, the original plantation house has been rebuilt and a farm workers' village has been re-created. It does a good job of showing what life was like for both the owners (a single family owned the land until 1960) and those who did all the hard labor over the centuries producing cotton, coffee, sugarcane, and cocoa. Cocoa, coconuts, and manioc are still grown on the estate using traditional agricultural methods. Guides show how coconuts are opened and roasted for use as oil and animal feed and how cocoa is fermented, dried, crushed by dancing on the beans, and finally, formed into chocolate sticks. Manioc roots (also called cassava) are grated, squeezed of excess water, dried, and turned into flour used in baking. The grounds are lovely for walking or hiking, and the views of mountains and Soufrière Harbour are spellbinding. More adventurous visitors can enjoy Soufrière Hotwire Rides, a zip-line excursion with eight stations, taking you under Petit Piton and through the adjacent rain forest. The large, open-air restaurant serves a creole buffet luncheon by reservation only. ☒ *2 miles (3 km) south of town* ☎ *758/459-7340* ⊕ *www.mornecoubarilestate.com; www.stluciaziplining.com* ☜ *$7, with lunch $15; zip line $69* ⊙ *Daily 8–5.*

★ **Fodor's Choice The Pitons.** Rising precipitously from the cobalt-blue Caribbean Sea just south of Soufrière Bay, these two

CLOSE UP

St. Lucia's Two Nobel Laureates

Sir W. Arthur Lewis won the Nobel Prize in Economics in 1979. Born in St. Lucia in 1915, Lewis graduated with distinction from the London School of Economics and went on to earn a PhD in industrial economics. His life interest—and his influence—was in economic development and the transformation and expansion of university education in the Caribbean. Lewis died in 1991 and was buried on the grounds of Sir Arthur Lewis Community College in St. Lucia.

Sir Derek Walcott was born in Castries in 1930. *Omeros*—an epic poem about his journey around the Caribbean, the American West, and London— contributed to his winning the Nobel Prize for Literature in 1992. Walcott is also a writer, playwright, and painter of watercolors. Today, in addition to spending time at his home in St. Lucia, he teaches poetry and drama at Boston University and lectures and gives readings throughout the world.

3

unusual mountains are a symbol of St. Lucia and also a UNESCO World Heritage Site. Covered with thick tropical vegetation, the massive outcroppings were formed by lava from a volcanic eruption 30 to 40 million years ago. They are not identical twins since—confusingly—2,619-foot Petit Piton is taller than 2,461-foot Gros Piton, though Gros Piton is, as the word translates, broader. It's possible to climb the Pitons, but it's a strenuous trip. Gros Piton is the easier climb, though the trail up even this shorter Piton is still very tough. Either climb requires the permission of the Forest & Lands Department and the use of a knowledgeable guide. ☎ *758/450–2231, 758/450–2078 for St. Lucia Forest & Lands Department* 🖫 *Guide services $45* ☉ *Daily by appointment only.*

Soufrière Tourist Information Centre. Head here for information about area attractions. Note that souvenir vendors station themselves outside some of the popular attractions in and around Soufrière, and they can be persistent. Be polite but firm if you're not interested. ✉ *Bay St.* ☎ *758/459–7200*

VIEUX FORT AND THE EAST COAST

Vieux Fort, on the southeastern tip of St. Lucia, is the location of Hewanorra International Airport, which serves all commercial jet aircraft arriving on and departing fromthe island. Although less developed for tourism than the island's north and west, the area around Vieux Fort and points north along the east coast are home to some of St. Lucia's unique ecosystems and interesting natural attractions.

WHAT TO SEE

Frégate Island Nature Reserve. A mile-long (1½-km) trail encircles the nature reserve, which you reach from the East Coast Road near the fishing village of Praslin. In this area boatbuilders still fashion traditional fishing canoes, called *gommiers* after the trees from which the hulls are made. The Amerindian people, who originally populated the Caribbean, used the ancient design. A natural promontory at Praslin provides a lookout from which you can view the two small islets, Frégate Major and Frégate Minor, and—with luck—the frigate birds that nest here from May to July. The only way to visit is on a guided tour, which includes a ride in a gommier to Frégate Minor for a picnic lunch and a swim; all trips are by reservation only and require a minimum of two people. Arrange visits through your hotel, a tour operator, or the St. Lucia National Trust; many tours include round-trip transportation from your hotel, as well as the tour cost. ⊠ *Praslin* ☎ *758/452–5005, 758/453–7656, 758/454–5014 for tour reservations* ⊕ *www.slunatrust.org* ⊠ *$18* ⊙ *Daily by appointment only.*

Mamiku Gardens. One of St. Lucia's largest and loveliest botanical gardens surrounds the hilltop ruins of the Micoud Estate. Baron Micoud, an 18th-century colonel in the French Army and governor-general of St. Lucia, deeded the land to his wife, Madame de Micoud, to avoid confiscation by the British during one of the many times when St. Lucia changed hands. Locals abbreviated her name to "Ma Micoud," which, over time, became "Mamiku." (The estate did become a British military outpost in 1796, but shortly thereafter was burned to the ground by slaves during the Brigand's War.) The estate is now primarily a banana plantation, but the gardens themselves—including several secluded or "secret" gardens—are filled with tropical flowers and plants, delicate orchids, and fragrant herbs. ⊠ *Vieux Fort Hwy., Praslin* ☎ *758/455–3729* ⊠ *$6; guided tour, $8* ⊙ *Daily 9–5.*

Maria Islands Nature Reserve. Two tiny islands in the Atlantic Ocean off St. Lucia's southeastern coast make up the reserve, which has its own interpretive center. The 25-acre Maria Major and the 4-acre Maria Minor, its little sister, are inhabited by two rare species of reptiles (the colorful Zandoli Terre ground lizard and the harmless Kouwes grass snake). They share their home with frigate birds, terns, doves, and other wildlife. There's a small beach for swimming and snorkeling, as well as an undisturbed forest, a vertical cliff covered with cacti, and a coral reef for snorkeling or diving. The St. Lucia Trust offers tours, including the boat trip to the islands, by appointment only; bring your own picnic lunch, as there are no facilities. ✉ *Vieux Fort* ☏ *758/452–5005, 758/453–7656, 758/454–5014 for tour reservations* ⊕ *www.slunatrust.org* ✉ *$35* ⊗ *Aug.–mid-May, Wed.–Sun. 9:30–5, by appointment only.*

Vieux Fort. St. Lucia's second-largest town is where you'll find Hewanorra International Airport. From the Moule à Chique Peninsula, the island's southernmost tip, you can see much of St. Lucia to the north and the island of St. Vincent 21 miles (34 km) to the south. This is where the waters of the clear Caribbean Sea blend with those of the deeper blue Atlantic Ocean. ✉ *Vieux Fort.*

BEACHES

Anse Chastanet. In front of the resort of the same name, just north of Soufrière, this palm-studded dark-sand beach has a backdrop of green hills, brightly painted fishing skiffs bobbing at anchor, and some of the island's best reefs for snorkeling and diving. The resort's gazebos are nestled among the palms; its dive shop, restaurant, and bar are on the beach and open to the public. **Amenities:** food and drink; toilets; water sports. **Best for:** snorkeling; sunset; swimming. ✉ *1 mile (1½ km) north of town, Soufrière.*

Anse Cochon. This dark-sand beach in front of Ti Kaye Village and part of the Marine Reserve is accessible only by boat or via Ti Kaye's mile-long, tire-crunching access road. The water and adjacent reefs are superb for swimming, diving, and snorkeling. Moorings are free, and boaters and swimmers can enjoy refreshments at Ti Kaye's beach bar. Snorkeling equipment is available at the dive shop on the beach. **Amenities:** food and drink; toilets; water sports. **Best for:** snorkeling; swimming. ✉ *3 miles (5 km) south of Anse la Raye.*

Embracing Kwéyòl

English is St. Lucia's official language, but most St. Lucians speak and often use Kwéyòl—a French-based Creole language—for informal conversations among themselves. Primarily a spoken language, Kwéyòl in its written version doesn't look at all like French; pronounce the words phonetically, though—*entenasyonnal* (international), for example, or the word *Kwéyòl* (Creole) itself—and you indeed sound as if you're speaking French.

Pretty much the same version of the Creole language, or patois, is spoken on the nearby island of Dominica. Otherwise, the St. Lucian Kwéyòl is quite different from that spoken in other Caribbean islands that have a French and African heritage, such as Haiti, Guadeloupe, and Martinique—or elsewhere, such as Louisiana, Mauritius, and Madagascar. The Kwéyòl spoken in St. Lucia and Dominica is mostly unintelligible to people from those other locations—and vice versa.

St. Lucia embraces its Creole heritage by devoting the month of October each year to celebrations that preserve and promote Creole culture, language, and traditions. In selected communities throughout the island, events and performances highlight Creole music, food, dance, theater, native costumes, church services, traditional games, folklore, native medicine—a little bit of everything, or *tout bagay,* as you say in Kwéyòl.

Creole Heritage Month culminates at the end of October with all-day events and activities on Jounen Kwéyòl Entenasyonnal, or International Creole Day, which is recognized by all countries that speak a version of the Creole language.

Anse des Pitons (*Jalousie Beach*). The white sand on this crescent beach, snuggled between the Pitons, was imported and spread over the natural black sand. Accessible through the Jalousie Plantation Sugar Beach resort property or by boat, the beach offers good snorkeling, diving, and breathtaking scenery. **Amenities:** food and drink; toilets; water sports. **Best for:** snorkeling; swimming. ⊠ *3 miles (5 km) south of Soufrière.*

Marigot Beach (*Labas Beach*). Calm waters rippled only by passing yachts lap a sliver of sand studded with palm trees on the north side of Marigot Bay. The beach is accessible by a ferry that operates continually from one side of the bay to the other, and you can find refreshments at adjacent

restaurants. **Amenities:** food and drink; toilets; water sports. **Best for:** swimming. ⊠ *Marigot Bay.*

Pigeon Point. At this small beach within the Pigeon Island National Landmark, on the northwestern tip of St. Lucia, there's a restaurant serving snacks and drinks; it's also a perfect spot for picnicking. **Amenities:** food and drink; toilets. **Best for:** snorkeling; swimming. ⊠ *Pigeon Island, Gros Islet* 🖃 *$5 park admission.*

★ **Fodors**Choice **Reduit Beach.** The long stretch of golden sand that frames Rodney Bay is within walking distance of many hotels and restaurants in Rodney Bay Village. The Rex St. Lucian hotel, which faces the beach, has a water-sports center, where you can rent sports equipment and beach chairs and take windsurfing or waterskiing lessons. Many feel that Reduit (pronounced red-wee) is the island's finest beach. **Amenities:** food and drink; toilets; water sports. **Best for:** snorkeling; swimming; walking; windsurfing. ⊠ *Rodney Bay.*

Vigie Beach (*Malabar Beach*). This 2-mile (3-km) strand runs parallel to the George F.L. Charles Airport runway in Castries and continues on past the Rendezvous resort, where it becomes Malabar Beach. **Amenities:** none. **Best for:** swimming. ⊠ *Adjacent to Vigie airport, Castries.*

WHERE TO EAT

Bananas, mangoes, passion fruit, plantains, breadfruit, okra, avocados, limes, pumpkins, cucumbers, papaya, yams, christophenes (also called chayote), and coconuts are among the fresh fruits and vegetables that grace St. Lucian menus. The French influence is strong, and most chefs cook with a creole flair. Resort buffets and restaurant fare include standards like steaks, chops, pasta, and pizza—and every menu lists fresh fish along with the ever-popular lobster.

Caribbean standards include callaloo, stuffed crab back, pepper-pot stew, curried chicken or goat, and *lambi* (conch). The national dish of salt fish and green fig—a stew of dried, salted codfish and boiled green banana—is, let's say, an acquired taste. A runner-up in terms of local popularity is bouyon, a cooked-all-day soup or stew that combines meat (usually pig tail), "provisions" (root vegetables), pigeon peas, dumplings, broth, and local spices. Soups and stews are traditionally prepared in a coal pot, a rustic clay casserole on a matching clay stand that holds the hot coals.

BEST BETS FOR DINING

With so many restaurants to choose from, how will you decide where to eat? Fodor's writers and editors have selected their favorite restaurants in the Best Bets lists below. The Fodor's Choice properties represent the "best of the best." Find the specific details about each restaurant in the reviews that follow.

Fodor's Choice★

Buzz, Coal Pot, Dasheene Restaurant and Bar, The Edge, Rainforest Hideaway, Tao

BEST VIEW
Boudreau, Chateau Mygo, Dasheene Restaurant and Bar, Coal Pot

BEST FOR FAMILIES
Doolittle's, Rowley's Café/Baguet Shop

MOST ROMANTIC
Apsara, Coal Pot, The Great House, Jacques Waterfront Dining, Rainforest Hideaway, Tao

BEST FOR LOCAL ST. LUCIAN CUISINE
Koko Cabana, Lifeline Restaurant at the Hummingbird, The Still

Chicken and pork dishes and barbecues are also popular here. Fresh lobster is available in season, which lasts from August through March. As they do throughout the Caribbean, local vendors set up barbecues along the roadside, at street fairs, and at Friday-night "jump-ups" and do bang-up business selling grilled fish or chicken legs, bakes (fried biscuits), and beer—you can get a full meal for less than $10. Most other meats are imported—beef from Argentina and Iowa, lamb from New Zealand. Piton is the local brew; Bounty, the local rum.

With so many popular all-inclusive resorts, guests take most meals at hotel restaurants—which are generally quite good, and in some cases, exceptional. It's fun when vacationing, however, to try some of the local restaurants, as well—for lunch when sightseeing or for a special night out.

What to Wear: Dress on St. Lucia is casual but conservative. Shorts are usually fine during the day, but bathing suits and immodest clothing are frowned upon anywhere but at the beach. In the evening the mood is casually elegant, but even the fanciest places generally expect only a collared shirt and long pants for men and a sundress or slacks for women.

THE NORTH: RODNEY BAY TO CAP ESTATE

Restaurant locations can be found on the Rodney Bay and Vigie to Pointe du Cap maps.

$$$ **Fodor's**Choice ✕**Buzz.** *Seafood.* Opposite the Royal St. Lucian hotel and Reduit Beach, Buzz is in Rodney Bay's "restaurant central." Starting with cool drinks (maybe a Buzz cooler) and warm appetizers (perhaps lobster and crab cakes, crispy calamari, or tempura shrimp) at the friendly bar, diners make their way to the dining room or the garden for some serious seafood or a good steak, baby back ribs, West Indian pepper-pot stew, or spicy lamb shanks. The seared yellowfin tuna, potato-crusted red snapper, and seafood creole are big hits, too. And there's a full vegetarian menu, as well. Fresh lobster is available in season (August–March). ⑤ *Average main: $24* ✉ *Reduit Beach Ave., Rodney Bay* ☎ *758/458–0450* ⊕ *www.buzzstlucia.com* ⚇ *Reservations essential* ⊗ *No lunch. Closed Mon., Apr.–Nov.*

$$$ ✕**Cap Grill.** *Steakhouse.* If you're in the mood for a perfectly cooked steak—or seafood or pasta—head for the St. Lucia Golf Resort & Country Club. Cap Grill, in its impressive clubhouse, serves breakfast and lunch daily, dinner from Thursday through Saturday, and Sunday brunch in air-conditioned comfort or alfresco on the dining porch. In either case, your table will overlook the golf course, which is floodlit at night. Golfers come for an early breakfast or an after-the-round lunch of Black Angus burgers, baguette sandwiches, fresh salads, or pasta specials. The Sports Bar is busy all afternoon. And you don't have to be a golfer to come for dinner. Start with beef or fish carpaccio or Caribbean ceviche, followed perhaps by garlic soup or shrimp and corn chowder, and then on to the steak: perfectly grilled 12- or 16-ounce New York strip or beautifully tender 8-ounce filet mignon. Or opt for roast duck breast, blackened mahimahi, rack of lamb, coconut shrimp, roasted pork tenderloin, or stuffed chicken breast. ⑤ *Average main: $28* ✉ *St. Lucia Golf Resort & Country Club, Cap Estate* ☎ *758/450–8523* ⊕ *www.stluciagolf.com* ⊗ *No dinner Sun.–Wed.*

$$$ ✕**The Charthouse.** *Steakhouse.* Since 1985, The Charthouse has been charcoal broiling U.S. Prime steaks and serving them to hungry St. Lucians and vacationers in an open-air, waterfront location on Rodney Bay. (For those who visit by sea, docking facilities are available at the restaurant.) Some prefer the hickory-smoked baby back ribs or the roast prime rib of beef—or even grilled seafood. In any case, it's all prepared

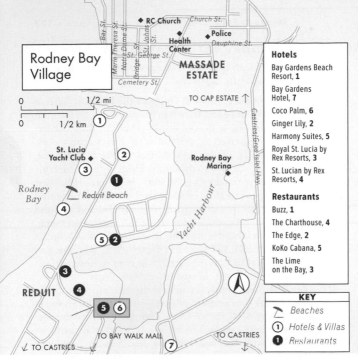

Hotels

Bay Gardens Beach
Resort, **1**

Bay Gardens
Hotel, **7**

Coco Palm, **6**

Ginger Lily, **2**

Harmony Suites, **5**

Royal St. Lucia by
Rex Resorts, **3**

St. Lucian by Rex
Resorts, **4**

Restaurants

Buzz, **1**

The Charthouse, **4**

The Edge, **2**

KoKo Cabana, **5**

The Lime
on the Bay, **3**

KEY

Beaches

① Hotels & Villas

❶ Restaurants

and served by a friendly staff, many of whom have been with the restaurant since it opened. Fresh lobster is delivered daily in season. After dinner, gentlemen (and audacious ladies) can choose from a wide variety of Cuban cigars. Take-out service is also available. ⑤ *Average main: $28 ⊠ Reduit Beach Ave., Rodney Bay ☎ 758/459–8115 ⊕ www.charthousestlucia.com ⚏ Reservations essential ⊗ No lunch.*

★ **Fodor's**Choice ✕ **The Edge.** *Eclectic.* The innovative Swedish
$$$$ chef Bobo Bergstrom, formerly the culinary director at Windjammer Landing and chef de cuisine at the famed Operakallaren in Stockholm, has brought "Eurobbean" cuisine to his own restaurant, which overlooks the harbor at Harmony Suites hotel. St. Lucian locals and visitors alike rave about chef Bobo's culinary feats, the excellent wine list, and the island's first sushi bar. The contemporary fusion style combines the chef's European heritage, Caribbean traditions and ingredients, and a touch of Asian influence. Among the dozen starters is a dreamy lobster bisque seasoned with saffron and paprika. Follow that with snapper braised in fennel bouillon, jerk-marinated-and-grilled beef tenderloin, or spice-glazed rabbit roulade. You might want to consider the five-course tasting menu. There's sure to

be a dish on the extensive menu (or at the sushi bar) that suits everyone in your party, but be sure to leave room for a fabulous dessert. Ⓢ *Average main: $39* ✉ *Harmony Suites, Reduit Beach Ave., Rodney Bay* ☎ *758/450–3343* ⊕ *www. edge-restaurant.com* ⌕ *Reservations essential.*

★ **Fodor's**Choice ✕ **Tao.** *Asian.* For exquisite dining, head for
$$$ Tao at the Body Holiday in Cap Estate. Perched on a second-floor balcony at the edge of Cariblue Beach, you're guaranteed a pleasant breeze and a starry sky while you enjoy fusion cuisine—Asian tastes with a Caribbean touch. Choose from appetizers such as seafood dumplings, sashimi salad, or miso-eggplant timbale, followed by tender slices of pork loin teriyaki, twice-cooked duck, wok-seared calves' liver, or tandoori chicken—the results are mouthwatering. Fine wines accompany the meal, desserts are extravagant, and service is superb. Seating is limited; hotel guests have priority, so reserve early. Ⓢ *Average main: $30* ✉ *The Body Holiday, Cap Estate* ☎ *758/457–7800* ⊕ *www.thebodyholi-day.com* ⌕ *Reservations essential* ⊘ *No lunch.*

$$$ ✕ **KoKo Cabana.** *Caribbean.* Poolside at the Coco Palm hotel in Rodney Bay, KoKo Cabana is an open-air Caribbean-style bistro and bar. Breakfast attracts mostly hotel guests, but the elegant yet casual restaurant attacts a wider range of clientele for lunch and dinner. Lunch is a good bet if you're poking around Rodney Bay, need a break from Reduit Beach, or are just looking for a good meal in an attractive spot. On Wednesday there's a special creole lunch buffet; for Sunday brunch, a barbecue buffet. In the evening the breezy dining room is where the magic really comes through. The exquisite French-inspired, creole-influenced dishes here include panfried snapper with orange and butter sauce and green fig Lyonnaise. Leave room for dessert—the trio of crèmes brûlées (mango and ginger, coconut, and seamoss and cinnamon) is the showstopper. And speaking of the show, a live band entertains every evening. Ⓢ *Average main: $28* ✉ *Coco Palm, Gros Islet* ☎ *758/456–2828* ⊕ *www.coco-resorts.com* ⌕ *Reservations essential.*

CASTRIES

★ **Fodor's**Choice ✕ **Coal Pot.** *French.* Popular since the early
$$$$ 1960s, this tiny (only 10 tables) waterfront restaurant overlooking pretty Vigie Cove is managed by local artist Michelle Elliott and her French husband, Xavier Ribot, who is also the chef. For a light lunch, opt for a bowl of creamy pumpkin soup, Greek or shrimp salad, or broiled fresh fish

with creole sauce. Dinner might start with a divine lobster bisque, followed by fresh seafood accompanied by one (or more) of the chef's fabulous sauces—ginger, coconut-curry, lemon-garlic butter, or wild mushroom. Heartier eaters may prefer duck, lamb, beef, or chicken laced with peppercorns, red wine, onion, or Roquefort sauce. ⑤ *Average main: $32* ✉ *Vigie Cove* ☎ *758/452–5566* ⊕ *www.coalpotrestaurant. com* ⚠ *Reservations essential* ⊙ *Closed Sun. No lunch Sat.*

$$$ ✕ **Jacques Waterfront Dining.** *Seafood.* Chef–owner Jacky Rioux creates magical dishes in his open-air garden restaurant, which overlooks Vigie Cove and was known for years as Froggie Jack's. The cooking style is decidedly French, as is Rioux, but fresh produce and local spices create a fusion cuisine that's memorable at either lunch or dinner. You might start with a bowl of creamy tomato-basil or pumpkin soup, a grilled portobello mushroom, or octopus and conch in curried coconut sauce. Main courses include fresh seafood, such as oven-baked kingfish with a white wine–and–sweet pepper sauce, or breast of chicken stuffed with smoked salmon in a citrus-butter sauce. The wine list is also impressive. ⑤ *Average main: $28* ✉ *Vigie Cove* ☎ *758/458–1900* ⊕ *www.jacquesrestaurant.com* ⚠ *Reservations essential* ⊙ *Closed Sun.*

MARIGOT BAY AND VICINITY

$$$ ✕ **Boudreau.** *Eclectic.* Simple and satisfying are words that come to mind when dining at Boudreau, the fine-dining restaurant at Discovery at Marigot Bay. The chef's passion for incorporating St. Lucian ingredients into the menu brings him to market regularly to choose the best fruits, roots, and greens to blend with fresh seafood and prime meats—or to create a vegetarian dish that's both filling and full of flavor. Seafood lovers may enjoy pan-roasted kingfish with tempura vegetables, mashed sweet potatoes, and maple mango sauce. Boudreau—which is rather casual at breakfast but becomes elegant at dinner—welcomes villa guests, yachties, and daytrippers alike. The open-air restaurant is named for Walter Boudreau, a schooner captain who built the original hotel where Discovery is now located. ⑤ *Average main: $28* ✉ *Discovery at Marigot Bay, Marigot Bay* ☎ *758/458–5300* ⊕ *www.discoverystlucia.com* ⚠ *Reservations essential.*

$$ ✕ **Chateau Mygo.** *Seafood.* Walk down a garden path to Chateau Mygo (a corruption of the word Marigot), pick out a table on the dockside dining deck, pull up a chair,

European-inspired Caribbean cuisine at The Edge in Rodney Bay

and soak up the waterfront atmosphere of what is argu-ably the prettiest bay in the Caribbean. The tableau is mesmerizing—and that's at lunch, when you can order a sandwich, burger, fish- or chicken-and-chips, salads, or grilled fish or chicken with peas and rice and vegetables. At dinner, chef–owner Doreen Rambally—whose family has owned and operated this place since the mid-1970s—draws on three generations of East Indian and creole family recipes. Beautifully grilled fresh tuna, red snapper, kingfish, mahimahi, and local lobster are embellished with flavors such as ginger, mango, papaya, or passion fruit, and then dished up with regional vegetables—perhaps callaloo, okra, dasheen, breadfruit, christophene, or yams. You can also have roast pork, beef, a chicken dish, or pizza—and you'll find the only sushi bar on St. Lucia's west coast. This is a very casual restaurant where locals, yachties, and frequent visitors know they'll get a delicious, reasonably priced meal right on the waterfront. And oh, that view! ⑤ *Average main: $20* ⊠ *Marigot Bay* ☎ *758/451–4772.*

$$ ×**Doolittle's.** *Seafood.* Named for the protagonist in the original (1967) *Dr. Dolittle* movie, part of which was filmed right here in Marigot Bay, Doolittle's is the inside–outside waterfront restaurant at the Marigot Beach Club & Dive Center on the north side of the bay. You can watch yachts quietly slip by as you enjoy your meal. The menu offers a broad range—light meals such as sandwiches, burgers, grilled chicken, and salads at lunchtime and, in the evening,

The Coal Pot restaurant in Vigie Marina, Castries

seafood, steak, chicken, and Caribbean specials such as curries and stews. Take the little ferry across the bay to reach Doolittle's. During the day, bring your bathing suit. The beach is just outside the restaurant's door. ⑤ *Average main: $20* ⊠ *Marigot Beach Club, Marigot Bay* 🕿 *758/451–4974* ⊕ *www.marigotbeachclub.com.*

★ **Fodor'sChoice** ✕ **Rainforest Hideaway.** *Eclectic.* Fusion fare—in
$$$$ this case, the exotic tastes and flavors influencing classical French cuisine—is presented by chef Noel Nugent at this romantic fine-dining hideaway on the north shore of pretty Marigot Bay. It's definitely worth the 20-minute-or-so drive from Castries. A little ferry whisks you to the alfresco restaurant, perched on a dock, where you're greeted with complimentary champagne. You'll be duly impressed by entrées such as balsamic-glazed roast quail, five-spice roast fillet of beef, or citrus-marinated wild salmon, accompanied by rich sauces, exotic vegetables, and excellent wines—not to mention the blanket of stars in the sky overhead and the live jazz several times a week. ⑤ *Average main: $35* ⊠ *Marigot Bay* 🕿 *758/286–0511* ⊕ *www.rainforesthideawaystlucia. com* 🕾 *Reservations essential* ⊗ *No lunch; closed Tues.; closed Sept.*

$ ✕ **Rowley's Café/Baguet Shop.** *Café.* Join the yachties and nearby hotel guests for breakfast, lunch, afternoon tea, an evening snack, or just dessert at this French bakery and café in the Marina Village on Marigot Bay. Open every day from 7 am to 7 pm, it offers freshly baked French bread,

crusty croissants, and delicious French pastries. Sandwiches are prepared on a baguette, croissant, or focaccia—your choice. Pair your favorite with a cup of cappuccino, mocha, or latte. Or hold the coffee until dessert, and pair your fruit tart, *pain au chocolat*, coconut flan, or another delicious pastry with a steaming cup of rich espresso. Eat in (well, outside on the dock) or take it out. Even if you eat in, you'll probably also want a baguette—or a bagful—to take out. ⑤ *Average main: $10* ✉ *Marina Village, Marigot Bay* ☎ *758/451–4275* ⚑ *Reservations not accepted.*

SOUFRIÈRE

$$$ ✕ **Apsara.** *Indian.* India has had an important historical influence on many islands in the Caribbean. To start, there's the heritage of its people (descendents of both indentured servants and wealthy businessmen), the colorful madras plaids, and the curry flavors that are a staple of Caribbean cuisine. At night, Anse Chastanet's Trou au Diable restaurant transforms itself into Apsara, an upscale dining experience where modern Indian cuisine is served in an extraordinarily romantic, candlelit, beachfront setting. The innovative menu, mixing East Indian and Caribbean cooking, produces food that's full of flavor but not too spicy, although you can opt for some dishes that are hotter than others. You might start with mulligatawny soup with cumin yogurt or vegetable samosas, followed by coconut-chili king prawns, pork vindaloo, or tandoori-roasted salmon, lamb chops, chicken, or lobster. Definitely order the naan bread, either plain or flavored with almond, coconut, or raisin. And for dessert, depending on your appetite, choose the mango, saffron, or seamoss-flavored *kulfi* (Indian-style ice cream) or go all the way with Apsara's Temptation (tandoori-baked pineapple with honey, saffron, and passion-fruit syrup, kulfi, and sun-blushed chili). ⑤ *Average main: $25* ✉ *Anse Chastanet* ☎ *758/459–7354* ⊕ *www.ansechastanet. com* ⚑ *Reservations essential* ⊘ *No lunch. Closed Tues.*

$$$ ✕ **Boucan.** *Caribbean.* Ahh . . . chocolate! Here at Boucan on the Rabot Estate, a working cocoa plantation and also home to Hotel Chocolat, you'll find that heavenly flavor infused into just about every dish: cacao gazpacho or citrus salad with white chocolate dressing for starters. The main course might be either red snapper or rib-eye steak marinated with roasted cacao nibs or dorado served with a red wine and cacao sauce. You get the picture. Dessert, of course, is the grand chocolate finale: chocolate tart,

Amazing views at Dasheene Restaurant in the Ladera Resort

meringue floating in a sea of chocolate crème anglaise, dark chocolate mouse...even cacao sorbet. Yum. ⑤ *Average main: $23* ✉ *Hotel Chocolat, Rabot Estate, West Coast Rd., 3 miles (5 km) south of Soufrière, Soufrière* ☎ *758/457–1624* ⚓ *Reservations essential.*

★ **Fodor's**Choice ✕**Dasheene Restaurant and Bar.** *Caribbean.* The
$$$ terrace restaurant at Ladera resort has breathtakingly close-up views of the Pitons and the sea between them, especially beautiful at sunset. The ambience is casual by day and magical at night. Executive chef Orlando Satchell describes his creative West Indian menu as "sexy Caribbean." Appetizers may include grilled crab claws with a choice of dips or silky pumpkin soup with ginger. Typical entrées are "fisherman's catch" with a choice of flavored butters or sauces, shrimp Dasheene (panfried with local herbs), grilled rack of lamb with coconut risotto and curry sauce, or pan-seared fillet of beef marinated in lime-and-pepper seasoning. Light dishes, pasta dishes, and fresh salads are also served at lunch—along with the view. ⑤ *Average main: $30* ✉ *Ladera, 2 miles (3 km) south of Soufrière* ☎ *758/459–7323* ⊕ *www.ladera.com.*

$$ ✕**Lifeline Restaurant at the Hummingbird.** *Caribbean.* The chef at this cheerful restaurant-bar in the Hummingbird Beach Resort specializes in French-creole cuisine, starting with fresh seafood or chicken seasoned with local herbs and accompanied by vegetables just picked from the Hummingbird's garden. Sandwiches and salads are also available. If you stop for lunch, sit outside by the pool for a magnifi-

cent view of the Pitons (you can also take a dip), and be sure to visit the batik studio and art gallery of proprietor Joan Alexander-Stowe, which is next to the dining room. ⑤ *Average main: $18* ✉ *Hummingbird Beach Resort, Anse Chastanet Rd.* ☎ *758/459–7985* ⊕ *www.istlucia.co.uk.*

$$ ✕ **The Still.** *Caribbean.* When you're visiting Diamond Waterfall and other attractions in Soufrière, this is a great lunch spot. The two dining rooms seat up to 400 people, so it's also a popular stop for tour groups and cruise passengers. The emphasis is on local cuisine using vegetables such as christophene, breadfruit, yam, and callaloo along with grilled fish or chicken, but there are also pork and beef dishes. All fruits and vegetables used in the restaurant are organically grown on the estate. Lunch is a buffet. ⑤ *Average main: $18* ✉ *The Still Plantation, Sir Arthur Lewis St.* ☎ *758/459–7261* ⊕ *www.thestillplantation.com* ⊙ *No dinner.*

WHERE TO STAY

Most people—particularly honeymooners—choose to stay in one of St. Lucia's many grand beach resorts, most of which are upscale and pricey. Several are all-inclusive, including the three Sandals resorts, two resorts owned or managed by Sunswept (The Body Holiday and Rendezvous), Morgan Bay Beach Resort, East Winds Inn, and Smugglers Cove Resort & Spa.

If you're looking for lodgings that are smaller and less expensive, St. Lucia has dozens of small inns and hotels that are primarily locally owned and frequently quite charming. They may or may not be directly on the beach. Luxury villa communities and independent private villas are another alternative in St. Lucia. Most of the villa communities are in the north near Cap Estate.

For expanded reviews, facilities, and current deals, visit Fodors.com.

PRIVATE VILLAS AND CONDOS

Luxury villa and condo communities are an important part of the accommodations mix on St. Lucia, as they can be an economical option for families, other groups, or couples vacationing together. Several communities have opened in recent years, and more are on the way. The villa units themselves are privately owned, but non-owners can rent individual units directly from the property managers for a vacation or short-term stay, much like reserving hotel

BEST BETS FOR LODGING

Fodor's offers a selective listing of quality lodging experiences, from the island's best boutique hotel to its most luxurious beach resort. Here, we've compiled our top recommendations based on the different types of lodging found on the island. The very best properties—in other words, those that provide a particularly remarkable experience—are designated in the listings with the Fodor's Choice logo.

Fodor's Choice★

The Body Holiday, Calabash Cove Resort & Spa, Cap Maison, Discovery at Marigot Bay, Jade Mountain, The Jalousie Planation Sugar Beach, Ladera, Sandals Grande St. Lucian Spa & Beach Resort

BEST BEACH RESORTS
The Body Holiday, Calabash Cove Resort & Spa,

BEST FOR HONEYMOONERS
Jade Mountain, Ladera, Sandals Grande St. Lucian Spa & Beach Resort

BEST FOR FAMILIES
Discovery at Marigot Bay, The Jalousie Plantation Sugar Beach, Cap Maison

accommodations. Units with fully equipped kitchens, up to three bedrooms, and as many baths run $200 to $2,500 per night, depending on the size and the season.

Local real-estate agencies will arrange vacation rentals of privately owned villas and condos that are fully equipped. Most private villas are in the hills of Cap Estate in the very north of the island, at Rodney Bay or Bois d'Orange, or in Soufrière among St. Lucia's natural treasures. Some are within walking distance of a beach.

All rental villas are staffed with a cook who specializes in local cuisine, and a housekeeper; in some cases, a caretaker lives on the property and a gardener and night watchman are on staff. All properties have telephones, and some have Internet access and fax machines. Telephones may be barred against outgoing overseas calls; plan to use a phone card or calling card. Most villas have TVs, DVDs, and CD players. All private villas have a swimming pool; condos share a community pool. Vehicles are generally not included in the rates, but rental cars can be arranged for and delivered to the villa upon request. Linens and basic supplies (such as bath soap, toilet tissue, and dish-washing detergent) are included. Pre-arrival grocery stocking can be arranged.

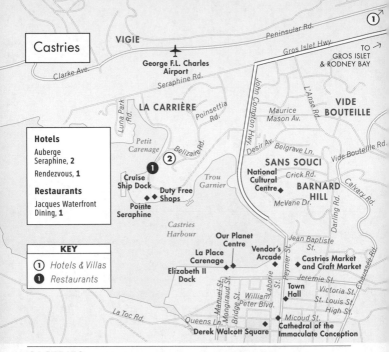

① ↗

TO ↗
GROS ISLET
& RODNEY BAY

Castries

VIGIE

Peninsular Rd.

Gros Islet Hwy

Clarke Ave.

George F.L. Charles
Airport

Seraphine Rd.

Luna Park Rd.

Poinsettia Rd.

John Compton Hwy

L'Anse Rd.

VIDE
BOUTEILLE

LA CARRIÈRE

Maurice
Mason Av.

Desir Av.

Belgrave Ln.

Vide Bouteille Rd.

Petit
Carenage

Belizaire Rd.

SANS SOUCI

Crick Rd.

Hotels
Auberge
Seraphine, **2**
Rendezvous, **1**

Restaurants
Jacques Waterfront
Dining, **1**

Cruise
Ship Dock

Trou
Garnier

National
Cultural
Centre ◆

Calvary Rd.

BARNARD
HILL

Darling Rd.

Chaussee Rd.

1

2

Duty Free
Shops ◆

McVane Dr.

Pointe
Seraphine ◆

Castries
Harbour

Our Planet
Centre

Jean Baptiste
St.

KEY
① *Hotels & Villas*
1 *Restaurants*

La Place
Carenage ◆

Vendor's
Arcade ◆

◆ Castries Market
and Craft Market

Teymier St.

Jeremie St.

Elizabeth II
Dock

Laborie St.

Victoria St.

St. Louis St.

Manuel St.

Mongiraud St.

Bridge St.

William
Peter Blvd.

Town
Hall

High St.

La Toc Rd.

Queens Ln.

Micoud St.

Derek Walcott Square

◆ Cathedral of the
Immaculate Conception

CASTRIES

Castries, the capital city, and the area north and just south of it are the island's most developed areas. About 15 minutes south of Castries, lovely Marigot Bay is both a yacht haven and a picture-pretty destination for landlubbers.

The capital, a busy commercial city of some 65,000 people, wraps around a sheltered bay. Morne Fortune rises sharply to the south of town, creating a dramatic green backdrop. The charm of Castries lies almost entirely in its liveliness, since four fires that occurred between 1796 and 1948 destroyed most of the colonial buildings. Freighters (exporting bananas, coconut, cocoa, mace, nutmeg, and citrus fruits) and cruise ships come and go frequently, making Castries Harbour one of the Caribbean's busiest ports.

WHAT TO SEE

Castries Market. Under a brilliant orange roof, the bustling **Castries Market** is at its liveliest on Saturday morning, when farmers bring their produce and spices to town—as they have for more than a century. Next door to the produce market is the **Craft Market,** where you can buy pottery, wood carvings, and handwoven straw articles. At the **Ven-**

Units with one to nine bedrooms and the same number of baths run $200 to $2,000 per night, depending on the size of the villa, the amenities, the number of guests, and the season. Rates include utilities and government taxes. Your only additional cost will be for groceries and staff gratuities. A security deposit is required upon booking and refunded after departure less any damages or unpaid miscellaneous charges.

Rental Contacts Discover Villas of St. Lucia. ✉ *Cap Estate* ☎ *758/484–3066* ⊕ *www.a1stluciavillas.com.* **Island Villas St. Lucia.** ✉ *Gros Islet* ☎ *758/458–4903, 866/978–8499 in the U.S.* ⊕ *www.island-villas.com/stlucia.php.* **Tropical Villas.** ✉ *Cap Estate* ☎ *758/450-8240* ⊕ *www.tropicalvillas.net.*

THE NORTH: RODNEY BAY TO CAP ESTATE

$$ 🏊 **Morgan Bay Beach Resort.** *All-inclusive.* An all-inclusive resort for singles, couples, and families alike, Morgan Bay Beach Resort offers both quiet seclusion on 22 acres surrounding a stretch of white-sand beach and tons of free sports and activities. **Pros:** family-friendly; lots to do; golf privileges nearby; great dining atmosphere at Morgan's Pier. **Cons:** resort is huge and can be very busy, especially when all rooms are filled; beach is small. ⑤ *Rooms from: $340* ✉ *Choc Bay, Castries* ☎ *758/450–2511* ⊕ *www.morganbayresort.com* ⇌ *345 rooms* ⑩ *All-inclusive.*

$ 🏊 **Bay Gardens Beach Resort.** *Resort.* One of three Bay Gardens properties in Rodney Bay Village, the family-friendly beach resort has a prime location directly on beautiful Reduit Beach. **Pros:** perfect location on St. Lucia's best beach; excellent value; stay at one, play at three resorts. **Cons:** popular place, so you need to book far in advance in season. ⑤ *Rooms from: $185* ✉ *Reduit Beach Ave., Rodney Bay* ☎ *758/457–8500, 877/629–3200 in the U.S.* ⊕ *www.baygardensbeachresort.com* ⇌ *36 rooms, 36 suites* ⑩ *Multiple meal plans.*

$ 🏊 **Bay Gardens Hotel.** *Hotel.* Independent travelers and regional businesspeople swear by this cheerful, well-run boutique hotel at Rodney Bay Village. **Pros:** excellent service; great value; Croton suites are a best bet. **Cons:** not beachfront; heavy focus on business travelers, so it's not exactly a vacation environment. ⑤ *Rooms from: $96* ✉ *Rodney Bay* ☎ *758/452–8060, 877/620–3200* ⊕ *www.baygardenshotel.com* ⇌ *59 rooms, 28 suites* ⑩ *Multiple meal plans.*

Cotton Bay Village

★ **Fodor's**Choice ⚅ **The Body Holiday.** *All-inclusive.* At this adults-
$$$$ only spa resort on picturesque Cariblue Beach—where
daily treatments are included in the rates—you can cus-
tomize your own "body holiday" online even before you
leave home. **Pros:** daily spa treatment included; excellent
dining; interesting activities such as archery (including free
instruction). **Cons:** extremely expensive; unremarkable
rooms; small bathrooms; lots of steps to the spa. ⑤ *Rooms
from: $1,162* ⊠ *Cariblue Beach, Cap Estate* ☎ *758/457–
7800* ⊕ *www.thebodyholiday.com* ⤳ *152 rooms, 3 suites*
⚏ *All-inclusive.*

★ **Fodor's**Choice ⚅ **Calabash Cove Resort & Spa.** *Resort.* The luxu-
$$$$ rious suites and private cottages at this inviting boutique
resort spill gently down a tropical hillside to the secluded
beach at Bonaire Bay, just south of Rodney Bay. **Pros:** stylish, sophisticated, and friendly; great food; wedding parties
can reserve the entire resort. **Cons:** the long, bone-crunching
dirt entrance road; its many steps may be difficult for those
with physical challenges. ⑤ *Rooms from: $445* ⊠ *Bonaire
Estate, Rodney Bay* ☎ *758/456–3500* ⊕ *www.calabashcove.
com* ⤳ *17 suites; 9 cottages* ⚏ *Multiple meal plans.*

★ **Fodor's**Choice ⚅ **Cap Maison.** *Resort.* This luxurious villa com-
$$$ munity on a seaside bluff overlooking Smugglers Cove has
22 units that can be configured as up to 49 rooms, junior
suites, and oversize one-, two-, or three-bedroom villa
suites. **Pros:** private and elegant; golf and tennis privileges
nearby; those rooftop plunge pools. **Cons:** a/c in bedrooms

only; beach access (the 62 steps) may be a consideration. ⑤ *Rooms from: $435* ✉ *Smugglers Cove Dr., Cap Estate* ☎ *758/457–8670, 888/765–4985 in the U.S.* ⊕ *www.cap-maison.com* ⇌ *10 rooms, 39 suites in 22 villas* ⊙ *Multiple meal plans.*

$ ⊞ **Coco Palm.** *Hotel.* This stylish boutique hotel in Rodney Bay Village also includes Coco Kreole, a cozy guesthouse at the edge of the property, and is right in the middle of the Rodney Bay Village action. **Pros:** excellent value; fabulous swim-up rooms; family suites. **Cons:** not directly on the beach; nightly entertainment can get noisy. ⑤ *Rooms from: $156* ✉ *Reduit Beach Ave., Rodney Bay* ☎ *758/456–2800, 877/655–2626 in the U.S.* ⊕ *www.coco-resorts.com* ⇌ *80 rooms, 12 suites* ⊙ *Multiple meal plans.*

$$ ⊞ **Cotton Bay Village.** *Resort.* Wedged between a quiet ocean beach and the St. Lucia Golf Resort & Country Club, these luxurious, individually designed and decorated colonial-style town houses and château-style villas surround a village center and a free-form lagoon pool. **Pros:** truly luxurious; very private; family-friendly. **Cons:** a/c in bedrooms only; bathrooms have showers only; rental car advised if you plan to leave the property. ⑤ *Rooms from: $313* ✉ *Cap Estate* ☎ *758/456–5700* ⊕ *www.cottonbayvillage.com* ⇌ *206 suites in 74 villas* ⊙ *No meals.*

$$$$ ⊞ **East Winds Inn.** *All-inclusive.* Guests keep returning to East Winds Inn, a small all-inclusive resort on a secluded beach halfway between Castries and Rodney Bay, where 7 acres of botanical gardens surround 13 duplex ginger-bread-style cottages, three ocean-view rooms, and a suite. **Pros:** long-established clientele is the best recommendation; lovely beach; excellent dining; peaceful and quiet. **Cons:** not the best choice for families (though children are welcome); very expensive. ⑤ *Rooms from: $890* ✉ *Labrelotte Bay* ☎ *758/452–8212* ⊕ *www.eastwinds.com* ⇌ *30 rooms* ⊙ *All-inclusive.*

$ ⊞ **Ginger Lily.** *Hotel.* A small, modern hotel with its own restaurant and a swimming pool, the Ginger Lily is smack in the middle of Rodney Bay Village scene and across the street from Reduit Beach. **Pros:** friendly service; good value; excellent location. **Cons:** few on-site activities. ⑤ *Rooms from: $220* ✉ *Reduit Beach Ave., Rodney Bay* ☎ *758/458–0300* ⊕ *www.gingerlilyhotel.com* ⇌ *9 rooms, 2 suites* ⊙ *Multiple meal plans.*

$ ⊞ **Harmony Suites.** *Hotel.* Harmony Suites guests are scuba divers, boaters, or others who don't need luxury but appreciate comfort and just like being on the waterfront. **Pros:**

Discovery at Marigot Bay

Cap Maison Resort & Spa

Sandals Halcyon Beach, lu-The Pierhouse Resta

Calabash Cove Resort & Spa

marina location; excellent on-site restaurant; waterfront suites. **Cons:** rooms are fairly basic; waterfront location not recommended for kids. ⑤ *Rooms from: $57* ⊠ *Reduit Beach Ave., Rodney Bay* ☎ *758/452–8756, 888/790–5264 in the U.S.* ⊕ *www.harmonysuites.com* ⊅ *30 suites* ⊚*No meals.*

$$$$ ⊡ **The Landings.** *Resort.* On 19 acres along the Pigeon Point Causeway at the northern edge of Rodney Bay, the Landings is so called because the property surrounds a private, 80-slip yacht harbor where residents can dock their own yachts literally at their doorstep. **Pros:** spacious, beautifully appointed units; perfect place for yachties to come ashore; personal chef service. **Con:** additional $30 per day "activities fee." ⑤ *Rooms from: $519* ⊠ *Pigeon Island Causeway, Gros Islet* ☎ *758/458–7300* ⊕ *www.landings.rockresorts. com* ⊅ *122 units* ⊚ *No meals.*

$$$$ ⊡ **Royal St. Lucia by Rex Resorts.** *Resort.* This luxurious all-suites resort on St. Lucia's best beach caters to every whim—for the whole family. **Pros:** great beachfront; roomy accommodations; family-friendly; convenient to restaurants, clubs, and shops. **Cons:** dated guest rooms and baths; expensive. ⑤ *Rooms from: $789* ⊠ *Reduit Beach Ave., Rodney Bay* ☎ *758/452–8351* ⊕ *www.rexcaribbean.com* ⊅ *96 suites* ⊚ *Multiple meal plans.*

★ Fodor'sChoice ⊡ **Sandals Grande St. Lucian Spa & Beach Resort.**
$$$$ *All-inclusive.* Grand, yes. And busy, busy, busy. Couples love this place—particularly young honeymooners and those getting married here—the biggest and splashiest of the three Sandals resorts on St. Lucia. **Pros:** excellent beach; lots of activities; dreamy spa; airport shuttle. **Cons:** the really long ride to and from Hewanorra; buffet meals are uninspired. ⑤ *Rooms from: $576* ⊠ *Pigeon Island Causeway, Gros Islet* ☎ *758/455–2000* ⊕ *www.sandals.com* ⊅ *271 rooms, 11 suites* ⊚ *All-inclusive.*

$$$$ ⊡ **Sandals Halcyon Beach St. Lucia.** *All-inclusive.* This is the most intimate and low-key of the three Sandals resorts on St. Lucia; like the others, though, it's beachfront, all-inclusive, for couples only, and loaded with amenities and activities. **Pros:** all the Sandals amenities in a more intimate setting; lots of dining and activity choices; exchange privileges (including golf) at two other Sandals properties. **Cons:** it's Sandals, so it's a theme property after all. ⑤ *Rooms from: $485* ⊠ *Choc Bay, Castries* ☎ *758/453–0222, 888/726–3257* ⊕ *www.sandals.com* ⊅ *169 rooms* ⊚ *All-inclusive.*

$$$$ ⊡ **Sandals Regency St. Lucia Golf Resort & Spa.** *All-inclusive.* One of three Sandals resorts on St. Lucia, this is the second-largest and distinguishes itself with its own 9-hole golf

Sandals Grande St. Lucian Spa & Beach Resort

course (for guests only). **Pros:** lots to do; picturesque location; on-site golf; airport shuttle. **Cons:** somewhat isolated; expert golfers will prefer the St. Lucia Golf Resort & Country Club, in Cap Estate. ⑤ *Rooms from: $491* ⊠ *La Toc Rd., Castries* ☎ *758/452–3081* ⊕ *www.sandals.com* ⇌ *212 rooms, 116 suites* ⦿ *All-inclusive.*

$$ 🏨 **Smugglers Cove Resort & Spa.** *All-inclusive.* This huge, all-inclusive, village-style resort has more food, fun, and features than you and your family will have time to enjoy in a week. **Pros:** family rooms sleep five; excellent children's program; superlative tennis facilities; nightly entertainment is family-friendly. **Cons:** busy, busy, busy; not the place for a quiet getaway; guest rooms are spread far and wide on the hillside. ⑤ *Rooms from: $325* ⊠ *Cap Estate* ☎ *758/457–4140, 855/719–321 in the U.S.* ⊕ *www.smugglersresort.com* ⇌ *257 rooms, 100 suites* ⦿ *All-inclusive.*

$ 🏨 **St. Lucian by Rex Resorts.** *Resort.* This 260-room, family-friendly resort on a long stretch of Reduit beachfront is surrounded by gardens. **Pros:** great beach and lots of water sports; excellent Rodney Bay Village location; easy access to sister hotel. **Cons:** standard rooms are pretty basic; the spa is not on-site. ⑤ *Rooms from: $195* ⊠ *Reduit Beach Ave., Rodney Bay* ☎ *758/452–8351* ⊕ *www.rexresorts.com* ⇌ *260 rooms* ⦿ *Multiple meal plans.*

$ 🏨 **Villa Beach Cottages.** *Rental.* Tidy housekeeping cottages with gingerbread-laced facades are steps from the beach at this family-run establishment 3 miles (5 km) north of the airport in Castries. **Pros:** directly on the beach; beautiful sunsets; peaceful and quiet. **Cons:** close quarters. ⑤ *Rooms from: $240* ✉ *Choc Bay, Castries* ☎ *758/450–2884* ⊕ *www. villabeachcottages.com* ✎ *20 units* ⫙ *No meals.*

$$ 🖭 **Windjammer Landing Villa Beach Resort.** *Resort.* As perfect for families as for a romantic getaway, Windjammer Landing offers lots to do yet still provides plenty of privacy. **Pros:** lovely, spacious units; beautiful sunset views; family-friendly, in-unit dining. **Cons:** some units have living rooms with no a/c; you'll want to rent a car if you plan to leave the property often, as it's far from the main road. ⑤ *Rooms from: $359* ✉ *Trouya Point Rd., Labrelotte Bay* ☎ *758/456–9000, 877/522–0722 in the U.S.* ⊕ *www.windjammer-landing.com* ✎ *41 suites, 72 villas* ⫙ *Multiple meal plans.*

GREATER CASTRIES

$ 🖭 **Auberge Seraphine.** *Hotel.* This is a good choice for independent vacationers who don't require a beachfront location or resort activities. **Pros:** nice pool; good restaurant. **Cons:** no beach; no resort activities. ⑤ *Rooms from: $125* ✉ *Vielle Bay, Pointe Seraphine, Castries* ☎ *758/453–2073* ⊕ *www.aubergeseraphine.com* ✎ *24 rooms* ⫙ *No meals.*

$$$$ 🖭 **Rendezvous.** *All-inclusive.* Romance is alive and well at this easygoing, all-inclusive couples resort, which stretches along the dreamy white sand of Malabar Beach opposite the George F.L. Charles Airport runway. **Pros:** convenient to Castries and Vigie Airport; great beach; romance in the air; popular wedding venue. **Cons:** no room TVs; occasional flyover noise. ⑤ *Rooms from: $838* ✉ *Vigie, Castries* ☎ *758/457–7900* ⊕ *www.theromanticholiday.com* ✎ *57 rooms, 35 suites, 8 cottages* ⫙ *All-inclusive.*

MARIGOT BAY TO ANSE LA RAYE

$ 🖭 **Inn on the Bay.** *B&B/Inn.* Renting just five rooms, Normand Viau and Louise Boucher, owners (since 1995) of this delightful aerie on the southern hillside at the entrance of Marigot Bay, treat you as their personal guests (adults only). **Pros:** the view; the value; the pleasant hosts; the personalized service. **Cons:** few, if any, amenities besides peace, quiet, and nature. ⑤ *Rooms from: $220* ✉ *Marigot Bay* ☎ *758/451–4260* ⊕ *www.saint-lucia.com* ✎ *5 rooms* ⫙ *Breakfast.*

$ 🖭 **Mango Beach Inn.** *B&B/Inn.* When the Marigot Bay ferry delivers you to the dock at Rainforest Hideaway restaurant, a small gate next to the bar opens to a stone staircase lead-

CLOSE UP

Bananas

More than 10,000 St. Lucian banana farmers produced 134,000 tons of the familiar fruit in the early 1990s, most of which was exported to Europe. By 2005, when the Caribbean nations had lost their preferential treatment in the European market, fewer than 2,000 banana farmers were producing about 30,000 tons. Nevertheless, you'll still see bananas growing throughout St. Lucia, especially in the rural areas around Babonneau in the northeast and south of Castries near Marigot Bay. As you pass by the banana fields, you'll notice that the fruit is wrapped in blue plastic. That's to protect it from birds and insects—because there's no market for an imperfect banana.

---

ing up to delightful Mango Beach Inn. **Pros:** spectacular views of Marigot Bay; beach, water sports, restaurants, and shopping nearby; attentive hosts; kid-friendly. **Cons:** tiny rooms; some bathrooms have showers only; negotiating the steps to the inn would be difficult for those with physical challenges. ⑤ *Rooms from: $140* ✉ *Marigot Bay* ☎ *758/451–4872* ⊕ *www.mangobeachmarigot.com* ⇨ *5 rooms* ⋈ *Breakfast.*

★ **Fodor's**Choice ⛰ **Discovery at Marigot Bay.** *Resort.* Five miles
$$$$ (8 km) south of Castries, this chic, ecofriendly villa resort climbs the hillside of what author James Michener called "the most beautiful bay in the Caribbean." **Pros:** peaceful and picturesque, with a stunning bay view; oversize villa accommodations; 12 ground-level units available for those with difficulty negotiating stairs. **Cons:** a/c in bedrooms only; you'll need a rental car to explore beyond Marigot Bay; nearby beach is pretty but tiny. ⑤ *Rooms from: $500* ✉ *Marigot Bay* ☎ *758/458–5300, 877/384–8037 in the U.S.* ⊕ *www.discoverystlucia.com* ⇨ *67 rooms, 57 suites* ⋈ *Multiple meal plans.*

$ ⛰ **Marigot Beach Club & Dive Resort.** *Resort.* Divers love this place, and everyone loves the location facing the little palm-studded beach at Marigot Bay. **Pros:** great value for divers; beautiful views of Marigot Bay; good casual dining; easy access to Marina Village. **Cons:** beach is tiny (though very inviting). ⑤ *Rooms from: $148* ✉ *Marigot Bay* ☎ *758/458–3323* ⊕ *www.marigotbeachclub.com* ⇨ *24 rooms, 3 villas* ⋈ *Breakfast.*

$$ 🏠 **Ti Kaye Village.** *Resort.* Rustic elegance is not an oxy-moron, at least at this upscale cottage community on the hillside up from Anse Cochon beach. **Pros:** perfect for a wedding, honeymoon, or private getaway; love those garden showers; good restaurant; excellent beach for snorkeling; dive shop on-site. **Cons:** far from anywhere; very bumpy 1.5-mile (2-km) dirt access road; all those steps to the beach; not a good choice for anyone with physical challenges; no kids under age 12. ⑤ *Rooms from: $325* ✉ *Anse Cochon* ☎ *758/456–8101* ⊕ *www.tikaye.com* ⮑ *33 rooms* 🍴 *Multiple meal plans.*

SOUFRIÈRE

$$$$ 🏠 **Anse Chastanet Resort.** *Resort.* This resort is magical—spec-tacular rooms, some with stunning Piton vistas beyond open fourth walls, peek out of the thick rain forest that cascades down a steep hillside to the sea. **Pros:** great for divers; Room 14B, which has a tree growing through the bathroom; the open-air Piton views. **Cons:** no pool; entrance road is difficult to negotiate; steep hillside certainly not conducive to strolling; some may miss in-room TVs, phones, and a/c. ⑤ *Rooms from: $495* ✉ *Anse Chastanet Rd.* ☎ *758/459–7000, 800/223–1108 in U.S.* ⊕ *www.ansechastanet.com* ⮑ *49 rooms* 🍴 *Multiple meal plans.*

$$ 🏠 **Fond Doux Holiday Plantation.** *Resort.* Ever wish you could stay in a cottage in the rain forest—with all (or at least most) of the conveniences of home? Here at Fond Doux, one of Soufrière's most active agricultural plantations, 10 historic homes salvaged from all around the island and meticulously disassembled have been rebuilt and refurbished on the estate. **Pros:** beautifully refurbished historic cottages; exotic and ecofriendly; striking location on an 18th-century plantation. **Cons:** a rental car is advised, as beach and local sights are a few miles away; not all cottages have a full kitchen where you can cook meals. ⑤ *Rooms from: $275* ✉ *Fond Doux Estate* ☎ *758/459–7545* ⊕ *www.fonddouxestate.com* ⮑ *10 cottages* 🍴 *Multiple meal plans.*

$$$$ 🏠 **Boucan by Hotel Chocolat.** *Hotel.* Anyone who loves choco-late will love this little cottage community just south of Soufrière and within shouting distance of the Pitons. **Pros:** small and sophisticated; chocolate lover's dream hotel; no service charge and no tipping expected. **Cons:** rental car advised; not for anyone allergic or less than thrilled by the idea of all that chocolate. ⑤ *Rooms from: $550* ✉ *Rabot Estate, West Coast Rd., 2 miles (3 km) south of town, Sou-*

JADE POOL, Saint Lucia. Jade Mountain Club

Jalousie Plantation

frière ☎ 758/457–1624, 800/757–7132 in the U.S. ⊕ www. thehotelchocolat.com ➫ 14 rooms ⊚ Multiple meal plans.

$ ☒ **Hummingbird Beach Resort.** B&B/Inn. Unpretentious and welcoming, this delightful little inn on Soufrière Harbour has simply furnished rooms—a traditional motif empha- sized by four-poster beds and African wood sculptures—in small seaside cabins. **Pros:** local island hospitality; small and quiet; good food. **Cons:** few resort amenities—but that's part of the charm. ⑤ Rooms from: $90 ⊠ Anse Chastanet Rd. ☎ 758/459–7985, 888/790–5264 in the U.S. ⊕ www. istlucia.co.uk ➫ 9 rooms, 2 with shared bath; 1 suite; 1 cottage ⊚ Multiple meal plans.

★ Fodor'sChoice ☒ **Jade Mountain.** Resort. This premium-class and $$$$ premium-priced hotel is a five-level behemoth stuck on the side of a mountain that slopes down to the sea. **Pros:** amaz- ing accommodations; huge in-room pools; incredible Piton views. **Cons:** sky-high rates; lack of in-room communica- tion and a/c; not appropriate for children or anyone with disabilities. ⑤ Rooms from: $1,200 ⊠ Anse Chastanet, Anse Chastanet Rd. ☎ 758/459–4000 ⊕ www.jademountainstlu- cia.com ➫ 28 suites ⊚ Multiple meal plans.

★ Fodor'sChoice ☒ **The Jalousie Plantation, Sugar Beach.** Resort. $$$$ Located on the most dramatic 192 acres in St. Lucia, Jal- ousie Plantation flows down Val des Pitons—the steep valley smack between the Pitons—on the remains of an 18th-century sugar plantation 2 miles (3 km) south of Sou- frière. **Pros:** incomparable scenery, service, and amenities; family-friendly; lots of activities, including complimentary scuba diving. **Cons:** very expensive; fairly isolated, so a meal plan makes sense; cottages are surrounded by thick foli- age, so bring mosquito spray. ⑤ Rooms from: $900 ⊠ Val de Pitons, 2 miles (3 km) south of town ☎ 800/235–4300, 758/456–8000 ⊕ www.jalousieplantation.com ➫ 11 rooms, 42 villas ⊚ Multiple meal plans.

★ Fodor'sChoice ☒ **Ladera.** B&B/Inn. One of the most sophis- $$$$ ticated small inns in the Caribbean, the elegantly rustic Ladera is perched 1,100 feet above the sea directly between the two Pitons. **Pros:** breathtaking Pitons vista; in-room pools; excellent cuisine. **Cons:** the hotel's communal infin- ity pool is not very big; open fourth walls and steep drops make this inappropriate for children (and also means no a/c); rental car advised. ⑤ Rooms from: $665 ⊠ West Coast Rd., 3 miles (5 km) south of town, Val de Pitons ☎ 758/459– 6600, 866/290–0978 in the U.S. ⊕ www.ladera.com ➫ 28 suites, 9 villas ⊚ Multiple meal plans.

3

A private in-suite plunge pool at Ladera Resort

$ 🔲 **La Haut Plantation.** *B&B/Inn*. It's all about the view—the Pitons, of course—and the appeal of staying in an intimate and affordable family-run inn. **Pros:** lovely for weddings and honeymoons but also for families with kids; stunning Piton views; excellent restaurant; excellent value. **Cons:** very quiet, especially at night, unless that's the point; bathrooms have showers only; vehicle recommended. Ⓢ *Rooms from: $100* ✉ *West Coast Rd., just north of town* ☎ *758/459– 7008, 888/790–5264 in the U.S.* ⊕ *www.lahaut.com* 🛏 *13 rooms* ❗ *Multiple meal plans.*

$$$$ 🔲 **Stonefield Estate Villa Resort & Spa.** *Resort*. One 18th-century plantation house and several gingerbread-style cottages dot this 26-acre family-owned estate, a tropical hillside with eye-popping views of Petit Piton. **Pros:** very private; beautiful pool; great sunset views from villa decks; lovely wedding venue. **Cons:** a rental car is recommended; you have to drive to off-site restaurants. Ⓢ *Rooms from: $545* ✉ *West Coast Rd., 1 mile (1½ km) south of Soufrière* ☎ *758/459–7037* ⊕ *www.stonefieldvillas.com* 🛏 *17 villas* ❗ *Multiple meal plans.*

VIEUX FORT

$$$$ 🔲 **Coconut Bay Beach Resort & Spa.** *All-inclusive*. The only resort in Vieux Fort, Coconut Bay is a sprawling (85 acres), family-friendly seaside retreat minutes from St. Lucia's Hewanorra International Airport. **Pros:** great for families;

perfect for windsurfers; friendly and sociable atmosphere. **Cons:** bathrooms have showers only; rough surf precludes ocean swimming; close to the airport but far from everything else. ⑤ *Rooms from: $659* ✉ *Vieux Fort* ☎ *758/459–6000* ⊕ *www.cbayresort.com* ✇ *254 rooms* ⑩ *All-inclusive.*

NIGHTLIFE AND THE ARTS

THE ARTS

★ **Fodor's**Choice **St. Lucia Jazz Festival.** Held in early May, the weeklong St. Lucia Jazz Festival is one of the premier events of its kind in the Caribbean. International jazz greats perform at outdoor venues on Pigeon Island and at various hotels, restaurants, and nightspots throughout the island; free concerts are also held at Derek Walcott Square in downtown Castries. ✉ *Pigeon Island, Gros Islet* ⊕ *www. stluciajazz.org.*

THEATER

Derek Walcott Center Theatre. The small, open-air Derek Walcott Center Theatre, next to The Great House restaurant in Cap Estate, seats 200 people for monthly productions of music, dance, and drama, as well as Sunday brunch programs. The Trinidad Theatre Workshop also presents an annual performance here. For schedule and ticket information, contact The **Great House** restaurant. ✉ *Next to The Great House, Cap Estate* ☎ *758/450–0551, 758/450–0450 for the Great House.*

NIGHTLIFE

Most resort hotels have entertainment—island music, calypso singers, and steel bands, as well as disco, karaoke, and talent shows—every night in high season and a couple of nights per week in the off-season. Otherwise, Rodney Bay is the best bet for nightlife. The many restaurants and bars there attract a crowd nearly every night.

BARS

Jambe de Bois. At this cozy Old English–style pub, there's live jazz on Sunday and violin on Thursday. ✉ *Pigeon Island, Gros Islet* ☎ *758/450–8166.*

Cocoa Tea

The homemade chocolate balls or sticks that vendors sell in the market are formed from locally grown and processed cocoa beans. The chocolate is used locally to make cocoa tea—a beverage that actually originated in Soufrière but has since become a popular drink wherever cocoa is grown throughout the Caribbean. The chocolate is grated and steeped in boiling water, along with a bay leaf and cinnamon stick. Sugar is added, along with a little milk or cream, and some vanilla. Some people add nutmeg, as well, and some cornstarch to make it thicker and more filling. Cocoa tea began as a breakfast treat but is now enjoyed with a slice of bread as a snack or even as a dessert. Be sure to bring some chocolate sticks or balls home with you. One sniff and you won't be able to resist buying a packet ($2–$4).

CASINOS

Treasure Bay Casino. St. Lucia opened its first casino in early 2011. You'll find more than 250 slot machines, along with 22 gaming tables (poker, blackjack, roulette, and craps) and a sports bar with 31 television screens. ⊠ *Bay Walk Shopping Mall, Rodney Bay* ☎ *758/459–2901* ⊕ *www.treasurebaystlucia.com* ☉ *Sun.–Thurs. 10 am–3 am, Fri.–Sat., 10 am–4 am.*

DANCE CLUBS

Rodney Bay has the most bars and clubs. Most dance clubs with live bands have a cover charge of $10 to $20 (EC$25 to EC$50), and the music usually starts at 11 pm.

Delirius. At Delirius, visitors and St. Lucians alike "lime" over cocktails at the horseshoe-shaped bar and at tables in the garden. The atmosphere is casual, the decor is contemporary, and the music (live bands or DJ) from the 1960s, '70s, and '80s. ⊠ *Reduit Beach Ave., Rodney Bay* ☎ *758/451–3354.*

Doolittle's. The music at Doolittle's changes nightly. Expect live bands and a mix of calypso, soul, salsa, steel band, reggae, limbo, and other music for dancing. ⊠ *Marigot Beach Club, Marigot Bay* ☎ *758/451–4974.*

STREET PARTIES

Anse La Raye "Seafood Friday". For a taste of St. Lucian village life, head for this street festival, held every Friday night. Beginning at 6:30 pm, the main street in this tiny fishing village—about halfway between Castries and Soufrière—is closed to vehicles, and the residents prepare what they know best: fish cakes, grilled or stewed fish, hot bakes (biscuits), roasted corn, boiled crayfish, and lobster (it's grilled before your eyes). Prices range from a few cents for a fish cake or bake to $10 or $15 for a whole lobster, depending on its size. Walk around, eat, chat with the local people, and listen to live music until the wee hours of the morning. ⊠ *Anse la Raye.*

★ **Fodor's**Choice **Gros Islet Jump-Up.** A Friday-night ritual for locals and visitors alike is to head to the Gros Islet Jump-Up, the island's largest street party. Huge speakers set up on the village's main street blast out Caribbean music all night long. Sometimes there are live bands. When you take a break from dancing, you can buy barbecued fish or chicken, rotis, beer, and soda from villagers who set up grills right along the roadside. It's the ultimate "lime" experience. ⊠ *Gros Islet.*

3

SHOPPING

The island's best-known products are artwork and wood carvings, straw mats, clay pottery, and clothing and household articles made from batik and silk-screened fabrics that are designed and produced in island workshops. You can also take home straw hats and baskets and locally grown cocoa, coffee, spices, sauces, and flavorings.

AREAS AND MALLS

★ **Baywalk Mall**, at Rodney Bay, is a 60-store complex of boutiques, restaurants, banks, a beauty salon, jewelry and souvenir stores, and the island's first casino.

Along the harbor in Castries, rambling structures with bright-orange roofs house several markets that are open from 6 am to 5 pm Monday through Saturday. Saturday morning is the busiest and most colorful time to shop. For more than a century, farmers' wives have gathered at the **Castries Market** to sell produce—which, alas, you can't import to the United States. But you can bring back spices (such as cocoa, turmeric, cloves, bay leaves, ginger, peppercorns, cinnamon sticks, nutmeg, and mace), as well as bottled hot-pepper sauces—all of which cost a fraction of what you'd pay back home. The **Craft Market**, adjacent to the produce market, has aisles and aisles of baskets and other handmade straw work, rustic brooms made from palm fronds, wood carvings, leather work, clay pottery, and souvenirs—all at affordable prices. The **Vendors' Arcade,** across the street from the Craft Market, is a maze of stalls and booths where you can find handicrafts among the T-shirts and costume jewelry.

Gablewoods Mall, on the Gros Islet Highway in Choc Bay, a couple of miles north of downtown Castries, has about 35 shops that sell groceries, wines and spirits, jewelry, clothing, crafts, books and overseas newspapers, music, souvenirs, household goods, and snacks.

Along with 54 boutiques, restaurants, and other businesses that sell services and supplies, a large supermarket is the focal point of each **J.Q.'s Shopping Mall;** one is at Rodney Bay and another is at Vieux Fort.

Marigot Marina Village in Marigot Bay has shops and services for boaters and landlubbers alike, including a bank, grocery store, business center, art gallery, assortment of boutiques, and French bakery and café.

Duty-free shopping areas are at **Pointe Seraphine,** an attractive Spanish-motif complex on Castries Harbour with more than 20 shops, and **La Place Carenage,** an inviting three-story complex on the opposite side of the harbor. You can also find duty-free items at Baywalk Mall, in a few small shops at the arcade at the Royal St. Lucia hotel in Rodney Bay, and, of course, in the departure lounge at Hewanorra International Airport. You must present your passport and airline ticket to purchase items at the duty-free price.

Vieux Fort Plaza, near Hewanorra International Airport in Vieux Fort, is the main shopping center in the southern part of St. Lucia. You'll find a bank, supermarket, bookstore, toy shop, and several clothing stores there.

SPECIALTY ITEMS

ART

Artsibit Gallery. The moderately priced works on display here are made by local painters and sculptors. ⊠ *Brazil and Mongiraud Sts., Castries* ☎ *758/452–7865.*

Caribbean Art Gallery. On offer here are original artwork by local artists, along with antique maps and prints and hand-painted silk. ⊠ *Rodney Bay Marina, Rodney Bay* ☎ *758/452–8071.*

Llewellyn Xavier. World-renowned St. Lucian artist Llewellyn Xavier creates modern art, ranging from vigorous oil abstracts that take up half a wall, to small objects made from beaten silver and gold. Much of his work has an environmental theme and is created from recycled materials. Xavier's work is on permanent exhibit at major museums in New York and Washington, D.C. Others are sold in gift shops throughout the island. Call to arrange a visit to his studio. ⊠ *Mount du Cap, Cap Estate* ☎ *758/450–9155* ⊕ *www.llewellynxavier.com.*

BOOKS AND MAGAZINES

Sunshine Bookshop. In addition to newspapers and magazines, Sunshine Bookshop carries novels and titles of regional interest, including books by the St. Lucian Nobel laureate Derek Walcott and other Caribbean authors. ⊠ *Gablewoods Mall, Castries* ☎ *758/452–3222.*

Valmont Books. This shop carries West Indian literature and picture books, as well as stationery. ⊠ *Jeremie and Laborie Sts., Castries* ☎ *758/452–3817.*

CLOTHES AND TEXTILES

The Bagshaws of St. Lucia. Using Sydney Bagshaw's original designs, this shop sells clothing and table linens in colorful tropical patterns. The fabrics are silk-screened by hand in the adjacent workroom. You can also find Bagshaw boutiques at Pointe Seraphine and La Place Carenage, as well as a selection of items in gift shops at Hewanorra Airport. Visit the workshop to see how the designs are turned into colorful silk-screened fabrics, which are then fashioned into clothing and household articles. It's open weekdays from 8:30 to 5, Saturday 8:30 to 4, and Sunday 10 to 1. Weekend hours may be extended if a cruise ship is in port. ⊠ *La Toc Rd., La Toc Bay, Castries* ☎ *758/451–9249.*

The Batik Studio. The superb batik sarongs, scarves, and wall panels here are designed and created on-site by Joan Alexander-Stowe. ⊠ *Hummingbird Beach Resort, Anse Chastanet Rd., Soufrière* ☎ *758/459–7985.*

Caribelle Batik. At Caribelle Batik, craftspeople demonstrate the art of batik and silk-screen printing. Meanwhile, seamstresses create clothing and wall hangings, which you can purchase in the shop. The studio is in an old Victorian mansion, high atop Morne Fortune, overlooking Castries. There's a terrace where you can have a cool drink and a garden full of tropical orchids and lilies. Caribelle Batik cre-

ations are featured in many gift shops throughout St. Lucia. ✉ *Howelton House, Old Victoria Rd., Morne Fortune, Castries* ☎ *758/452–3785* ⊕ *www.caribellebatikstlucia.com.*

Sea Island Cotton Shop. High-quality T-shirts, Caribelle Batik clothing and other resort wear, and colorful souvenirs are all for sale here. ✉ *Baywalk Mall, Rodney Bay* ☎ *758/458–4220* ⊕ *www.seaislandstlucia.com* ✉ *Gablewoods Mall, Choc Bay, Castries* ☎ *758/451–6946.*

GIFTS AND SOUVENIRS

Caribbean Perfumes. Using exotic flowers, fruits, tropical woods, and spices, Caribbean Perfumes blends a half dozen lovely scents for women and two aftershaves for men. The reasonably priced fragrances, all made in St. Lucia, are available at the perfumery (in the garden adjacent to the restaurant) and at many hotel gift shops. ✉ *Jacques Waterfront Dining, Vigie Marina, Castries* ☎ *758/453–7249* ⊕ *www.caribbeanperfumes.com.*

Noah's Arkade. Hammocks, wood carvings, straw mats, T-shirts, books, and other regional goods are available here. ✉ *Jeremie St., Castries* ☎ *758/452–2523* ✉ *Pointe Seraphine, Castries* ☎ *758/452–7488.*

HANDICRAFTS

Choiseul Arts & Crafts Centre. You can find locally made clay and straw pieces at the Choiseul Arts & Crafts Centre. It's on the southwest coast, halfway between Soufrière and Vieux Fort; many of St. Lucia's artisans come from this area. ✉ *La Fargue* ☎ *758/454–3226.*

Eudovic Art Studio. Head to this workshop and studio for trays, masks, and abstract figures sculpted by Vincent Joseph Eudovic from local mahogany, red cedar, and eucalyptus wood. ✉ *Goodlands, Morne Fortune, Castries* ☎ *758/452–2747* ⊕ *www.eudovicart.com.*

Zaka. At Zaka, you may get a chance to talk with artist and craftsman Simon Gajhadhar, who fashions totems and masks from driftwood and other environmentally friendly sources of wood—taking advantage of all the natural nibs and knots that distinguish each piece. Once the "face" is carved, it is painted in vivid colors to highlight the exaggerated features and provide expression. Each piece is unique. ✉ *Malgretoute, on the road to Jalousie Plantation, Soufrière* ☎ *758/457–1504* ⊕ *www.zaka-art.com.*

SPORTS AND ACTIVITIES

BIKING

Although the terrain is pretty rugged, two tour operators have put together fascinating bicycle and combination bicycle-hiking tours that appeal to novice riders as well as those who enjoy a good workout. Prices range from $60 to $100 per person.

Bike St. Lucia. This company takes small groups of bikers on Jungle Biking tours along trails that meander through the remnants of the 18th-century plantation that's part of the Anse Chastanet estate in Soufrière. Stops are made to explore the French colonial ruins, study the beautiful tropical plants and fruit trees, enjoy a picnic lunch, and take a dip in a river swimming hole or a swim at the beach. There's a training area for learning or brushing up on off-road riding skills. If you're staying in the north, you can arrange a tour that includes transportation to the Soufrière area. ✉ *Anse Mamin Plantation, adjacent to Anse Chastanet, Soufrière* ☎ *758/457–1400* ⊕ *www.bikestlucia.com.*

Palm Services Bike Tours. To start a Palm Services tour, participants first take a jeep or bus across the central mountains to Dennery, on the east coast. After a 3-mile (5-km) ride through the countryside, bikes are exchanged for shoe leather. The short hike into the rain forest ends with a picnic and a refreshing swim next to a sparkling waterfall—then the return leg to Dennery. All gear is included, and the tours are suitable for all fitness levels. ✉ *Rodney Bay* ☎ *758/458–0908* ⊕ *www.adventuretoursstlucia.com.*

BOATING AND SAILING

Rodney Bay and Marigot Bay are centers for bareboat and crewed yacht charters. Their marinas offer safe anchorage, shower facilities, restaurants, groceries, and maintenance for yachts sailing the waters of the eastern Caribbean. Charter prices range from $400 to $500 per overnight or $1,750 to $10,000 per week, depending on the season and the type and size of vessel, plus $250 extra per day if you want a skipper and cook.

Bateau Mygo. The customized, crewed charters from Bateau Mygo are on a 38-foot catamaran, for either a couple of days or a week. ✉ *Chateau Mygo Villas, Marigot Bay* ☎ *758/458–3957* ⊕ *www.bateaumygo.com.*

Destination St. Lucia (DSL) Ltd. For its bareboat yacht charters, DSL's vessels include a 42-foot catamaran and monohulls ranging in length from 32 to 50 feet. ⊠ *Rodney Bay Marina, Rodney Bay* ☎ *758/452–8531* ⊕ *www.dsl-yachting.com.*

Moorings Yacht Charters. Bareboat and crewed catamarans and monohulls ranging from Beneteau 39s to Morgan 60s are what you can get from this company. ⊠ *Marigot Bay Marina, Marigot Bay* ☎ *758/451–4357, 800/952–8420* ⊕ *www.moorings.com.*

DIVING AND SNORKELING

Depending on the season and the particular trip, prices range from about $40 to $60 for a one-tank dive to $175 to $260 for a six-dive package over three days and $265 to $450 for a 10-dive package over five days. Dive shops provide instruction for all levels (beginner, intermediate, and advanced). For beginners, a resort course (pool training), followed by one open-water dive, runs from $90 to $120. Snorkelers are generally welcome on dive trips and usually pay $50 to $65, which includes equipment and sometimes lunch and transportation.

★ **Fodor's Choice Anse Chastanet,** near the Pitons on the southwest coast, is the best beach-entry dive site. The underwater reef drops from 20 feet to nearly 140 feet in a stunning coral wall.

A 165-foot freighter, *Lesleen M,* was deliberately sunk in 60 feet of water near **Anse Cochon** to create an artificial reef; divers can explore the ship in its entirety and view huge gorgonians, black coral trees, gigantic barrel sponges, lace corals, schooling fish, angelfish, sea horses, spotted eels, stingrays, nurse sharks, and sea turtles.

Anse La Raye, midway up the west coast, is one of St. Lucia's finest wall and drift dives and a great place for snorkeling.

Superman's Flight is a dramatic drift dive along the steep walls beneath the Pitons. At the base of **Petit Piton** a spectacular wall drops to 200 feet, where you can view an impressive collection of huge barrel sponges and black coral trees; strong currents ensure good visibility.

At the **Pinnacles,** four coral-encrusted stone piers rise to within 10 feet of the surface.

A large brain coral off the coast of St. Lucia

DIVE OPERATORS
Dive Fair Helen. This PADI center offers half- and full-day excursions to wreck, wall, and marine reserve areas, as well as night dives. ⊠ *Marigot Bay Marina, Marigot Bay* ☎ *758/451–7716, 888/855–2206 in U.S. and Canada* ⊕ *www.divefairhelen.com.*

Scuba St. Lucia. Daily beach and boat dives and resort and certification courses are available from this PADI Five Star facility, and so is underwater photography and snorkeling equipment. Day trips from the north of the island include round-trip speedboat transportation. ⊠ *Anse Chastanet Resort, Anse Chastanet Rd., Soufrière* ☎ *758/459–7755, 888/465–8242 in the U.S.* ⊕ *www.scubastlucia.com.*

Island Divers. Found at the edge of the Soufriere Marine Park at Anse Cochon, with two reefs and an offshore wreck accessible from shore, Island Divers has a convenient location for boat dives, PADI certification, and specialty courses. A day package includes hotel transfers, lunch at Ti Kaye's beachside bar and grill, a two-tank dive, and the use of snorkel gear for the day. ⊠ *Ti Kaye Village, Anse Cochon* ☎ *758/456–8110* ⊕ *www.islanddiversstlucia.com.*

FISHING

Among the deep-sea creatures you can find in St. Lucia's waters are dolphin (the fish, also called dorado or mahimahi), barracuda, mackerel, wahoo, kingfish, sailfish, and white and blue marlin. Sportfishing is generally done on a catch-and-release basis, but the captain may permit you to take a fish back to your hotel to be prepared for your dinner. Neither spearfishing nor collecting live fish in coastal waters is permitted. Half- and full-day deep-sea fishing excursions can be arranged at either Vigie Marina or Rodney Bay Marina. A half day of fishing on a scheduled trip runs about $85 per person to join a scheduled party for a half day or $500 to $1,000 for a private charter for up to six or eight people, depending on the size of the boat and the length of time. Beginners are welcome.

Captain Mike's. The captain's fleet of Bertram powerboats (31 to 38 feet) accommodate as many as eight passengers for half-day or full-day sport-fishing charters; tackle and cold drinks are supplied. ⊠ *Vigie Marina, Castries* ☎ *758/452–7044* ⊕ *www.captmikes.com.*

Hackshaw's Boat Charters. In business since 1953, Hackshaw's Boat Charters runs charters on boats that include the 31-foot *Blue Boy* and the 50-foot, custom-built *Lady Hack* and *Lady Anne.* ⊠ *Vigie Marina, Castries* ☎ *758/453–0553, 758/452–3909* ⊕ *www.hackshaws.com.*

Mako Watersports. Mako takes fishing enthusiasts out on the well-equipped six-passenger *Annie Baby.* ⊠ *Rodney Bay Marina, Rodney Bay* ☎ *758/452–0412.*

GOLF

St. Lucia has only one 18-hole championship course: **St. Lucia Golf Resort & Country Club**, which is in Cap Estate. **Sandals Regency Golf Resort and Spa** has a 9-hole course for its guests.

St. Lucia Golf Resort & Country Club. The island's only public course is at the northern tip, with wide views of both the Atlantic and the Caribbean. The 18-hole championship course is 6,836 yards and par 71. Its clubhouse's fine-dining restaurant, the Cap Grill, serves breakfast, lunch, and dinner; the Sports Bar is a convivial meeting place any time of day. You can rent clubs and shoes and arrange lessons at the pro shop and perfect your swing at the 350-yard driving range. Greens fees are approximately $105 for 9 holes and

$145 for 18 holes, including carts, which are required; club and shoe rentals are available. Reservations are essential. Complimentary transportation from your hotel or cruise ship is provided for parties of three or more people. The St. Lucia Golf Open, a two-day spring tournament, is open to amateurs; it's a handicap event, and prizes are awarded. ⌧ *Cap Estate* ☎ *758/452–8523* ⊕ *www.stluciagolf.com.*

GUIDED TOURS

Taxi drivers are well informed and can give you a full tour and often an excellent one, thanks to government-sponsored training programs. From the Castries area, full-day island tours cost $40 to $75 per person for up to four people, depending on the route and whether entrance fees and lunch are included. If you plan your own day, expect to pay the driver $40 per hour plus tip.

Jungle Tours. This company specializes in rain-forest hiking tours for all levels of ability. You're required only to bring hiking shoes or sneakers and have a willingness to get wet and have fun. The cost is $95 per person and includes lunch, fees, and transportation via an open Land Rover truck. ⌧ *Cas en Bas, Gros Islet* ☎ *758/715–3438* ⊕ *www. jungletoursstlucia.com.*

St. Lucia Helicopters. Now you can get a bird's-eye view of the island. A 10-minute North Island tour ($85 per person) leaves from Pointe Seraphine, in Castries, continues up the west coast to Pigeon Island, then flies along the rugged Atlantic coastline before returning inland over Castries. The 20-minute South Island tour ($140 per person) starts at Pointe Seraphine and follows the western coastline, circling beautiful Marigot Bay, Soufrière, and the majestic Pitons before returning inland over the volcanic hot springs and tropical rain forest. A complete island tour combines the two and lasts 30 minutes ($175 per person). ⌧ *Pointe Seraphine, Castries* ☎ *758/453–6950* ⊕ *www. stluciahelicopters.com.*

St. Lucia Heritage Tours. The Heritage Tourism Association of St. Lucia (HERITAS), a volunteer group that represents local sites and institutions, puts together "authentic St. Lucia experiences" that focus on local culture and traditions. Groups are kept small, and the tours can be tailored to your interests. Some of the unusual sites visited include a 19th-century plantation house surrounded by nature trails, a 20-foot waterfall hidden away on private property, and a living museum presenting Creole practices and traditions. Plan on paying $75 per person for a full-day tour. ⊠ *Pointe Seraphine, Castries* ☎ *758/451–6058* ⊕ *www. heritagetoursstlucia.org.*

Sunlink Tours. This huge tour operator offers dozens of land, sea, and combination sightseeing tours, as well as shopping tours, plantation, and rain-forest adventures via jeep safari, deep-sea fishing excursions, and day trips to other islands. Prices range from $35 for a half-day shopping tour to $140 for a full-day land-and-sea jeep safari to Soufrière. ⊠ *Reduit Beach Ave., Rodney Bay* ☎ *758/456–9100* ⊕ *www. sunlinktours.com.*

HIKING

The island is laced with trails, but you shouldn't attempt the more challenging ones—especially those that are deep in the rain forest—on your own.

St. Lucia Forest & Lands Department. Trails under this department's jurisdiction include the Barre de L'Isle Trail, the Des Cartiers Rain Forest Trail, and the Edmund Rain Forest Reserve Trail. It also provides guides, who explain the plants and trees you'll encounter and keep you on the right track. Seasoned hikers climb the Pitons, the two volcanic cones rising 2,461 feet and 2,619 feet, respectively, from the ocean floor just south of Soufrière. Hiking is recommended only on Gros Piton, which offers a steep but safe trail to the top. The first half of the hike is moderately difficult; reaching the summit is challenging and should be attempted only by those who are physically fit. The view from the top is spectacular. Tourists are also permitted to hike Petit Piton, but the second half of the hike requires a good deal of rock climbing, and you'll need to provide your own safety equipment. Hiking either Piton requires permission from the St. Lucia Forest & Lands Department and a guide. ☎ *758/468–5649, 758/450–2078.*

HORSEBACK RIDING

Creole horses, a breed native to South America and popular on the island, are fairly small, fast, sturdy, and even-tempered animals suitable for beginners. Established stables can accommodate all skill levels. They offer countryside trail rides, beach rides with picnic lunches, plantation tours, carriage rides, and lengthy treks. Prices run about $60 for one hour, $70 for two hours, and $85 for a three-hour beach ride and barbecue. Transportation is usually provided between the stables and nearby hotels. Local people sometimes appear on beaches with their steeds and offer 30-minute rides for $10 to $15; ride at your own risk.

Atlantic Shores Riding Stables. The two-hour trail rides from Atlantic Shores can take place on the beach and through the countryside. Beginners are welcome. ⊠ *Savannes Bay, Vieux Fort* ☎ *758/285–1090.*

International Pony Club. The beach-picnic ride from the International Pony Club includes time for a swim—with or without your horse. Both English- and Western-style riding are available. ⊠ *Beauséjour Estate, Gros Islet* ☎ *758/452–8139, 758/450–8665.*

Trim's National Riding Stable. At the island's oldest riding stable there are four sessions per day, plus beach tours, trail rides, and carriage tours to Pigeon Island. ⊠ *Cas-en-Bas, Gros Islet* ☎ *758/450–8273.*

SEA EXCURSIONS

★ **Fodor's**Choice A day sail or sea cruise from Rodney Bay or Vigie Cove to Soufrière and the Pitons is a wonderful way to see St. Lucia and a great way to get to the island's distinctive natural sights. Prices for a full-day sailing excursion to Soufrière run about $100 per person and include a land tour to the Diamond Botanical Gardens, lunch, a stop for swimming and snorkeling, and a visit to pretty Marigot Bay. Two-hour sunset cruises along the northwest coast cost $45 to $60 per person.

Brig Unicorn. The 140-foot tall ship *Brig Unicorn*, used in the filming of the TV miniseries *Roots* and the movie *Pirates of the Caribbean,* is a 140-foot replica of a 19th-century sailing ship. Day trips along the coast are fun for the whole family. Several nights each week a sunset cruise, with drinks and a live steel band, sails to Pigeon Point and back. ⊠ *Vigie Marina, Castries* ☎ *758/452–8644.*

Captain Mike's. Customized sightseeing or whale-watching trips ($45 per person) can be arranged for small groups (four to six people) through Captain Mike's. ⊠ *Vigie Marina, Castries* ☎ *758/452–7044* ⊕ *www.captmikes.com.*

Endless Summer. On *Endless Summer,* a 56-foot "party" catamaran, you can take a day trip along the coast to Soufrière—hotel transfers, tour, entrance fees, lunch, and drinks included—for

Des Cartiers Rain Forest

$100 per person. A half-day swimming and snorkeling trip is also available. For romantics, there's a weekly sunset cruise, with dinner and entertainment. ✉ *Rodney Bay* ☎ *758/450–8651* ⊕ *www.stluciaboattours.com.*

Mystic Man Tours. This company operates glassbottom boat, sailing, snorkeling whale- and dolphin-watching tours—all great family excursions. ✉ *Bay St., Soufrière* ☎ *758/459–7783* ⊕ *www.mysticmantours.com.*

Rodney Bay Ferry. There are two departures daily to Pigeon Island from this company. The cost of $50 per person round-trip includes the entrance fee to the island and lunch; snorkeling equipment can be rented for $12. ✉ *Rodney Bay Marina, Rodney Bay* ☎ *758/452–8816.*

WINDSURFING AND KITEBOARDING

Windsurfers and kiteboarders congregate at Anse de Sables Beach in Vieux Fort, at the southeastern tip of St. Lucia, to take advantage of the blue-water and high-wind conditions that the Atlantic Ocean provides.

Reef Kite and Surf Centre. You can rent equipment or take lessons from certified instructors in windsurfing and kite-surfing at this water-sports center. Windsurfing equipment rental is $45 for a half day; $60 for a full day. Kitesurfing equipment rental is $60 for a half day; $80 for a full day. A three-hour beginning windsurfing course costs $90, including equipment. For kiteboarding, the three-hour starter course costs $180, including equipment and safety gear. Kitesurfing is particularly strenuous, so participants must be excellent swimmers and in good physical health. ✉ *Anse de Sables, near Coconut Bay Beach Resort, Vieux Fort* ☎ *758/454–3418.*

Travel Smart Barbados and St. Lucia

WORD OF MOUTH

"[In St. Lucia, d]o make sure to arrange a rental car with 4-wheel drive . You need a working spare tire as well. The roads are mountainous, twisting, two-lane, dangerous and hair-raising, and that is the main highway. Once off the highway the roads are steep, unpaved, rutted and impassible without 4-wheel drive. "

—rainesilver

GETTING HERE AND AROUND

Barbados and St. Lucia are two popular resort destinations in the eastern Caribbean's southern arc. St. Lucia is situated between Martinique to the north and St. Vincent to the south. Barbados is about 100 miles (160 km) farther east of the rest of the Windward Islands. The two islands are about 20 or 30 minutes apart by air.

▮ AIR TRAVEL

BARBADOS

You can fly nonstop to Barbados from Atlanta (Delta), Charlotte (US Airways), Dallas-Ft. Worth (American), Miami (American), New York–JFK (American and JetBlue), and Philadelphia (US Airways).

American Eagle flies nonstop from San Juan, so many American Airlines customers transfer there instead of in Miami. Caribbean Airlines offers connecting service from Fort Lauderdale, Miami, and New York via Port of Spain, Trinidad, but this adds at least two hours to your flight time even in the best of circumstances and may not be the best option for most Americans. Barbados is also well connected to other Caribbean islands via LIAT. Mustique Airways and SVG Air connect Barbados to St. Vincent and the Grenadines, and many passengers use Barbados as a transit hub, often spending the night each way. RedJet flies between Barbados and Guyana, Jamaica, and Trinidad.

Not all airlines flying into Barbados have local numbers. If your airline doesn't have a local contact number on the island, you may have to pay for the call.

Airline Contacts American Airlines/American Eagle ☎ 246/428–4170 ⊕ www.aa.com. **Caribbean Airlines** ☎ 246/428–1650, 800/744–2225 ⊕ www.caribbean-airlines.com. **Delta** ☎ 800/221–1212 ⊕ www.delta.com. **JetBlue** ☎ 877/596–2413 ⊕ www.jetblue.com. **LIAT** ☎ 246/434–5428, 888/844–5428 ⊕ www.liatairline.com. **Mustique Airways** ☎ 246/428–1638 ⊕ www.mustique.com. **RedJet** ☎ 246/827–2727 ⊕ www.flyredjet.com. **SVG Air** ☎ 246/247–3712 ⊕ www.svgair.com. **US Airways** ☎ 800/622–1015 ⊕ www.usairways.com.

AIRPORTS AND TRANSFERS

Grantley Adams International Airport (BGI) is a stunning, modern facility located in Christ Church Parish, on the south coast. The airport is about 15 minutes from hotels situated along the south or east coast, 45 minutes from the west coast, and about 30 minutes from Bridgetown. If your hotel does not offer airport transfers, you can take a taxi or a shared van service to your resort.

Airport Contacts Grantley Adams International Airport (BGI). ✉ Christ Church, Barbados ☎ 246/428–7101.

ST. LUCIA

American Airlines flies non-stop from Miami to Hewanorra (UVF), with connecting service from New York and other major cities via American Eagle from San Juan to George F. L. Charles Airport (SLU) in Castries. Delta flies nonstop from Atlanta to UVF. Jet-Blue flies nonstop to UVF from New York (JFK). US Airways flies nonstop to UVF from Philadelphia and Charlotte. Air Caraïbes flies from Guadeloupe and Martinique; LIAT flies from several neighboring islands.

Airline Contacts

Air Caraïbes ☎ 758/453-0357 ⊕ www.aircaraibes-usa.com. **American Airlines/American Eagle** ☎ 758/459-6500, 758/452-1820, 800/744-0006 ⊕ www.aa.com. **Delta** ☎ 758/484-5594 ⊕ www.delta.com. **JetBlue** ☎ 877/766-9614, 888/844-5428 ⊕ www.jetblue.com. **LIAT** ☎ 888/844-5428, 758/452-3056 ⊕ www.liatairline.com. **US Airways** ☎ 758/454-8186 ⊕ www.usairways.com.

AIRPORTS AND TRANSFERS

St. Lucia has two airports. Hewanorra International Airport (UVF), which accommodates large jet aircraft, is at the southeastern tip of the island in Vieux Fort. George F.L. Charles Airport (SLU), also referred to as Vigie Airport, is at Vigie Point in Castries, which is in the northwestern part of the island, and accommodates only small prop aircraft due to its location and runway limitations.

Some large resorts—particularly the all-inclusive ones—and pack-age tour operators provide round-trip airport transfers. That's a significant amenity if you're landing at Hewanorra, as the one-way taxi fare for the 60- to 90-minute ride (depending on whether you're headed to Soufrière or Castries) is expensive—$65 to $75 for up to four passengers. Taxis are always available at the airports.

If you land at George F. L. Charles Airport, it's a short drive to resorts in the north and about 20 minutes to Marigot Bay but more than an hour to Soufrière.

Some people opt for a helicopter transfer between Hewanorra and either Castries or Soufrière, a quick 7- to 10-minute ride with a beautiful view at a one-way cost of $145 per passenger. Helicopters operate in daylight hours only and carry up to six passengers.

Airport Contacts George F.L. Charles Airport (SLU). ✉ Vigie, Castries, St. Lucia ☎ 758/452-1156. **Hewanorra International Airport** (UVF). ✉ Vieux Fort, St. Lucia ☎ 758/454-6355. **St. Lucia Helicopters** ☎ 758/453-6950 ⊕ www.stluciahelicopters.com.

▌ BOAT AND FERRY TRAVEL

BARBADOS

No ferries provide interisland service to or from Barbados at this writing.

ST. LUCIA

Visitors combining a visit to St. Lucia with a visit to Martinique, Dominica, or Guadeloupe may opt for the L'Express des Iles fast ferry, a modern, high-speed catamaran that calls in Castries four days a week. The trip between St. Lucia and Fort de France, Martinique, takes 1½ hours; Roseau, Dominica, 3½ hours; and Point à Pitre, Guadeloupe, 5½ hours.

When cruise ships are in port in Castries, a water taxi shuttles back and forth between Pointe Seraphine on the north side of the harbor and La Place Carenage on the south side of the harbor for $2 per person each way.

For visitors arriving at Rodney Bay on their own or chartered yachts, Rodney Bay Marina is an official port of entry for customs and immigration purposes. A regularly scheduled ferry travels between the marina and the shopping complex daily on the hour, from 9 to 4, for $5 per person round-trip.

Ferry Contacts L'Express des Iles 🕿🕿 *758/456–5000* ⊕ *www.express-des-iles.com.* **Rodney Bay Ferry** 🕿 *758/452–8816.*

▌ BUS TRAVEL

BARBADOS

Bus service is efficient and inexpensive. Blue buses with a yellow stripe are public, yellow buses with a blue stripe are private, and private "Zed-R" vans (so called for their ZR license plate designation) are white with a maroon stripe. All buses travel frequently along Highway 1 (St. James Road) and Highway 7 (South Coast Main Road), as well as inland routes. The fare is Bds$1.50 (75¢) for any one destination; exact change in either local or U.S. currency is

appreciated. Buses run about every 20 minutes. Small signs on roadside poles that say "To City" or "Out of City," meaning the direction relative to Bridgetown, mark the bus stops. Flag down the bus with your hand, even if you're standing at the stop. Bridgetown terminals are at Fairchild Street for buses to the south and east and at Lower Green for buses to Speightstown via the west coast.

ST. LUCIA

Privately owned and operated minivans constitute St. Lucia's bus system, an inexpensive and efficient means of transportation used primarily by local people. Minivan routes cover the entire island and run from early morning until approximately 10 pm. You may find this method of getting around most useful for short distances—between Castries and the Rodney Bay area, for example; longer hauls can be uncomfortable. The fare between Castries and Gablewoods Mall is EC$1.25; Castries and Rodney Bay, EC$2; Castries and Gros Islet, EC$2.25; Castries and Vieux Fort (a trip that takes more than two hours), EC$7; Castries and Soufrière (a bone-crushing journey that takes even longer), EC$10. Minivans follow designated routes (signs are displayed on the front window); ask at your hotel for the appropriate route number for your destination. Wait at a marked bus stop or hail a passing minivan from the roadside. In Castries, minivans depart from the corner of Micoud and Bridge streets, behind the markets.

In addition to the driver, each minivan usually has a conductor, a young man whose job it is to collect fares, open the door, and generally take charge of the passenger area. If you're sure of where you're going, simply knock twice on the metal window frame to signal that you want to get off at the next stop. Otherwise, just let the conductor or driver know where you're going, and he'll stop at the appropriate place.

▌ CAR TRAVEL

BARBADOS
Barbados has good roads, but traffic can be heavy on the highways, particularly around Bridgetown. Be sure to keep a map handy, as the road system in the countryside can be very confusing—although the friendly Bajans are always happy to help you find your way. Drive on the left, British-style. When someone flashes headlights at you at an intersection, it means "after you." Be especially careful negotiating roundabouts (traffic circles). The speed limit is 30 mph (50 kph) in the country, 20 mph (30 kph) in town. Bridgetown actually has rush hours: 7 to 9 and 4 to 6. Park only in approved parking areas; downtown parking costs Bds75¢ to Bds$1 per hour.

Car Rentals: Most car-rental agencies require renters to be between 21 and either 70 or 75 years of age and to have a valid driver's license and major credit card. Dozens of agencies rent cars, jeeps, or minimokes (small, open-sided vehicles). Rates are about $60 per day for a minimoke to $85 or more per day for a four-wheel-drive vehicle (or $225 to $400 or more per week) in high season. Most firms also offer discounted three-day rates, and many require at least a two-day rental in high season.

A local driver's permit, which costs $5, is obtained through the rental agency. The rental generally includes insurance, pickup and delivery service, maps, 24-hour emergency service, and unlimited mileage.

Car-Rental Contacts Coconut Car Rentals ⊠ Bayside, Bay St., Bridgetown, St. Michael, Barbados ☎ 246/437–0297 ⊕ www.coconut-cars.com. **Courtesy Rent-A-Car** ⊠ Grantley Adams International Airport, Christ Church, Barbados ☎ 246/431–4173, 246/431–4160 ⊕ www.courtesyrentacar.com. **Drive-a-Matic Car Rental** ⊠ CWTS Complex, Barbados ☎ 246/422–3000, 800/581–8773 ⊕ www.carhire.tv.

ST. LUCIA
Roads in St. Lucia are winding and mountainous, except north of Castries, making driving a challenge for timid or apprehensive drivers and exhausting for everyone else. You drive on the left, British-style. Seat belts are required, and speed limits are enforced, especially in and around Castries.

To rent a car you must be at least 25 years old and provide a valid driver's license and a credit card. If you don't have an international driver's license, you must buy a temporary St. Lucia driving permit ($20 [EC$54]) at the car-rental office, the immigration office at either airport, or the Gros Islet police station. Car-rental rates are usually quoted in U.S. dollars and range from $50 to $80 per day or $300 to $425 per week.

Car-Rental Contacts
Avis ⊠ *Vide Bouteille, Castries, St. Lucia* ☎ *758/452–2700* ⊕ *www.avisstlucia.com* ⊠ *Vieux Fort, St. Lucia* ☎ *758/454–6325* ⊠ *Vigie, St. Lucia* ☎ *758/452–2046.* **Cool Breeze Jeep/Car Rental** ⊠ *Soufrière, St. Lucia* ☎ *758/459–7729* ⊕ *www.coolbreezecarrental. com.* **Courtesy Car Rental** ⊠ *Bois d'Orange, Gros Islet, St. Lucia* ☎ *758/452–8140* ⊕ *www.cour-tesycarrentals.com.* **Hertz** ⊠ *Cap Estate, St. Lucia* ☎ *758/450–0222* ⊕ *www.hertz.com.*

▮ CRUISE SHIP TRAVEL

BARBADOS
Up to eight ships at a time can dock at Bridgetown's Deep Water Harbour, on the northwest side of Carlisle Bay. The cruise-ship terminal has duty-free shops, handicraft vendors, a post office, a telephone station, a tourist information desk, and a taxi stand. To get downtown, follow the shoreline to the Careenage. It's a 15-minute walk or a $4 taxi ride.

Taxis await ships at the pier. Drivers accept U.S. dollars and appreciate a 10% tip. Taxis are unmetered and operate at an hourly rate of $35 to $40 per carload (up to three passengers). Most drivers will cheerfully narrate an island tour. You can rent a car with a valid driver's license, but rates are steep—$60 to $85 per day during

the high season—and some agencies require a two-day rental at that time. Note, too, that driving is on the left, British-style.

ST. LUCIA
Most cruise ships dock at the capital city of Castries, on the island's northwest coast, at either of two docking areas: Pointe Seraphine, a port of entry and duty-free shopping complex, or Port Castries (Place Carenage), a commercial wharf across the harbor. Ferry service connects the two piers. Smaller vessels occasionally call at Soufrière, on the island's southwest coast. Ships calling at Soufrière must anchor offshore and bring passengers ashore via tender. Tourist information booths are at Pointe Seraphine, at Place Carenage, and along the waterfront on Bay Street in Soufrière. Downtown Castries is within walking distance of the pier, and the produce market and adjacent crafts and vendors' markets are the main attractions. Soufrière is a sleepy West Indian town, but it's worth a short walk around the central square to view the French colonial architecture; many of the island's spectacular natural sights are in or near Soufrière.

Taxis are available at the docks in Castries. Although they are unmetered, the standard fares are posted at the entrance to Pointe Seraphine. Taxi drivers are well informed and can give you a full tour—often an excellent one—thanks to government-sponsored training programs. From the Castries area, full-day island tours for up to four people cost $40 to $75 per person, depending on the route and whether entrance fees and lunch are included; sightseeing trips to Soufrière cost around $175. If you plan your own day, expect to pay the driver at least $40 per hour plus a 10% tip. Whatever your destination, negotiate the price with the driver before you depart—and be sure that you both understand whether the rate is quoted in EC or U.S. dollars.

I TAXI TRAVEL

BARBADOS

Taxis operate 24 hours a day. They aren't metered but charge according to fixed rates set by the government. They carry up to three passengers, and the fare may be shared. Sample one-way fares from Bridgetown are $20 to Holetown, $25 to Speightstown, $20 to St. Lawrence Gap, and $35 to Bathsheba. Drivers can also be hired for an hourly rate of about $35–$40 for up to three people.

ST. LUCIA

Taxis are unmetered, although fares are fairly standard. Sample fares for up to four passengers are Castries to Rodney Bay, $20; Rodney Bay to Cap Estate, $10; Castries to Cap Estate, $25; Castries to Marigot Bay, $30; Castries to Anse La Raye, $40; Castries to Soufrière, $90; and Castries to Vieux Forte, $75. Always ask the driver to quote the price *before* you get in, and be sure that you both understand whether it's quoted in EC or U.S. dollars. Drivers are generally careful, knowledgeable, and courteous. Drivers can also be hired for an hourly rate of about $40 per hour for up to three people.

ESSENTIALS

▮ ACCOMMODATIONS

In Barbados most people stay either in luxurious enclaves on the fashionable west coast—north of Bridgetown—or on the action-packed south coast with easy access to small, independent restaurants, bars, and nightclubs. A few inns on the remote southeast and east coasts offer ocean views and tranquillity, but those on the east coast don't have good swimming beaches nearby. Prices in Barbados are sometimes twice as high in season as during the quieter months. Most hotels include no meals in their rates; some include breakfast, many offer a meal plan, others require you to purchase the meal plan in the high season, and a few offer all-inclusive packages.

Great resorts run the gamut—from unpretentious to knock-your-socks-off—in terms of size, intimacy, amenities, and price. Many are well suited to families. A few small, cozy inns may be found in the east and southeast regions of the island. Families and long-term visitors may choose from a wide variety of condos (everything from busy time-share resorts to more sedate vacation complexes). Villas and villa complexes can be luxurious, simple, or something in between.

Nearly all of St. Lucia's resorts and small inns are tucked into lush surroundings on secluded coves, unspoiled beaches, or forested hillsides in three locations along the calm Caribbean (western) coast. They're in the greater Castries area between Marigot Bay, a few miles south of the city, and Labrelotte Bay in the north; in and around Rodney Bay and north to Cap Estate; and in and around Soufrière on the southwest coast near the Pitons. There's only one resort in Vieux Fort, near Hewanorra. The advantage of being in the north is that you have access to a wider range of restaurants and nightlife; in the south you may be limited to your hotel's offerings—albeit some of the best—and a few other dining options in and around Soufrière.

Most people choose to stay in one of St. Lucia's many beach resorts, the majority of which are upscale and fairly pricey. Several are all-inclusive, including three Sandals resorts, two Sunswept resorts (The Body Holiday and Rendezvous), Morgan Bay Beach Resort, East Winds Inn, and Smugglers Cove Resort & Spa. Others may offer an all-inclusive option. If you are looking for something more intimate and perhaps less expensive, a locally owned inn or small hotel is a good option; it may or may not be directly on the beach. Luxury villa communities that operate like hotels are a good alternative for families. Several are in the north in or near Cap Estate.

HOTEL AND RESTAURANT PRICES

Prices in the restaurant reviews are the average cost of a main course at dinner or, if dinner is not served, at lunch; taxes and service charges are generally included. Prices in the hotel reviews are the lowest cost of a standard double room in high season, excluding taxes, service charges, and meal plans (except at all-inclusives). Prices for rentals are the lowest per-night cost for a one-bedroom unit in high season.

∎ COMMUNICATIONS

INTERNET

BARBADOS

Barbados began an initiative in November 2011 to provide free WiFi access throughout the island. As that effort continues, more and more hotspots are becoming available. Most hotels and resorts provide free WiFi and one or more Internet terminals for guest use. You'll also find Internet cafés in and around Bridgetown, in Holetown on the west coast, and at St. Lawrence Gap on the south coast. Rates range from $2 for 15 minutes to $8 or $9 per hour.

Contacts Bean-n-Bagel Internet Cafe ✉ *St. Lawrence Gap, Dover, Christ Church, Barbados* ☎ *246/420–4604* ✉ *West Coast Mall, Holetown, St. James, Barbados* ☎ *246/432–1103* ✉ *The Wharf, Bridgetown, St. Michael, Barbados* ☎ *246/436–7778.*

ST. LUCIA

Many hotels and resorts in St. Lucia offer free or inexpensive WiFi and Internet terminals for

guest use. WiFi hotspots are located in several bars and restaurants at The Marina Village at Marigot Bay. Internet cafés can be found in and around Rodney Bay Marina and in Soufriere. LIME maintains a public Internet kiosk at Pointe Seraphine, in Castries, that accepts major credit cards or cash.

Contacts Cost Less Rent a Car & Internet Cafe ✉ *Rodney Bay, St. Lucia* ☎ *758/450–3416.*

Diamondnet Internet Cafe ✉ *Excelsior Plaza Mall, Town Square, Soufrière, St. Lucia* ☎ *758/457–1444.*

PHONES

BARBADOS

The area code for Barbados is 246. Local calls from private phones are free; some hotels charge a small fee. For directory assistance, dial 411. U.S. visitors can dial 1-800 CALL USA (225–5872) to call home from any phone; it's less expensive than using a calling card, a credit card, or calling collect. Calls from pay phones cost Bds25¢ for five minutes. Prepaid phone cards, which can be used throughout Barbados and other Caribbean islands, are sold at shops, attractions, transportation centers, and other convenient outlets.

Most U.S. cell phones will work in Barbados, though roaming charges can be expensive. Renting a cell phone or buying a local SIM card for your own unlocked phone may be a less expensive alternative if you're planning an extended stay or expect to make a lot of local calls. A cell phone can be rented for as little as $5 a day (minimum one-week rental); prepaid cards in varying denominations and top-off services are available at several locations throughout the island.

Contacts Digicel ✉ *The Courtyard, Hastings, Christ Church, Barbados* ☎ *246/467–7000.*

LIME ✉ *Carlisle House, Hincks St., Bridgetown, St. Michael, Barbados* ☎ *800/804–2994.*

ST. LUCIA
The area code for St. Lucia is 758. You can make direct-dial overseas and interisland calls from St. Lucia, and the connections are excellent. You can charge an overseas call to a major credit card with no surcharge; from public phones and many hotels, dial 811 to charge the call to your credit card. Some hotels charge a small fee (usually about EC$1) for local calls. Many retail outlets sell phone cards to use for either local or international calls from any touch-tone telephone (including pay phones) in St. Lucia. Cell phones may be rented from LIME or Digicel offices in Castries, Gablewoods Mall, Baywalk Mall in Rodney Bay, and Vieux Fort, or you can purchase a local SIM card for $20 (which includes an $8 call credit) in those same locations. The cards may be topped up at hundreds of business locations around the island.

Contacts Digicel ☎ *758/456–3400, 758/456–3444.* **LIME** ☎ *758/453–9000.*

▌ EATING OUT
Barbados prides itself on its many wonderful restaurants, many of which can compete with top-notch dining experiences anywhere in the world. On the west coast, excellent restaurants are concentrated in St. James Parish along Highway 1, particularly in and around Holetown. In fact, 1st Street and 2nd Street in Holetown are lined with restaurants that offer a variety of cuisines and prices that range from inexpensive to plan ahead! On the south coast, St. Lawrence Gap is the mother lode of Barbados restaurants, with about 20 possible choices lining both sides of the street (or "gap").

The bulk of St. Lucia's restaurants—both casual and classy—are concentrated in Rodney Bay Village, although some excellent dining establishments are in the Vigie area of Castries and in pretty Marigot Bay. In Soufrière, the best dining is in small hotels and inns, which always welcome nonguests for both lunch and dinner.

MEALS AND MEALTIMES
Resort breakfasts are frequently lavish buffets that offer tropical fruits and fruit juices, cereal, fresh rolls and pastries, hot dishes (such as codfish, corned-beef hash, and potatoes), and prepared-to-order eggs, pancakes, and French toast. Lunch could be a sit-down meal at a beachfront café or a picnic at a secluded cove. But dinner is the highlight, often combining the expertise of internationally trained chefs with local know-how and ingredients.

Of course, you'll want to take advantage of the weekend evening street parties in both Barbados (Oistins) and St. Lucia (Gros Islet and Anse La Raye), where you can buy and try local food barbecued right before your eyes and accompanied by music and conviviality—a wonderful experience for the whole family.

Expect breakfast to be served from 7:30 am to 10 am; lunch from noon to 2 pm or so; and dinner from 7 pm to about 10 pm. Some restaurants have specific mealtimes; others serve continuously all day long.

Unless otherwise noted, the restaurants listed in this guide are open daily for lunch and dinner.

PAYING

Major credit cards (American Express, MasterCard, and Visa) are accepted in most Caribbean restaurants. We note in reviews when credit cards are not accepted. Price charts for restaurants are included in each destination chapter's Planner.

RESERVATIONS AND DRESS

It's always a good idea to make a reservation if you can. In some small or pricey restaurants, it's required. We mention specifically only when reservations are essential (there's no other way you'll ever get a table) or when they are not accepted. For very popular restaurants, book as far ahead as you can (often 30 days), and reconfirm as soon as you arrive. Large parties should always call ahead to check the reservations policy. We mention dress only for the very few restaurants where men are required to wear a jacket or a jacket and tie. Shorts and T-shirts at dinner and beach attire or bare feet anytime are universally frowned upon in restaurants throughout the Caribbean.

WINES, BEER, AND SPIRITS

Mount Gay and Cockspur are the most popular local rum brands in Barbados, "the birthplace of rum"; Bounty and Chairman's Reserve, in St. Lucia. Some distilleries are open to the public for tours, tastings, and duty-free shopping.

Both islands also have their own breweries—Banks in Barbados and Piton in St. Lucia. Both are light, refreshing beers—perfect for hot summer afternoons at the beach.

Those who prefer a nonalcoholic drink will love the fresh fruit punch, lime squash, or Ting—a carbonated grapefruit drink from Jamaica that's often available in Barbados and St. Lucia. For something unusual and purely local, try mauby, a strong, dark, rather bitter beverage made from the bark of a tree; ginger beer; sea moss, a reputed aphrodisiac made from a combination of seaweed, sweetener, milk, and spices; and coconut water, the liquid inside a green "jelly coconut" often sold on the street by a "jellyman" who, for $1 or so, will nip off the top of the coconut with his sharp machete so you can drink the coconut water inside.

▮ ELECTRICITY

The electric current throughout Barbados is 110 volts, 50 cycles, U.S. standard.

The electric current on St. Lucia is 220 volts, 50 cycles, with a square, three-pin plug (U.K. standard). You'll need a transformer to convert voltage and a plug adapter to use most North American appliances; dual-voltage computer and phone chargers or other appliances will still need a plug adapter, which you can often borrow from the hotel. More and more hotels and resorts have added 110-volt outlets for general use but sometimes only for electric razors. Many hotels and resorts also provide iPod docking stations.

▮ EMERGENCIES

BARBADOS
Emergency Services
Ambulance ☎ *511.* **Divers' Alert Network** ☎ *246/684–8111, 246/684–2948.* **Fire** ☎ *311.* **Hyperbaric Chamber in Barbados** ☎ *246/436–5483 to treat decompression illness in divers.* **Police** ☎ *211 emergencies, 246/430–7100 nonemergencies.*

EMBASSIES
Contacts Embassy of the United States ✉ *Wildey Business Park, Wildey, St. Michael, Barbados* ☎ *246/227–4000.*

ST. LUCIA
Ambulance and Fire
Ambulance and Fire ☎ *911.*
Police ☎ *999.*

▮ HEALTH

Dengue fever is one of the common viral diseases transmitted to humans by the bite of mosquitoes, and the Caribbean—including the islands of Barbados and St. Lucia—is one of the regions of the world that is considered a "risk area" by the CDC. No vaccine is available to prevent dengue fever, but travelers are advised to protect against mosquito bites by using insect repellent and protective clothing when in swampy or forested areas.

HIV is also a growing problem throughout the Caribbean, and visitors to the region should take appropriate precautions to prevent contracting the virus.

Tap water in both Barbados and St. Lucia is generally safe to drink, although bottled water is always available if you prefer.

The major health risk in the Caribbean is sunburn or sunstroke. Protect your skin, wear a hat, and use sunscreen.

Swimming on the windward (Atlantic Ocean) side of either island is unsafe—even for experienced swimmers. Tricky currents, powerful waves, strong undertows, and rocky bottoms can be extremely dangerous—and lifeguards are nonexistent.

Watch out for black, spiny sea urchins that live on the rocky sea floor in both shallow and deep waters. Stepping on one is guaranteed to be painful for quite some time, as the urchin releases its spikes into the offending body. To remove a spike, simply pull it out and apply an antiseptic. To remove an embedded spike, first apply some warm oil (preferably olive oil) to soften and dilate the skin and then remove the spike with a sterile needle.

The worst insect problem may well be the tiny "no-see-ums" (sand flies) that appear after a rain, near swampy ground, and at the beach around sunset. If you're hiking through the rain forest in St. Lucia, however, wear long pants and a shirt with long sleeves—just in case.

On the west coast of Barbados in particular, beware of the manchineel tree, which grows near the beach, looks like a beautiful shade tree, and has fruit that looks like little green apples—that are poisonous—and bark and leaves that can burn the skin if you touch them; even the droplets of water that might reach your skin can burn you if you seek protection under the tree during a shower.

Do not fly within 24 hours of scuba diving.

MEDICAL INSURANCE AND ASSISTANCE

Consider buying trip insurance with medical-only coverage. Neither Medicare nor some private insurers cover medical expenses anywhere outside the United States. Medical-only policies typically reimburse you for medical care (excluding that related to pre-existing conditions) and hospitalization abroad, as well as medical evacuation.

Another option is to sign up with a medical-evacuation assistance company. A membership in one of these companies provides doctor referrals, emergency evacuation or repatriation, 24-hour hotlines for medical consultation, and other assistance. International SOS Assistance Emergency and AirMed International provide evacuation services and medical referrals. MedjetAssist offers medical evacuation.

Medical Assistance Companies AirMed International ☎ 800/356–2161 ⊕ www.airmed.com. **International SOS** ☎ 215/942–8000 ⊕ www.internationalsos.com. **MedjetAssist** ☎ 800/527-7478 ⊕ www.medjetassist.com.

Medical-Only Insurers International Medical Group ☎ 800/628–4664 ⊕ www.imglobal.com. **Wallach & Company** ☎ 800/237-6615, 540/687-3166 ⊕ www.wallach.com.

■ HOURS OF OPERATION

BARBADOS

Banks are open Monday through Thursday 8–3, Friday 8–5 (some branches in supermarkets are open Saturday morning 9–noon). At the airport, the Barbados National Bank is open from 8 am until the last plane leaves or arrives, seven days a week (including holidays). Most stores in Bridgetown are open weekdays from 8:30 or 9 to 4:30 or 5, Saturday from 8:30 to 1 or 2. Stores in shopping malls outside Bridgetown may stay open later. Some supermarkets are open daily 8–6 or later.

ST. LUCIA

Banks are open Monday through Thursday 8–2, Friday 8–5; a few branches in Rodney Bay are also open Saturday 9–noon. Post offices are open weekdays 8:30–4:30. Most stores are open weekdays 8:30–4:30, Saturday 8–12:30; Gablewoods Mall shops are open Monday through Saturday 9–7; J.Q.'s Shopping Mall shops are open weekdays 9–7 and Saturday 9–8; Pointe Seraphine shops are open weekdays 9–5, Saturday 9–2. Some hotel gift shops may be open on Sunday.

■ MAIL

BARBADOS

An airmail letter from Barbados to the United States or Canada costs Bds$2.80 for a half ounce, Bds$3.80 for one ounce; an airmail postcard costs Bds$2.80. When sending mail to Barbados, be sure to include the parish name in the address. The General Post Office in Cheapside, Bridgetown, is open weekdays 7:30–5; branches in each parish are open weekdays 8–3:00; the Sherbourne Conference Center branch is open weekdays 8:15–4:30 during conferences.

ST. LUCIA

The General Post Office is on Bridge Street in Castries and is open weekdays 8:30–4:30; all towns and villages have branches. Postage for airmail letters to the United States, Canada, and the United Kingdom is EC95¢ per ½ ounce; postcards are EC65¢.

■ MONEY

BARBADOS

The Barbados dollar is pegged to the U.S. dollar at the rate of Bds$1.98 to $1. The U.S. dollar (not coins) is widely accepted, although you are likely to get your change in local currency. Major credit cards and traveler's checks are also widely accepted. Barbados National Bank has a branch at Grantley Adams International Airport open daily from 8 am until the last plane lands or departs. ATMs are available 24 hours a day throughout the island and dispense only local currency. All prices quoted in this book are in U.S. dollars unless otherwise indicated as Bds$.

ST. LUCIA

The official currency is the Eastern Caribbean dollar (EC$) at the exchange rate is EC$2.67 to $1. The U.S. dollar (not coins) is accepted nearly everywhere—although you may get your change in local currency. Major credit cards and traveler's checks are also widely accepted. ATMs dispense only local currency. All prices quoted in this book are in U.S. dollars unless otherwise indicated as EC$

▪ PASSPORTS AND VISAS

To enter either Barbados or St. Lucia, all visitors must have a valid passport and a return or ongoing ticket.

▪ SAFETY

Although crime isn't a significant problem in either Barbados or St. Lucia, take the same precautions you would at home—lock your door, secure your valuables, and don't carry too much money or flaunt expensive jewelry on the street or beach.

▪ TAXES

BARBADOS

A departure tax ($31.50) is automatically included in your airfare. An 8.75% government tax is added to all hotel bills. A 10% service charge is often added to hotel bills and restaurant checks. A 17.5% V.A.T. is imposed on restaurant meals, admissions to attractions, and merchandise sales (other than those that are duty-free). Prices are often tax-inclusive; if not, the V.A.T. will be added to your bill.

ST. LUCIA

A departure tax of $26 (EC$68) is automatically included in your airfare. A V.A.T. (value-added tax) of 15%, introduced in September

2012, applies to most goods and services, although a reduced rate of 8% will apply to hotel accommodations through April 30, 2013. Duty-free goods, fuel, local transportation services, and many groceries are exempted from the V.A.T. Most restaurants and some hotels also add a service charge of 10% in lieu of tipping.

▪ TIME

Barbados and St. Lucia are both in the Atlantic Standard Time zone, which is one hour later than Eastern Standard Time and four hours earlier than GMT. As is true throughout the Caribbean, neither island observes daylight saving time, so Atlantic Standard is the same time as Eastern Daylight Time during that period (March through October).

▪ TIPPING

BARBADOS

If no service charge is added to your bill, tip waiters 10% to 15% and maids $2 per room per day. Tip bellhops and airport porters $1 per bag. Taxi drivers and tour guides appreciate a 10% tip.

ST. LUCIA

If no service charge is added to your bill, tip waiters 10%–15%. Tip porters and bellhops $1 per bag and hotel maids $2 per night, although many of the all-inclusive resorts have a no-tipping policy. Taxi drivers and tour guides also appreciate a 10% tip.

▌TRIP INSURANCE

Comprehensive trip insurance is valuable if you're booking a very expensive or complicated trip (particularly to an isolated region) or if you're booking far in advance. Comprehensive policies typically cover trip cancellation and interruption, letting you cancel or cut your trip short due to illness or, in some cases, acts of terrorism in your destination. Such policies might also cover evacuation and medical care. (For trips abroad you should have at least medical-only coverage. *See Medical Insurance and Assistance under Health.*) Some policies also cover you for trip delays due to bad weather or mechanical problems, as well as for lost or delayed luggage.

Another type of coverage to consider is financial default—that is, when your trip is disrupted because a tour operator, airline, or cruise line goes out of business. Generally, you must buy this when you book your trip or shortly thereafter; also, it's available only if your operator doesn't appear on a list of excluded companies.

Always read the fine print of your policy to make sure that you're covered for the risks that most concern you. Compare several policies to be sure you're getting the best price and range of coverage available.

Insurance Comparison Sites
Insure My Trip.com ☎ 800/487–4722 ⊕ www.insuremytrip.com.
SquareMouth.com ☎ 800/240–0369 ⊕ www.squaremouth.com.

Comprehensive Travel Insurers
Allianz Travel Insurance
☎ 800/284–8300 ⊕ www.allianztravelinsurance.com. **Chartis Travel Guard** ☎ 800/826–4919 ⊕ www.travelguard.com. **CSA Travel Protection** ☎ 800/711–1197 ⊕ www.csatravelprotection.com. **HTH Worldwide** ☎ 610/254–8700 ⊕ www.hthworldwide.com. **Travel Insured International** ☎ 800/243–3174 ⊕ www.travelinsured.com. **Travelex Insurance** ☎ 800/228–9792 ⊕ www.travelex-insurance.com.

▌VISITOR INFORMATION

BARBADOS
Barbados Tourism Authority
✉ Harbour Rd., Bridgetown, St. Michael, Barbados ☎ 246/427–2623 ⊕ www.visitbarbados.org ✈ Grantley Adams International Airport, Christ Church, Barbados ☎ 246/428–5570 ✉ Cruise-Ship Terminal, Deep Water Harbour, Bridgetown, St. Michael, Barbados ☎ 246/426–1718.

ST. LUCIA
St. Lucia Tourist Board ☎ 212/867–2950 in New York, 800/456–3984 ⊕ www.saintlucianow.com.

▌WEDDINGS

BARBADOS
Barbados makes weddings relatively simple for nonresidents, as there are no minimum residency requirements. Most resorts—and many smaller hotels and inns—offer wedding packages and have on-site wedding coordinators to help you secure a marriage license and plan a personalized ceremony and reception. Alternatively, you may wish to have your wedding

at a scenic historic site or botanical garden, on the grounds of a restored great house, or at sunset on a quiet beach.

To obtain a marriage license, which often can be completed in less than a half hour, both partners must apply in person and present valid passports to the Ministry of Home Affairs (located in the General Post Office building, Cheapside, Bridgetown, ☎ 246/228–8950, and open 8:15–4:30 weekdays). If either party was previously married and widowed, you need to present a certified copy of the marriage certificate and a death certificate for the deceased spouse; if either party is divorced, you need a certified copy of the official divorce decree. Nonresidents of Barbados must pay a fee of $75 (Bds$150) plus a stamp fee of $12.50 (Bds$25)—plus $10 (Bds$20) for the marriage certificate. A notarized parental consent is required if either party is under the age of 18. Finally, you must make arrangements for an authorized marriage officer (a magistrate or minister) to perform the ceremony.

ST. LUCIA

St. Lucia may be *the* most popular island in all of the Caribbean for weddings and honeymoons. Nearly all of St. Lucia's resort hotels and most of the small inns offer attractive wedding-honeymoon packages, as well as coordinators to handle the legalities and help plan a memorable event. Several resorts, including the three Sandals resorts on St. Lucia, offer complimentary weddings to couples booking a minimum-stay honeymoon. The most striking setting, though, may be between the Pitons at the Ladera or Jalousie, Sugar Beach resorts—or at one of the nearby resorts that also offer spectacular Piton views, such as Jade Mountain, Anse Chastanet, or several smaller properties. Alternatively, botanical gardens, historical sites, waterfalls, or breezy boat trips are all romantic settings for the special event.

There is no waiting period to get married in St. Lucia. You can marry on the same day that you arrive if you apply for a "special" marriage license, pay a $200 special marriage license fee, and have all the necessary documents mailed in advance. You must present valid passports, birth certificates, a divorce decree if either party is divorced, an appropriate death certificate if either party is widowed, and a notarized parental consent if either party is under the age of 18. Most couples opt for the standard marriage license, which costs $125 and requires three days of residence on the island prior to the wedding ceremony. In either case, special or standard, you can expect additional registrar and certificate fees amounting to about $40.

INDEX

Photo Credits

1, Gavin Hellier/age fotostock. 4, Barbados Tourism Authority. Chapter 1 Experience Barbados and St. Lucia: 6-7, Benjamin Howell/iStockphoto. 8 (top), Saint Lucia Tourism Board. 8 (bottom), Barbados Tourism Authority. 9 (left), Barbados Tourism Authority/Mike Toy. 9 (right), Saint Lucia Tourism Board. 14 (left), Barbados Tourism Authority/Jim Smith. 14 (right), Saint Lucia Tourism Board. 15 (top left), Barbados Tourism Authority/Jim Smith. 15 (bottom left), ben.ramirez/Flickr. 15 (right), Saint Lucia Tourism Board. 16(left), Sandy Lane Hotel. 16 (right), Kristine Dear. 17 (top left), Barbados Tourism Authority/Harold Davis. 17 (bottom left), Ladera. 17 (right), Saint Lucia Tourism Board. 18, Barbados Tourism Authority. 19, Jim Smith/Barbados Tourism Authority. 20, Barbados Tourism Authority/Jim Smith. 21, Ramunas I Dreamstime.com. 22, Jim Smith/Barbados Tourism Authority. 23, melissa bouyounan/Shutterstock. 25, Barbados Tourism Authority/Craig Lenihan. 26, Mrs. Joan Devaux/ Diamond Botanical Gardens and Waterfall, Soufriere, St. Lucia. Chapter 2 Barbados: 27, John Miller / age fotostock. 34, Barbados Tourism Authority/Andrew Hulsmeier copyright 2008. 38, Barbados Concorde Experience. 41, Walter Bibikow / age fotostock. 46, Shirley Kilpatrick/ Alamy. 50, St. Nicholas Abbey. 55, Barbados Tourism Authority. 61, Brown Sugar Restaurant. 66, Julie Webster.72, Ingolf Pompe / age fotostock. 76 (top), Coral Reef Club. 76 (bottom), Sweetfield Manor. 77 (top), Addison Cumberbatch/Willie Alleyne Photography. 77 (bottom left), Hilton Barbados. 77 (bottom right), Sandy Lane Hotel. 80-81, PetePhipp/ Travelshots / age fotostock. 84-85, Barbados Tourism Authority/Mike Toy. 87, graham tomlin/Shutterstock. 89, World Pictures / age fotostock. 91, Roy Riley / Alamy. 92, david sanger photography / Alamy. 97, Barbados Tourism Authority/ Ronnie Carrington. 103, MAT/Shutterstock. Chapter 3 St. Lucia: 107, Colin Sinclair / age fotostock. 116-117, Ian Cumming / age fotostock. 120, Helene Rogers / age fotostock. 125, Ian Cumming / age fotostock. 134-135, Ian Cumming /age fotostock. 141, The Edge Restaurant, St Lucia West Indies. 142, Coal Pot. 144, Ladera. 148, Cotton Bay Village. 150 (top), The Leading Hotels of the World. 150 (bottom), leonardo.com. 151 (top), Sandals Resorts. 151 (bottom), Mikael Lamber. 153, Sandals Resorts. 155, Ian Cumming / age fotostock. 158 (top), Saint Lucia Tourism Board. 158 (bottom), Christian Horan. 160, Ladera. 166, Gavin Hellier / age fotostock. 170, Stephen Frink Collection / Alamy. 175, M. Timothy O'Keefe/ Alamy.

ABOUT OUR WRITER

Jane E. Zarem characterizes herself as a globe-trotting writer, intrepid researcher, fastidious editor, and curious soul with a positive outlook, mature view, and big-picture perspective. Notwithstanding the sheer enthusiasm for her work, she loves the chance to kick back in the Caribbean each year on her updating missions to Barbados, St. Lucia, and several other islands for *Fodor's Caribbean*.

Jane's love affair with the Caribbean began several decades ago, when she joined a 10-day Windjammer cruise that called on islands that, at the time, she never knew existed: Tortola, Virgin Gorda, Nevis, St. Kitts, St. Maarten, Saba, St. Barth's. Tourism hadn't yet hit those island paradises, and most claimed more goats than people. Times have changed.

She has since made more than 80 trips to the Caribbean and has visited Barbados and St. Lucia—two of her favorite islands—more than a dozen times each. She has stared at the awesome east coast of Barbados and swum between the Pitons in St. Lucia. She has visited historic great houses and wandered through St. Lucia's Diamond Botanical Gardens. She has explored shops and markets in both Bridgetown and Castries, off-roaded along the northern tip of Barbados, and sailed along the west coast of St. Lucia. She's also met wonderful people on both islands, who have welcomed her back with a big hug and a broad smile on each subsequent visit.

Jane has been a freelance travel writer for more than 25 years. Her very first travel-writing assignment involved updating the Connecticut chapter of Fodor's *New England* in the late 1970s. Since then, she has worked on many Fodor's guides, contributed travel articles to various newspapers and magazines, written travel and other business-related newsletters, and contributed numerous articles and research reports to trade magazines and other organizations. Most significantly, she has been a contributor to *Fodor's Caribbean* since 1994, writing and updating the Grenada and St. Vincent and the Grenadines chapters, along with Barbados and St. Lucia.

Acknowledgments
Writing this third edition of *In Focus Barbados and St. Lucia* was a natural assignment for her and, she will tell you, "a labor of love." She could not have accomplished it, though, without the assistance of the good people at the Barbados Tourism Authority and the St. Lucia Tourist Board, who have coordinated her trips to the respective islands over the many years that she has focused on these wonderful destinations.